LEEDS UNITED

C000245664

Dedicated to Lesley Anne Edwards, B.Sc.

LEEDS UNITED

THE SECOND COAT

GARY EDWARDS

MAINSTREAM PUBLISHING
EDINBURGH AND LONDON

Reprinted, 2007

Copyright © Gary Edwards, 2005
All rights reserved
The moral right of the author has been asserted

First published in Great Britain in 2005 by
MAINSTREAM PUBLISHING COMPANY
(EDINBURGH) LTD
7 Albany Street
Edinburgh EH1 3UG

ISBN 9781845960193

No part of this book may be reproduced or transmitted in any form or by any other means without permission in writing from the publisher, except by a reviewer who wishes to quote brief passages in connection with a review written for insertion in a magazine, newspaper or broadcast

A catalogue record for this book is available from the British Library

Typeset in Baskerville and Frutiger

Printed in Great Britain by
William Clowes Ltd, Beccles, Suffolk

Acknowledgements

Once again, I would like to thank Wub (Lesley) for her unswerving loyalty and support. She's always been there to put her hand over my glass when I've wanted 'just one more'. So, for that, Wub . . . er . . . thanks. As usual, I'm indebted to Neil Jeffries for his invaluable advice. It must be noted, too, that none of these books would have surfaced had it not been for the constant encouragement from Alan Osborne. Thanks also to Paul Dews and Steve Riding from the *Yorkshire Evening Post* for their continued support and to Frank Rounding, who unlocked some distant memories deep in my decaying memory bank. Grateful thanks go to ex-pat Dave Redshaw, as well as to Dave Shack, Robert Endeacott, Chris Tams, Kev Morgan and Andy Starmore. A massive thank you to Leeds United's Gary Kelly, to TV presenter Nicki Chapman, to actor Ralph Ineson and to Radio One's very own Chris Moyles.

Thanks go to Dave 'Para' Brown, Lee Dyson and Paul Sodermark for their own unique accounts of life watching Leeds United.

This time around I had *two* computer experts helping me along. Thank you Vicky (Spoon) and Kippax's Webmaster Ken Radcliffe.

As usual, thanks to Bill Campbell, Graeme Blaikie, Doug Nicholl, Paul Murphy and all the team at Mainstream Publishing.

Finally, my sincere thanks to Malcolm Glazer for providing the one silver lining in an otherwise mediocre season.

Contents

Foreword

I can't remember when I first met Gary Edwards but that's OK because if he'd had as many beers as I had, the chances are he won't either. I do, however, remember the first time it dawned on me what a nutter-cum-national treasure he is. I was editing *Leeds Leeds Leeds* when I took a call from Gary Inman, one of the magazine's many excellent freelance writers. Now Gary Inman has been around the world, he's driven fast cars, ridden fast bikes and maybe even met a few fast women, so when he called raving about how *Leeds Leeds Leeds* simply had to make more room to fit in his profile of this guy Edwards, I knew he was extraordinarily excited. It was a breathless phone call, punctuated by fits of laughter and giggling at both ends of the line, as he recounted some of the stories he'd heard minutes earlier from the horse's mouth, as it were. (Not that I'm saying Gary Edwards looks like a horse, you understand. Certainly not. He's more of a bear: a bear that's halfway through eating a grey squirrel.)

'He's seen every Leeds game since 1968!' raved Inman. 'And I mean every game – even the friendlies! He divorced a woman after two and a half weeks because she bought red saucepans. He hates that lot over the Pennines so much he won't even say their name, and when the Queen knighted Alex Ferguson he took down his picture of her and hung it in his under-the-stairs cupboard.' I was now laughing so much, people in the office were giving me funny looks.

I already knew that Gary Edwards was on a mission to rid the world of red paint – and as a professional decorator would go over it in white for free. And I knew about his utter devotion to Leeds United – that's why I'd commissioned the interview. But I had no idea what a unique and amusing character he was. If someone tells me they want to introduce me to someone who's seen every Leeds game since 1968, I'll expect to meet an anorak with very few real friends. But Gary Edwards is no anorak, and he makes friends wherever he goes.

So, Gary Inman's feature spawned a regular column by Gary Edwards in the magazine, and when that got a bit close to the mark, and one of Peter Ridsdale's cronies objected, the column spawned the seed of his first book, called *Paint it White*. It took a lot of arm-twisting by a lot of people to get him to write that, but we can all be grateful that he did. Not least because so many people loved it that they walked up to him and told him so – and in the telling quizzed him about other tales he'd left out. Gary Edwards is a modest chap and, therefore, a bit embarrassed that this quizzing meant he was eventually persuaded to write another one. I say: don't be so bloody bashful! If you live life like Gary Edwards does, there's always another funny story to tell.

I'm now proud to count Gary as a friend, because, even among that magnificent legion that is the fan-base of Leeds United, he is special. So, I raise a glass to book two and to Gary himself: nutter, national treasure, painter, decorator, funny man, Leeds fan. Not necessarily in that order.

Neil Jeffries
Editor of Leeds Leeds Leeds,
the official club magazine of Leeds United AFC

1

The Green Academy

> If I had ever been blessed with having a son, I was going to call him 'Leeds'. The highlight of any day would have been calling him in for his tea.

Ever since I was a kid, I've never wanted a day to end. Obviously, I've wished the odd minute away: such as the 1968 Fairs Cup final, when Leeds were beating Ferencváros, hanging on a knife-edge at 1–0 on aggregate; or the 1975 European Cup semi-final in Barcelona; or even the slender 2–1 victory in a European Cup play-off match against Stuttgart in 1992, also in Barcelona. But, overall, I hate it when the day finally comes to a close. I vividly remember Ma having to put a large, thick blanket up at my bedroom window to block out the light summer evenings, so I'd go to sleep.

Many a time, Ma would come in, and I'd made a tent under the covers (oooh matron) so I could read my *Beano* by torchlight. With the *Beano* confiscated, I would lie there and drift off at around four or five in the morning. I would be wide awake an hour later, up and ready for school.

You would think that sleeping would have been easy considering the running about I did every night. Young footballers from the whole estate would gather on the Green – our Wembley – surrounded by our houses. Between twenty and thirty lads and one lass, Gloria King, would gather after tea for the team picking. Two mediocre players would select the teams. Andy Robinson and

Graham Denton were usually the first to be picked. Graham moved up to Scotland when he was about 20 and went on to play in the Scottish First Division, but, to be fair, he could have played at a much higher level. Andy chose the army over football, although he did buy himself out years later so he could resume watching Leeds United.

I would be picked next because I was a goalie, and nobody liked going in goal. The other side would play with a 'drop back' goalie, because their keeper – Dave 'Snapper' Capper – would still be having his tea. He lived the nearest to the Green but was always last out. He was about ten years old and weighed about fifteen stone. Usually, the next to be picked would be Gloria 'Glozz' King. Glozz had an older brother Melvyn and a younger brother Malcolm, but she would be picked before either of these two. She didn't hold back in the tackle and had a sweet right foot. Once the teams were picked, two jumpers were dropped at either end for goalposts and we were off. Melv King was always the oldest lad on the pitch. He was, and still is, a great lad. He would take off his glasses, put them under one of the jumpers and look around to see who was on his side. Not that it mattered: if you went anywhere near him with the ball, he would clatter you.

'Melv! I'm on your side!' Kev Spencer would shout. 'Put your bleedin' glasses on!' Billy Anderson would be helpless with laughter. Occasionally, we were graced by the presence of Tommy Jackson, by far and away the best footballer on the estate. He was always long gone with the ball before Melv came charging in.

Stan 'Rastus' Richardson would be sulking because he'd been put in goal until Snapper had finished his tea. Rastus (who was given his nickname by my Auntie Ann) always had the proverbial green 'number 11' on his upper lip and his sleeves were always like stiff cardboard from all the snot wiped on them. After ten minutes, four goals had flown past Rastus, and by now he was sat on his arse with his teddy well out.

'Snapper!' his teammates would shout at his open front door, 'Come on, hurry up!'

Snapper would come charging out like an oversized superhero. His jumper would be well up over his huge belly, but you would still be able to see what he'd had for his tea all down the front of it. In fact, more often than not, he'd still have a sandwich in his hand. Snapper wasn't the most agile athlete I've ever seen, but his huge, bulky frame made it enormously difficult to get the ball past him.

Snapper has left the area now, but I bet he still likes his food. Only a few years before he moved on, he was seen on the bench outside The Royal Oak eating fish and chips. He'd clearly had a few too many bevvies: when he threw up, he did so into his supper bag but was that pissed he carried on eating. It took him a little longer, but he managed to finish it.

When we were all about seven or eight, a shady-looking bloke would park his van not far from the Green. Hooked up to the van at the rear was an old wooden roundabout-type thing, with wooden horses and cars and stuff like that. For a threepenny bit, or a bag of old clothes, you could ride for about five minutes, with the man operating it by use of an old starting handle. As a special treat he would shout, 'Right, now the Chinese way!' and with that we were all propelled backwards. Afterwards, we would climb off, thoroughly giddy, and for the first few minutes everyone would be staggering about, bumping into each other.

Our usual game of football on the Green was put on hold one afternoon in 1966. It was the day of the World Cup final at Wembley between England and West Germany. The Green was deserted, as everyone was glued to their televisions. At the final whistle, the whole estate erupted: England had won the cup, and scores of kids descended onto the Green. 'I'm Geoff Hurst!' everyone was shouting. 'I'll be Martin Peters, then,' another would shout. I was Jack Charlton, even though I was in goal. He was the only Leeds player in the England team, and so I had to be him. Snapper was Gordon Banks, and he'd had spaghetti hoops for his tea. We picked the teams and, after a 15-minute row as to who was going to be England, we kicked off. Kev Higgins led the German team, and Gordon Banks was their goalie. We replayed the World Cup final for weeks, and we even had a cup. It was a picture of the Jules Rimet Cup, cut out of a football book and pasted onto cardboard.

The games were intense. One time, Colin Booth was preparing to take a corner, with time running out. He missed the ball, kicking one of the kerbstones that surrounded the Green instead. He was in agony and was rolling about crying. The tragic thing was that Col had a trial at Elland Road the following day for Leeds United, but he had broken his toe. It was months before he got another chance, but by then he seemed to have lost interest and wasn't successful. He chose to play rugby after that.

I had decided that all I wanted to do was watch Leeds United, so, despite a couple of promising trials, a career in football was not an option for me. I still loved playing football, and, a few years later, I got my chance once again. Mr Roberts, at number 29, was the secretary of a pub side from nearby Garforth. The Podger was a fairly new pub and had quite a successful side. I had just left school and was about to start a new job. John had seen me throwing myself around between the jumpers and asked me if I would play for them for two weeks while their goalie was on holiday. As it turned out, I played in every game for the next four years.

Around that time – 1972 – Leeds United were in their pomp, and Elland Road was buzzing. Leeds had disposed of Liverpool, among others, in the FA Cup, and had now beaten Tottenham Hotspur in the quarter-final. Leeds had set a new trend before each game, by parading in Admiral tracksuit tops bearing their names across the shoulders. Old hat now, but Leeds did it first. The team would come out earlier than their opponents and do special warm-up routines under the watchful eye of trainer Les Cocker. Each player also wore tassled stocking tabs with their team number on. The opposing fans hated it, but there was no doubt that it made an impression on the opposing side. The chant of 'Super Leeds' rang from the stands, beginning in the Gelderd End and spreading around the ground, as Leeds tore into their opponents from the start of each game and totally outclassed teams week after week.

All this hadn't gone unnoticed by the management team at The Podger. At the start of the following season, our chairman, Eric Batty, arrived at our pre-season training with tracksuits for the whole squad. Each one had our own name on it, and we felt the business. As with Leeds, it showed in our game as we romped to a league title triumph. The following season, we reached the final of the league cup against Scholes at Micklefield. In the final minute, we were awarded a penalty with the score at 1–1. Alan Buchanan Thursfield, our best player by far, stepped up to take the kick. To this day, the ball is still in the air. The game went to extra time and we lost 2–1. Of course, all these years later, no one mentions it to him.

Our final game of the 1975–76 season was a crucial one away at

Burley, near Leeds: we just needed a point to clinch the league title. On the same evening, Leeds United were away in a fixture that, quite frankly, meant nothing to either side. Ronnie Dean, our manager, could not understand why I travelled to Leicester, instead of being at Burley for one of our most important games for years. The Podger won 1–0, and Leeds lost 2–1. I arrived back at the pub in time to have a drink out of our new trophy.

At the end of each season, it was customary for the winning teams to attend an official awards ceremony where each team would officially receive their trophy. This particular year, it was held at the Mecca nightclub in the Merrion Centre in Leeds. Over recent years, fights had broken out between rival teams, and the league warned each team that their behaviour would be monitored: any bad behaviour would not be tolerated. When the time came for us to receive our trophy, our captain, Dennis Ruddick, walked across to the top table. As he was coming back to our table, he raised the cup aloft, and we all cheered loudly. At this point, the lid fell off, and, as it made contact with the floor, Dennis's right foot connected with it, resulting in a perfect half-volley. The spinning lid travelled 15 yards towards the West Leeds Railwaymen table, hitting one of their players full in the face and immediately drawing blood. The inevitable brawl followed, and, as the committee members sat there shaking their heads, a player from another table was hurled across the top table completely felling two of the committee and their chairs. It just wasn't this chap's night: seconds later, Keith Mathews had to pick up his pint as the poor guy then came flying across our table. The funny thing was that when the evening came to an abrupt end, players from all teams were outside the club laughing and joking among themselves, including those who, only minutes earlier, had been locked in combat. Some teams, including ours, were severely reprimanded, but nothing too serious came of it – apart from having to move the venue for the following season's presentations.

That following season, the team moved lock, stock and barrel to The Royal Oak in Kippax. Apart from a couple of additions, the management and the players remained the same. Royal Oak FC went on to have many happy seasons, and it was a very close-knit club with a very good social side. John Roberts remained the pillar of the club, organising events and evenings. Sadly, John died in 1982, shortly after an accident at work; he was only 55. I was very close to John and, indeed, his whole family, especially his wife Ada, who took over John's secretarial obligations at the club. I missed John so much. I had never experienced anything like it before in my life.

A few years later, The Royal Oak were progressing nicely in the coveted Barkston Ash Cup, a prestigious trophy contested by sides from all over West Yorkshire, including many clubs from leagues much higher than our own. Amazingly, we reached the semi-final and were paired with Bramham Lions, a very classy outfit indeed. Even more amazingly, and much to the annoyance of the Lions, we won 2–1 to reach the final of the trophy that every team in the competition dreamt of winning. The champagne and beer were flowing big style that night in the Oak . . . The atmosphere was superb, with all the players' wives and girlfriends joining in the celebrations.

Julie Cryer was in the pub that night. I have known Julie all my life: she grew up on the same estate as me, and her husband Richard is a season ticket holder at Elland Road. Julie is a medium – a very good one – who travels all over the country and has made countless TV appearances. Many Leeds players are said to be among her clients. When we were kids, our mums told us about Julie and her 'special gift'. To be honest, I always kept my distance: she could 'talk to the dead' and that scared the shit out of me.

That particular night in the Oak, she was staring at me. I kept looking away, but eventually she came over and said, 'Hi, Gary, can I have a word?' I left the main group, and we walked over to the back of the pub. I noticed Gary Noble watching me out of the corner of his eye. It was like I was being taken away by an evil spirit, and I could do nothing about it. Julie spoke quietly. 'John's here,' she said.

'Oh shit,' I gulped. I looked around and then asked pathetically, 'Where?'

'He's over there, by the trophy cabinet.' My whole body was covered in goose bumps. 'He's doing something with his hands,' she said. 'I can't see what . . . Oh, I think he's peeling an apple or an orange?'

I nearly freaked there and then. Every half-time, while Ronnie Dean and, later, Kenny Smith gave the team-talk, John would be cutting and dishing out the oranges. He did this religiously at every game. She hadn't finished with me yet: 'He's holding his arm out by his waist. He's saying that he's very proud of the team, but if we win the cup, it is too tall to fit in his cupboard.' She was right. How did she know? 'He's gone now,' she said suddenly.

On another occasion, Julie was at our house giving a reading to our lass, Lesley (Wub), and my daughter Vicky (Spoon). When she'd finished she came into the lounge where I was: I sat upright immediately. She began staring at the large picture of Winston Churchill above the fireplace. 'He's got very piercing eyes,' she said, without looking away. Christ, I thought, she's gonna bring Winnie here. But no . . . 'I hope you don't mind,' she said to me, 'I've got a David here.' Now, I've seen this type of thing on the telly, but it was here, happening in my own house! 'He passed over after a short illness,' she went on. 'He's holding his throat. He is saying the name Andy, but you will know him by another name.'

My goose bumps were back. Dave Johnson, who came to Leeds games with us, had died of throat cancer a few months prior to this. His brother Andy also came with us but was always known to everyone as Sid. I was stunned and could only mumble, 'Well, at least Dave won't have to pay to watch Leeds these days.'

This was the late 1980s, and Julie told me that a return to the top division was imminent. Sure enough, Leeds were promoted in 1990. I still see Julie and Rich occasionally at various Northern Soul get-togethers. As yet, Julie hasn't predicted an escape from Leeds' current plight.

Gypsy Rose Lee was another famous medium, who, in 1967, got a call from Don Revie. Don was extremely superstitious, and he believed that a curse laid by gypsies on the site of Elland Road, long before football was played there, was the cause of United's failure to win any silverware. Rose Lee arrived from Scarborough and, amid huge publicity, duly exorcised Elland Road. The following year, Leeds United won their first two trophies, adding their first league title the year after that. Spooky, eh?

Continuing with the supernatural theme, I used to live in an old house on Helena Street in Kippax, which was definitely haunted. The lady who owned it when it was first built had died in the bath, and, although I never saw her drifting round the house, all sorts of 'bumps in the night' occurred. Spoon was only about four years old when she came into our bedroom one night to tell us that Fred, our dog, was on her bed. Fred had died four months earlier. Another time, when my dad's house was being renovated, he stayed at ours for a while. A very short while. My dad, the famous country singer 'Eddie Stevens', would not subscribe to ghost stories. Until he stayed with us, that is. One night, while we were away overnight, pictures began falling off the wall; biscuits helped themselves out of their packets in the cupboards; and the kitchen door appeared to be locked even though there was no lock on the door. Minutes later, it opened by itself. Now, whether this had anything to do with me having a hearse parked at the front of the house, as well as one at the back, I don't know, but my good old dad didn't stay after that night.

One of those hearses was my trusty old Austin. Now, I can say with some authority that hearses are real passion wagons. However, one encounter in this particular Austin ended with me more than a tad embarrassed. Wub and I christened it one chilly night in a park in Leeds, and, once we had both climbed into the back, I closed the door behind us. On the side of the hearse was a sign I had retrieved from an old bus. It read, 'No Standing'. With the deed done, I went to open the door. To my horror, there was no handle on the inside. Well there wouldn't be, would there? Not many people climb out of the back of a hearse. I had to unceremoniously climb through the glass panels at the front, dressed only in my fetching Y-fronts. Those pegs that hold the coffin in position come in handy, though. You can set them to your own requirement, and they help tremendously with the propulsion – if you get my drift!

I would also use the hearse for football. We would often scare the opposition to death, as I drove it into the local park on a crisp Sunday morning, and an entire football team would emerge from the back of it.

There are die-hard fans, even at amateur level, and Neil 'Geordie' Malloch was one of them. He would come out to watch us every Sunday without fail, come rain or, occasionally, shine. Kevin Denton was another such fan. It has to be said that Kev wasn't exactly at the head of the queue when the brains were being dished out, but he has this knack of making you think that he was further to the front of the queue than you were. Weird.

Once, we were playing at Cutsyke near Castleford. It was pouring down with rain, and the ball was kicked out of play, where it ended up in an adjoining field. Kev attempted to retrieve the ball but got caught in the barbed-wire fence. The more he struggled, the tighter he became entangled. He was becoming very angry, and, as he struggled and the rain continued to fall, 22 players, a ref and about 55 spectators waited patiently for Kev to turn 'Hulk' green. Finally, our captain Barry Hope, and some other lads, freed a very irate and wet Kev.

It was clearly a day for off-the-field entertainment. Glenn Parkinson, our manager, told John Robertshaw to get 'warmed up'. Within seconds, John was sat in his van with the engine running and the heater on full blast.

Another memorable encounter I had with Kev happened one New Year's Eve. I was attending a house party hosted by Kev's and Gord's parents: it was an annual event, which was always well attended. The house was on the corner of the Green. This particular year, I was having a whisky with Gord's dad, Jock. Suddenly, and without warning, I felt the overwhelming urge to throw up. Anxious to avoid embarrassment, I hurried out of the lounge and made for the stairs to go to the bathroom. I didn't quite make it that far, and my suit was soon decorated with my evening's food and drink. I certainly wouldn't like this to happen in my own home so I was really embarrassed – so much so that when Wub came to see if I was OK, I told her to open the front door so that I could leave without anyone seeing me. Just my luck, the door was stuck and, apparently, hadn't opened for years. Determined not to walk back through the lounge, I went into one of the back bedrooms. 'Where are you going?' asked Wub.

'I'm going to jump out of the window,' I replied.

'Don't be stupid!' she said, but I was adamant that this was the only way out. She disappeared downstairs. As I eased my way up onto the windowsill, with the window open, Kev appeared. 'Hello, what are you doing?' he asked.

'Hello, Kev. Oh, I'm just going to jump out of the window.'

As if he saw this sort of thing every day, Kev just said, 'Oh, OK.'

It was a struggle though. As I was squat on the windowsill with my arse and one leg hanging out of the open window, I was having difficulty getting my last leg out through it.

'You'll have to push me, Kev,' I said. He never batted an eyelid.

'OK,' he said. With that, he pushed my remaining leg, and I flew out of the window and plummeted two storeys onto the patio below. I dusted myself down and walked home, avoiding all forms of human life. By the time Wub returned home, I had showered and washed the suit. I asked her what had been said at the party: 'Oh, Kev came down and told everyone he'd helped push you out through the window.' When asked why, he had replied, 'I don't know, really, he just asked me to push him.' The following lunchtime, New Year's Day, I walked into The Royal Oak taproom to a thunderous rendition of the *Superman* theme tune.

After a few more successful seasons under manager Kenny Smith, The Royal Oak Football Club folded. Ada sadly died a couple of years ago and only recently our original chairman, Eric Batty, passed away. That in effect drew a line under that chapter of my life.

However, I did play for a couple of other teams: The Commercial was one and I briefly went on loan to Swillington, before finally hanging up my boots and gloves at the age of 40 in 1996. My last game was played in a tranquil setting beneath the cooling towers of Ferrybridge Power Station. I took over as secretary and spent the rest of my days on the touchline, sharing the odd whisky flask with big Frank Hope, Barry's brother, who had retired the year before.

After The Royal Oak team split up, most of the lads went to play for The Moorgate. Kenny Smith, with his able assistant Les Moran, went on to manage The Moorgate, and I'm happy to report that the elusive Barkston Ash Cup was finally captured in 1997. After duly celebrating the cup victory with a few stouts, Ken was walking home past my dad's house. He noticed that one of Dad's goats, Jenny, had jumped over the garden wall. Although still tethered, she was now stood on the pavement. Without a moment's thought, Ken bent down and picked her up to put her back over the wall. Whilst being awkwardly cradled in his arms, Jenny lifted her head back and headbutted Ken straight in the face. Ken, although slightly shaken, continued to stagger home to his bewildered wife, Carol.

Today, there is a new bunch of kids occupying the Green, and every time I drive past, on my way to my Ma's, I'm happy to see that, even in these not so good times, the Leeds United shirt is prominent.

2

The Next Generation

> At the next game of football, anywhere in the world, there could be a little 'Gary Edwards' just starting out. That's a scary thought.

Just around the corner from the Green is the bus stop for the number 163 into Leeds. It was an hour's journey back in the day, and, quite frankly, it hasn't improved much since. The bus still takes about three-quarters of an hour, as it meanders about 20 miles instead of making a direct trip. However, about ten others and I would regularly make this journey to watch our heroes at Elland Road. I began doing this around 1966, and then, in 1967, when Leeds were away, we would catch the bus the other direction into Castleford, from where we would board a Wallace Arnold coach bound for Burnley, Newcastle, Leicester or wherever Leeds were playing that day.

Since I was about nine or ten, I had sat on the Green on match days and watched the older lads from the estate return from the Leeds United game, be it home or away. Dinger, Simmo, Buller, Shog, Wagger, Griff and others would walk past the Green and tell us the score. John Hiddon always brought me a programme back. Nearly 40 years on, John still goes to Elland Road. Once Leeds United are in your heart, it's for ever.

Gord Findlay and Jimmy Blackburn were a couple of years older than me (and still are as far as I know) and were the next in line for the Leeds United experience. I, along with the Next Generation, wasn't going to be far behind them. There was a long adventure ahead, and I was almost ready. There was a smattering of lads supporting other clubs. Among them were, dare I say, manchester united (I will not capitalise their name), Chelsea, Everton, Man City and some even stranger clubs. But as with most things, sensible people grow out of such fads.

The local celebrity in those days was my jackdaw, Jack. I had him for about four or five years after a local man known only as 'Big Dave' gave him to me. He had found Jack alone in long grass in the nearby Billy Wood. Jack was only a baby, and Big Dave reckoned he'd fallen out of his nest. Whatever happened, he was alone. I looked after Jack, and Dad partitioned part of his aviary to accommodate our new arrival. Although the door to his part of the aviary was never closed – so he was free to fly off whenever he chose – he would return each night. As I walked about the estate, he would be perched on my shoulder. He loved egg and beans, which my Ma would leave for him on the coal bunker behind our house. He also loved his regular trips down to the fish shop.

I knew Jack was a Leeds fan. It was always evident on Saturday, as we climbed onto the 163 into Leeds. He would leave my shoulder and 'escort' the bus for about a mile before he could be seen veering off and heading back to find new friends to play with until we returned from the match. I always wished I could take him to the match.

After the game we would return home, and within minutes Jack would arrive for his evening meal on the coal bunker. My mates and I would sit on the grass and watch him as we relived every kick we had just seen at Elland Road. Regularly, people would call and ask if I had their pen. Jack would cheekily swoop and pinch pens, and anything else that was shiny, out of people's top pockets. My bedroom windowsill was often laden with treasure.

Inside the house, we also used to have a mynah bird. It was the best talking bird I have ever heard. The only snag was that we bought it from an Italian family and half its vocabulary was in Italian. Nevertheless, its speech was so clear. Many a time, one of the lads would call for me when the door would be half-open, and, after hearing a knock, the mynah bird would shout, 'Hello'. We would sit there quietly laughing as the bird and our caller would have a two-minute conversation. Unfortunately, the mynah bird, like Jack, never made it to Elland Road.

One of my first vivid memories of Elland Road was when I went to a game against Everton with my cousin Steve. We paid our three bob to get into the Lowfields Road side, and then Steve pointed over to what he called the 'Scratching Shed'. I had heard about the Shed and its fearsome reputation, and here I was looking at it in person. I was mesmerised. Steve interrupted my thoughts. 'Right, come on,' he said. I did as I was told and went with him. We arrived at the fence separating the Lowfields from the Shed: it then dawned on me what we were going to do. We were going over. 'I'll climb over first', Steve whispered. 'You follow straight away and then we run into the middle.' I gulped as he scaled the fence and landed on the other side in the Shed: I was surprised to see people in the Shed help him down. I took a deep breath and began my assault. As I was straddled at the top, a policeman grabbed my foot. I was about 12 years old, and I was shitting myself. Time seemed to stand still as he shouted, 'Where are you going, son?'

'My cousin's just gone in there,' I stuttered.

'If your cousin jumped off a cliff, would you follow him?' the copper asked.

Without thinking, I replied, 'Yes,' and wrestled free, before landing on the other side.

'Run!' shouted Steve, and we disappeared into the middle of the crowd. We must have missed the first 20 minutes of the match as we crouched down to escape capture. When we finally bobbed up, I could just see the tops of the players' heads.

'What have we come in here for?' I asked, somewhat puzzled as to why we had left a perfect viewing spot down the side.

''Cos this is where the Leeds fans stand, and it's dearer in here.' I didn't know how to reply to that, so I didn't.

The Scratching Shed was a unique place. It was full of characters of all shapes and sizes. Over the next few weeks, I gathered more and more information about the various individuals who occupied that famous part of the ground.

Just seeing the white-shirted Leeds players that day was magical. Leeds manager, Don Revie, had adopted the all-white strip from the

Spanish giants, Real Madrid. Many believe this was a contributing factor to Leeds' rise to the top. A Leeds player at that time was Rod Johnson, who now lives near me in Kippax. Years later he told me that when he moved from Leeds United to Doncaster Rovers in 1968, they also adopted all white as their away strip. It didn't have the same effect as at Leeds. Nor did it have the same effect when Rod moved on to Rotherham, who had also adopted an all-white strip when playing away games. In 1972, Bradford City signed Rod, and, lo and behold, all white became their preferred away kit. Rod was soon made captain of the side, and he laughed when he recalled an occasion when he led his all-white team out at Chesterfield. 'I was stood in the tunnel chatting with my teammates,' he told me. It had been raining and the pitch looked heavy. City needed points badly, and Rod told his team that just because they were in all white and on a muddy pitch that didn't mean they couldn't get stuck in. They got the nod to enter the field. 'Right! Come on lads, make 'em have it!' Rod shouted as he ran out of the tunnel. Rod was carrying a ball, and just as he was about to step onto the pitch he tossed it in the air. As he looked up at the ball, he tripped over a small wooden plinth that had been placed next to the playing area. Rod ended up lying face down on the muddy pitch, as his giggling teammates ran round him and disappeared to one of the goalmouths. I forgot to ask Rod if City won that day.

Anyway, back to my first memories of the Shed. That day, I gazed at the amazing characters that were shouting on their heroes all around me. It was, really, all quite bizarre. There was a lad who played a guitar, whose name I found out later was Keith Penniker, and this would begin the chanting. People with tambourines would accompany him, along with a bloke – who looked uncannily like Jesus Christ – playing merrily on his flute.

This carnival atmosphere, however, hid the real intensity in the Shed. The Shed was known throughout the country as a hostile area for away fans and the regular chants bore this out. One such example was, 'We are the Shed, we are the Shed, everybody knows that we are the Shed! You come in alive, you go out dead, you've just been the victim of the Mighty Shed!' Despite this often-aggressive behaviour, I always felt very safe and secure. However, I suppose I did use to wear a gigantic woollen Leeds hat and scarf.

Over the years, people came and went, but the bulk of the characters remained year after year. There was a large bloke who always wore a Glasgow Rangers hat and a big blue woolly jumper. He never missed a Leeds game, home or away, and he was as hard as nails. I believe his name was Davy Welch: quite an unfortunate name for a Scot. Another regular, who was known as Alki Mick, was from the Seacroft area of Leeds. He always got two pints from the bar: both for himself. He used to have long, straight, greasy hair and always wore the same brown corduroy jacket, with a Leeds badge sewn onto the breast pocket.

'Wilkie' was the first one I remember as being an identikit hooligan. He was always dressed very smartly in a suit. His sharp appearance, however, hid a very sinister character. He was always in the thick of the action but somehow managed to evade capture or injury. This would be almost impossible these days.

In the late '60s, when Yorkshire still had a coal industry, pit helmets were the required fashion accessory. Hundreds of white painted helmets, decorated with the team colours and slogans, would fill the Shed. However, the musical instruments had all but disappeared by then, and only the lone flute remained. The accompaniment of choice was now the noisy wooden rattle, which had been around throughout the '60s. 'Old Jack' would lead the chanting from his usual vantage point on the barrier. Years later, our very own 'Collar' (Roy Coles to his doctor) would take the reins from Jack, and, from that day to this, Collar's antics on the barrier remain legendary.

In 1968, the open Gelderd Road end of the ground was revamped. It received new terracing and a roof. This immediately signalled a mass exodus from the Shed, as thousands of Leeds fans changed ends. The first game in front of the new Kop was the first leg of the Inter-Cities Fairs Cup final against Ferencváros, but once the domestic season got under way it caused a few problems at first. Away fans such as Stoke, Sunderland, Wolves and Liverpool, unaware of the home fans' occupation, entered the turnstiles of what, up to now, had been the 'away' end. Sporadic scuffles occurred, as the Gelderd End's new occupants informed their guests that they were in the wrong part of the ground. News quickly spread throughout the country of the new arrangements, and away fans eventually began to use the allocated Shed. A number of Leeds fans, however, didn't want to leave the Shed and often confronted confused travelling fans.

One evening at Elland Road was surreal, to say the least, and left both home and away fans bemused. It was August 1968, and Leeds were about to enter into battle with Sunderland. With both sets of fans exchanging obscenities from opposite ends of the ground, the loudspeaker interrupted the pleasantries: 'Good evening, ladies and gentlemen, welcome to Elland Road. Tonight we have a very special treat for you. Please put your hands together for . . . Lulu!' She walked out onto the centre spot and, before 38,000 supporters, sang her latest single, 'I'm a Tiger'.

Jack the jackdaw was hovering above as a group of us walked down to the bus stop. We were going to Castleford to catch our Wallace Arnold coach to Burnley. Because of the hairs growing on my chin, it was becoming increasingly difficult to get half fare, but, for the time being, I was just about getting away with it. Although it was just a short distance over the Pennines to Burnley, there was no M62 back then, and the journey took about two hours. We'd made a similar trip a month earlier, when a bunch of us travelled in my dad's Thames Dormobile to the FA Cup semi-final against Everton at Old Trafford. In the van that day was my uncle Frank and my cousin Jean, along with around eight or nine lads from our estate. Despite easily being the best team, a mistake near the end by Gary Sprake forced Jack Charlton to give away a penalty and we lost 1–0.

The game at Burnley was our last league match of the season but again we lost: this time 3–0. It meant that Leeds had lost their last four games of the season: an extremely rare occurrence. After the game, as we made our way to our coach, four of us were confronted by about twenty Burnley fans. We quickly weighed up the odds: there were five times as many of them, and they were twice as old as us. We legged it. We arrived safely back at the coach park but couldn't see anything of Stan 'Rastus' Richardson. When the Burnley fans had disappeared, we began to gingerly retrace our steps to look for Rastus. We'd hardly left the coach park when we saw Rastus happily walking towards us with a burger in his hand. Rastus liked his food more than most, and, whilst we were being chased, he'd spied a burger bar and stopped for one.

Amazingly, this had gone unnoticed by the pursuing Burnley mob, and they ran straight past him as he queued hungrily for a burger.

It used to be pretty unnerving at Newcastle too. The entrance to the coach park (a disused cattle market) was just a narrow gap, and, if you were going through it, the Geordie conclusion was that you were a Leeds fan, and that invariably meant at least a kick up the arse.

One game I always looked forward to was the one against Blackpool. They had been a great side in the past, but had endured a few seasons in the old Second Division since getting relegated in 1967. Now, in the 1970–71 season, they were back in the top-flight, and the Leeds fans couldn't wait for the trip to the seaside.

Hundreds of us got off the train and made our way to the promenade. Although it was mid-March, the holiday season was just about getting under way: a few hardy souls had braved the spring sunshine and were camped on the beach in their deckchairs. Leeds fans were everywhere as 'football specials' regularly pulled into the train station. I was two weeks away from my 16th birthday, and I was as proud as Punch as I walked down the sea front amongst hordes of Leeds fans. Holidaymakers and locals scattered as this menacing chant of 'Leeds! Leeds! Leeds!' filled the air.

Soon it was our turn to scatter as four police cars and a police van arrived. I had been walking behind Gord but lost him in the confusion that followed. I instinctively followed a mob across the road and ended up in the 2/11 store. That's not the shop opening hours: that's how much everything was – two shillings and eleven pence! 'Just mingle with the shoppers till the coppers have gone,' someone said. This was bizarre. I had not caused any trouble, and neither, to be honest, had I seen any, but here we were hiding in a shop like major criminals. Eventually, I did more than 'mingle': I bought Ma a small brass ornament for 2s and 11d. She still has it today, bless her.

It wasn't long before the Leeds contingent had regrouped and was, once again, walking down the front, this time with a heavy police escort around us. It was no Pleasure Beach for us; it was straight to the ground. I had found Gord and was walking behind him again, watching his every move. We were near to the front of our group, and a police dog handler was threatening the Leeds fans with his snarling Alsatian. The dog was going berserk and was almost turning inside out as it barked and slavered all over everybody. Just then, Gord moved to the front. 'What's up, little fella – won't he feed you?' he said to the dog. The dog seemed a little surprised by this, and the copper didn't seem to know how to respond either. In an attempt to gain back his respect, he let a bit of slack off the dog lead. 'Go, boy!' he ordered and pointed the dog at Gord. Amazingly, Gord didn't flinch and once again talked to the animal. 'Poor little pooch, what's the matter then?' He leant over the dog and put his arm out to stroke it. The dog was now totally confused, and it swung its huge head around and bit the copper. The Leeds fans, as you can imagine, fell about laughing. Gord discreetly stepped back into the middle of the group, and the disgraced policeman retreated, as one of his colleagues took charge of the front of the group. Several of the other officers were also having difficulty in keeping a straight face, and I'll bet there were many things said about it back at the police station.

Leeds fans half-filled Bloomfield Road, and a goal by Peter Lorimer earned a 1–1 draw. A few of us had booked a hotel for the night, and, after a couple of hours sampling the delights of the Blackpool experience, we returned to watch *Match of the Day* in the hotel's television room. We weren't the only Leeds supporters in the hotel, and we all gathered around the TV. Ours was the main match, and the first words came from commentator Barry Davies: 'Leeds fans arrived in their thousands early this morning, and it wasn't long before they were tipping holiday makers out of their deckchairs and writing the words "Leeds United" in the sand.'

Blackpool were the first team I ever saw Leeds play, back in 1966, and I have always had a soft spot for them. Unfortunately, Blackpool were relegated again after that 1971 season and have never returned to top-flight football since.

Sadly, my jackdaw died in his sleep in 1971, and, as I travelled to West Ham with Nigel Pashley, I felt awful. I could not get thoughts of Jack out of my head. I imagined every blackbird I saw out of the coach window to be Jack. I have to admit, as I stood and watched the match, my thoughts were still back home. When I did arrive home, Ma said Big Dave had heard about Jack's demise, and I was to go see him the next day. When I saw Big Dave, as if to order, he said that he had a magpie if I wanted it. Feeling that it probably wasn't the right thing to do, I declined.

My passion for Leeds, though, was as strong as ever, and to fund my activities I used to go with my dad to work on Sundays, as well as chopping wood and selling bags of firewood around the estate. One morning, before a Liverpool home game, I was chopping wood near the coal bunker that Jack used to feed atop. My sister Julie and I had an argument about something. Instinctively, I jumped up and chased her towards our back door. 'I'm going to smash every one of your Gilbert O'Sullivan records!' I shouted. As she ran into the house, she closed the door behind her. However, I carried on, and, as the door shut, my right arm went crashing straight through the glass pane. Blood splattered all over the kitchen as our Julie shouted, 'Gary! Your arm. Oh God, look at your arm!' It was dripping with blood and bits were hanging out all over. I was rushed to the hospital.

I looked at the clock as the doctor began sewing my arm back together. I had refused a general anaesthetic, in case I woke up and the match had finished, but, of course, I hadn't told him the reason. As it turned out, I didn't have to. My big-mouthed dad said, 'Looks like you're going to miss the game, old son.' The doctor looked at me and, in a strong Scottish accent, said, 'No, no. You won't be able to play football for some time, laddie.'

I stuttered, 'Oh, no . . . I'm only going to watch . . .' Dr McKendrick finished the last of my 17 stitches. He was our family doctor back in Kippax, and, more importantly, he was a season ticket holder at Elland Road. As the nurse bandaged my arm, Dr McKendrick washed his hands. He had a reputation of being a hard and unsympathetic doctor, and he was widely thought of as quite an intimidating figure. Ma and Dad had differing opinions of him. Ma didn't like him one bit. She thought he was a bully. Dad, on the other hand, said he was 'hard but fair'. I was on my dad's side here. Once, when Dad was in hospital, the whole ward was waiting for the doctor's daily visit. On this particular occasion – a Saturday – it was the turn of Dr McKendrick. Over an hour later, Dr McKendrick arrived and began his rounds. Dad saw him hand a patient what looked like a football programme. It later transpired that Dr McKendrick had just got back from an away match at Wolves and was being kind to someone who had missed the game.

With this in mind, I felt slightly optimistic as he hung up his towel. He looked at Dad. 'If you think he's OK in a couple of hours, he can go. But only if you think he's OK,' he said. Then he turned into a villain again: 'Right, nurse, you can give him his injection.' To this day I hate needles, but back then I was absolutely petrified. The nurse turned into the pantomime witch as she took out a needle that, I swear, looked like one of Carlton Palmer's legs. But if this was what it took, then so be it. It hurt – God, did it hurt – but my face never altered. For the next two hours, I fought the drowsiness, and, at 2 p.m., I asked Dad what he thought. Half an hour later I took up my place in the West Stand.

I hated it in the West Stand. We had sat there for two years after my Dad had bought two season tickets from the *Yorkshire Evening Post.* In 1970, the only guaranteed way to purchase an FA Cup final ticket was with a season ticket. With about four league games left, many season tickets appeared in the classifieds at inflated prices. The ticket system then was that you would collect match-numbered tokens printed on the front page of Leeds' home-match programmes and also produce away programmes as proof of your loyalty. However, as there were only about 18,000 tickets allocated to Leeds, even a full sheet of tokens and every away programme didn't guarantee a ticket for the final.

As extra insurance, I queued all night at Elland Road for another ticket, on top of the one guaranteed by my season ticket. I must admit, though, it wasn't a chore. I used to love the atmosphere of queuing all night. Hundreds of people in sleeping bags with flasks, beer and food braved the wintry elements. Although not many slept. People would chat away with one another and compare away programmes. I even had vouchers from games in Norway, Hungary and Belgium – as did many others – but no one was guaranteed a priceless ticket. It was 3 a.m., and a 50-a-side football match was going on in the West Stand car park, utilising the grass banking as an extra bit of pitch. I calculated that there were about a hundred people in the queue in front of me. It snaked down the back of the West Stand, round the back of the Gelderd End (which, in effect, was the warmest place to be as it was under cover), all the way up Lowfields Road and back along the Shed. As things turned out, only a quarter of the people behind the Gelderd End received tickets: the rest were disappointed. Things turned ugly as thousands of disappointed fans clashed with police near the old ticket office behind the West Stand, which is now replaced by the Leeds United Banqueting Suite. The biggest disappointment of the whole affair for me was that, after all his efforts of attending every round, my Dad had to go into hospital and missed the final.

It's puzzling how people around you stop going to matches, and you don't notice for perhaps a year or so. This happened with me in the early '70s. Although a few of the lads were still going, a lot had dropped off. It was around this time that I began to travel to away games from Leeds rather than from Castleford. For home games, Dad and I would go into Leeds early and have fish and chips with my grandma, who lived in the Gipton area of Leeds. Grandma, my Dad's mam, loved it when we went there, and she always gave me a pound for 'a pie'. Invariably, that pound went in my 'European travel tin'. I would often stay at Grandma's after I had travelled alone to a midweek away game. The next morning I would get a bus direct from hers to my school at Garforth.

It was around this time that I became aware that my Dad was losing interest in the game or, more to the point, felt that he'd done his bit and it was now time for me to move on. I eventually drifted off and began to get the coach to away games from Leeds on my own.

A line of Wallace Arnold coaches would be parked at The Calls, near the Corn Exchange in Leeds. Fans would just queue and get the next bus in line. This way you had no way of knowing who you would be travelling with to any given match. On one of my first trips, I sat next to a chap who continually smoked cigars. He was a nice bloke who chatted away as we travelled down to Southampton. His name was Ray Sanderson, and I was to find out he was one of United's biggest fans, travelling to every game. This was the sort of fan I wanted to be with. As we talked, I couldn't help but notice the heavy tobacco stains on his old moustache. He was a real character, and I listened to him for hours. After I took a swig out of his whisky flask, we became firm friends. From then on, I made sure I travelled on the same coach as Ray and a couple of friends who travelled with him. The group gradually grew larger in numbers, and the atmosphere got better and better each week. For an FA Cup tie at Cardiff in 1972, the coaches were to leave at midnight the night before the game. After a couple of hours in various Leeds pubs, we boarded the bus for the long haul south. A blind man and his son, who were regular travellers, told us that because of heavy rain in Wales the game might have to be postponed. The coach organisers announced that they were waiting for an announcement on the condition of the pitch before setting off. A midnight inspection proved inconclusive. Inspections throughout the night ended with an announcement, at around 5 a.m., that the game was going ahead. Ironically, we had sat on the coach all night. As we headed out of Leeds, Ray took out his whisky flask and tapped it. 'We may have to replenish at the next stop,' he told me.

Other regulars in those days were John Walker from Belle Isle in Leeds and a lad called Paul Taylor, who came from Hunslet. Many girls travelled too, including Colleen Johnson and Chris Harrison from Seacroft. Other stalwarts were Ester, Carol and Maureen. One legend among all Leeds fans, male or female, is a good friend of mine, Heidi. Married to 'The Captain', Heidi is still an ever present to this day.

A nice chap by the name of Phil Beeton also tagged along, and years later he was to marry Chris. The couple are known these days, of course, for their work on the committee of the Leeds United Supporters Club (LUSC). A young man called Eric Carlile was quite an experienced traveller too.

A few years later, a group of us got together and arranged our own travel to away games. From that group two official branches of the supporters club were eventually formed. Richard Binns and John Peckham were instrumental in forming what are now known as the Fullerton Park and Griffin branches. However, I moved on to join up with another group of lads, from deep in the heart of Leeds, who frequented The Viaduct. Another couple of years down the line, of course, saw the Kippax Branch born. Ray Sanderson joined the Fullerton Branch, but we remained good friends and travelled together on many European nights in the late '60s and early '70s. Sadly, Ray passed away a couple of years ago.

Not long after we all went our separate ways, I was driving my dad's work's van round Leeds. With my van fully loaded for the day's deliveries, I happened to pass by the main bus station. There I noticed a coach with a Leeds flag up at the back window. Immediately I investigated: it was the Fullerton Branch. I was told they were heading up to Dundee for that night's friendly. I'd thought it was the night after and planned to travel up in the car with John and Paul. 'Can you wait ten minutes?' I shouted. 'I'm coming with you.' I shot back to the factory in Swinegate and drove straight into the loading bay. One of the other drivers, Pete, said, 'Christ, that was quick.' I explained about going to Scotland and asked where my Dad was. He was my immediate boss at the time and, if he hadn't have been, I would have been out of a job on the spot. He wasn't happy but agreed to let me 'double up' the next day. Within minutes I was on the coach heading for the A1.

I'd met Paul Taylor in 1970 when we'd travelled on the same plane to Oslo for Leeds United's first-ever game in the European Cup. Part-timers SK Lyn Oslo were Leeds' first opponents. We flew out for the second leg with the tie finely poised at 10–0 to Leeds. I had a little bit of stubble on my chin, and I was a little worried as we touched down. My plane ticket, and match ticket for that matter, had me down as a junior, and I'd already had a few funny looks as I checked in back in England. Thankfully, they waved me through; frankly, they seemed more interested in two Leeds players, Terry Hibbitt and Rod Belfitt. There seemed to be some discrepancy with Hibbitt's travel documents, and trainer Les Cocker was with them trying to sort it out. They were still arguing when we walked past them and through Customs. They must have got whatever it was sorted out, because the following evening both players took to the field against the Norwegian outfit. It was almost déjà vu as I'd been to a similar ground months earlier in the FA Cup. Leeds had played another part-time side, Sutton United, in the previous season's fourth round. Although Sutton's ground was slightly larger, there were definite similarities between the two. The incident at the airport had certainly made an impression on Hibbitt and Belfitt, as both players scored twice in front of about 8,000 spectators. Leeds ran out 6–0 winners, ironically the same score as at Sutton the year before.

Over the years, I lost touch with Paul, and so I was amazed when I bumped into him at a recent away fixture at Reading. He now lives near Newbury racecourse and still gets to as many Leeds games as he can.

We reminisced about our times at Elland Road in the '70s. A familiar sight in those days was a line of small turquoise invalid cars beside the pitch. They were situated directly behind the corner flags, and, during one particular game, one of the occupants had to be warned by the police. Every time the opposition were about to take a corner-kick, this occupant would sound his horn. It really was piss funny. Every time, the player involved would turn round and glare at this innocent-looking face peering out through the small windscreen. After the umpteenth time, the police ordered the vehicle away from the corner. As he was driving to his next allocated position, a small group of busmen, who used to congregate underneath the Lowfields/Gelderd floodlight pylon, began wolf whistling and jeering. This resulted in a further defiant blast of the horn from the invalid car. The whole crowd roared with laughter as the sergeant, desperately trying to keep a straight face, wagged his finger at the driver.

The first game of the 1972–73 season was a disaster for the Leeds team and fans alike. Leeds were playing Chelsea at Stamford Bridge, and things weren't going well for us on the pitch. Goalkeeper David Harvey had been injured, and Peter Lorimer had to go in goal. Inevitably, despite a great fight, Leeds went down 4–0. Off the pitch we, the Leeds fans, had to endure our own fight. The Chelsea end was also called the Shed, and, after a barrier gave way, hundreds of the Chelsea fans were allowed to sit and watch the game on the grass verge behind the goal. However, with things on the pitch distracting most people, including the police, the Chelsea fans made their way to our end in small groups. Before long, the police were surprised to discover that hundreds of Chelsea fans were now sitting in front of the wall at our end. Every time Chelsea scored, some of them would jump over the wall and disappear into the crowd. It was not long until they were all mingled in with us. I turned to Stan, who had been standing next to me, and said, 'This is gonna get a bit naughty, mate, watch your back.' To my surprise, a cockney voice answered, 'Too facking right, mate.'

Stan had, surprise, surprise, gone for a burger, and I was now joined by a couple of very nice Chelsea skinheads. Nigel Pashley was on my left, and, before I said anything else, I turned to make sure he was still there. He was, but it wasn't looking good.

Inevitably, I received a smack over the back of the head, but before it had a chance to get really ugly, most of the Leeds fans had managed to form groups and were able to 'escort' our visitors out of our end. The police finally woke up, and the rowdy element were marched back to where they had come from.

THE NEXT GENERATION

In 1974, our beloved Scratching Shed at Elland Road was demolished. I still have a brick from the dearly loved structure at my home. The Shed was replaced by the South Stand. Thousands of Leeds fans made this their end, so, in effect, Leeds fans held both ends of the ground.

There was an occasion, in a 1975 European Cup tie, when the Gelderd End had to ask the South Stand a favour. It was the third round against Anderlecht, and thick fog had descended on Elland Road. It was impossible to see the opposite end of the field, but when the crowd roared at the South Stand end it was obvious that Leeds had scored.

'Who scored? Who scored?' chanted the Gelderd End. 'Super MacQueen! Super MacQueen!' came back the immediate response. We had to watch the goal on TV later, in The Royal Oak taproom. A big fan of the South Stand was the infamous 'Butter' from Kippax. It was at the time of our Lambretta days, and Butter had 'Kippax Scooter Boys' tattooed on one arm and 'South Stand Boys' on the other.

Meanwhile, the Gelderd End was packed to the rafters at every home game. Collar had firmly established himself as 'King of the Kop', and he was the one who was the first to 'split' the Kop into two bodies. On occasion, I would lead the other half, but I was only the reserve: his regular partner was Paul Mathews. They would teeter on the barrier and, with outstretched arms, divide the Kop down the middle. The 'right side' and 'left side' were now ready to follow Collar's instructions. 'We are the Champions! Champions of Europe!' was one of the first songs to benefit from 'stereo'. It wasn't just confined to Elland Road either. One evening, we were on our way home from a game at Anfield and were listening to Radio One on the coach. Suddenly the driver was asked to turn it up. John Peel was on. 'I have just been to watch my beloved Liverpool tonight,' he announced. 'We beat Leeds 3–0, but I have never in my life seen support like it. For almost half an hour, the Anfield Kop was silent as Leeds fans, led by two lads perched on the barrier, bellowed out a chant claiming them to be the "Champions of Europe". It really was quite incredible.' Take a bow Collar and Paul, and God bless John.

By the time Leeds lifted their second League Championship, in 1974, support for Leeds in the Kippax and surrounding areas was growing by the day.

3

Never Take it as Red

It is illegal to own a red car in Shanghai. And we like to think *we're* civilised.

As the title of my previous book would suggest, I love white, but, almost as importantly, I hate red. Let's not beat about the bush: this is purely because it's the preferred colour of manchester united. I am the owner of a small decorating company that refuses to paint anything red. We have painted houses from red to white completely free of charge. Our company stationery declares, 'Red paint removed in an instant'.

This naturally extends into my personal life. I once returned a watch because it had a red second hand. Even Leeds United seem to agree with me. They sold Alan Smith to manchester united, because they discovered that he was red. There are many mysteries in life: why on earth didn't the Sheriff of Nottingham and his men look for Robin Hood in the autumn? How is it possible to become a general in the Kamikaze Army? And, most importantly, how on earth can someone from Yorkshire support manchester united?

I have made it my mission to remove all things red from the world. On one particular assignment, I was with Ian Padgett. Ian is a Jehovah's Witness but a splendid fellow nonetheless. However, he never swears at any time. I once took him to a pub called The Nags Head in Leeds. The pub is now closed, but it was famous for its 'down-to-earth' clientele. Oh, and they swore a lot. He liked the pub very much and we had a laugh, but I must say that his non-swearing approach didn't quite fit in with the regular banter. 'Flippin' 'eck' was lost on most of the regulars, many of whom had never even heard the expression before. When we left the Nag's, not even a 'bloody hell' had passed Ian's lips.

On this particular job, on the outskirts of Leeds, we had arrived to spray a red brick terrace house to a much more suitable shade of white. Because of the nature of paint spraying, many hours were spent masking off the doors and windows and even any cars in the vicinity, if the owners could not be located. One car was parked directly outside the house and, unable to find the driver, we thoroughly covered it in clean dust sheets and masking tape. We were to use a large industrial paint sprayer, into which we poured around ten gallons of white exterior paint. Attached to the machine was a thick, 10-ft-long hose with a spray gun at the other end, which, unbeknown to us, had the valve open. We laid the hose down, stretching it from the pavement, up the garden path, to the front door. Once the machine was filled with paint, Ian flicked the switch to 'on'. Just then we noticed a small kink in the hose close to the machine, and Ian bent down to straighten it out. Suddenly, as he picked up the hose, it began to fill with paint at a quite furious rate. So furious, in fact, that it lifted off the ground, and within seconds it was flying about all over the place like a huge angry snake. As we both frantically grappled with the hose, which by now seemed to have a mind of its own, it reared up and doubled back down the path and headed straight towards the sheeted car. It crashed into the car and, as if truly alive, rose up above it and spewed out gallons of white paint. Luckily, as everything had been covered with sheets, it was just a matter of bringing the beast under control. Easier said than done. With the scene reminiscent of a classic Laurel and Hardy sketch, and with Ian rolling around the floor with the wriggling hose, he completely lost it. And no, it wasn't flippin' 'eck this time. The air was thick with expletives as he belted out words that even made me blush. Effin' and blindin' at the top of his voice, he chased the hose, which now looked like a giant sea serpent gliding up the garden path. I was helpless with laughter and was literally crying as he jumped onto the gun end. After taking a final few spurts of paint in the face, he finally managed to turn off the jet. As the defeated hose lay lifeless, I looked at the house wall and joked, 'Well, at least half of the job is done.' Ian didn't hear me. He was now kneeling in the front garden, with hands clasped, looking up at the heavens. He looked remarkably like Ned Flanders from *The Simpsons*. I gave thanks myself. Now that's what I call 'Painting it White'.

I had another memorable encounter with a hose – this time a fire hose. In December 2003, I was invited by my local fire station to come along and paint one of their gleaming red fire engines – white. Newspaper cameras clicked away, and a crowd gathered as, armed with a tin of white paint and a brush, I began to rid the world of yet more red. Two firemen attempted to stop me as I edged closer. Of course, it was just a publicity stunt. Whisky manufacturers Whyte and Mackay had heard of my exploits concerning the colour red, and, as the sponsors of Leeds United, they thought it would be a good way to promote themselves and the club.

One item of red that I will tolerate is the poppy. For obvious reasons, I feel it necessary to wear a red poppy every year. A white one on this occasion, I feel, would be inappropriate. A very good friend of mine, Demon Barber Kev Higgins, is a prominent member of the Kippax Parish Council, as too are fellow Leeds fans Prem Gunga and Paul Cooper. Recently, at the Remembrance Sunday parade at the cenotaph in Kippax, a crowd gathered to remember those who died for their country. The cenotaph itself stands in its own garden next to the local rugby field. Kev stood alongside the vicar, and dozens of others with heads bowed, as the two minutes' silence began. A minute later, the silence was interrupted when from the adjoining rugby match a loud voice shouted, 'Knock his fuckin' 'ead off!' As Kev struggled to keep a straight face, the vicar whispered in his ear, 'I trust you can have a word in that department, Kevin?'

A big part of my job involves designing and painting wall murals, both inside and outside of buildings. The one ingredient never used, of course, is red paint. One job presented a particularly awkward obstacle. The local dentist's surgery wanted a large mural painted on the walls of the children's crèche area. Postman Pat, complete with his cat and van, was the order of the day. A postman's van is, of course, red. 'This could be tricky,' I thought.

After a couple of days, the mural was almost complete. The van was the only thing that remained to do. My reputation had preceded me, and a small crowd of customers and nurses had gathered to witness me paint the van red. I fiddled around with other bits and generally 'played for time' until the electrician, who was working in a downstairs office, walked in. He looked at the mural and said, 'This is it, yes?' I nodded. With that he opened a tin of red paint, which he had brought with him, and, as he whistled, happily painted in the van. I could hear the disappointed groans from my audience. I had had a word with the electrician the previous day and had asked him to help me out of a potentially embarrassing situation.

Once, I even persuaded my local post office to have their exterior changed from the traditional red to a lovely shade of green. Jurgen and Karen Smith, the owners, were very pleased with the end result. And, of course, it came at a specially discounted rate.

Another time, when I was doing a 70-ft trawler scene on the gable end of Phil Pepper's fish shop in the Kippax high street, I must have heard the words, 'I hope you're not using any red' a million times. Of course I wasn't. And I painted the letters 'LUFC', tucked away discreetly on the ship's main mast, too.

I also do several Leeds United murals on bedroom walls each month, and, although I do undertake to do other teams, I won't if they involve red. One team, of course, is definitely off-limits.

Many Leeds fans, quite rightly, proudly fly the St George's flag alongside Leeds banners at games, and this caused a small problem when I did a large mural at The Viaduct pub in Leeds. The pub is a popular gathering place for Leeds United fans from all over the world. Les Hince, the landlord and a Leeds fan, asked me to paint a Leeds crowd scene on the beer garden wall. Many Leeds lads and lasses brought along photos of themselves and their flags to be included in the mural. Many were of the St George's flag with the Leeds emblem on them, but, as I don't possess any red paint whatsoever, they were quite impossible to execute. I am immensely patriotic and wear a St George's badge but only on 23 April each year. Even without the red of England, the mural did attract quite a lot of media attention both local and national.

The Viaduct beer garden is a smallish area with around a dozen benches and tables on paving stones. One cold day, I was up the ladder painting the mural when I heard the pub door open. As it was cold there was no one in the garden, so I looked round to see who it was. A small woman dressed in scruffy old clothes, and a regular on the streets of Leeds, was standing there. She always wears a dirty old woollen hat and looks like the diminutive comedian of years ago Charlie Drake.

'Hello love,' I said, and carried on with my work. Realising that it had gone very quiet, I looked round again. I was horrified at what I saw. She had dropped her trousers, followed by her extremely large red Y-fronts, and was taking a dump on the ground. I was convinced someone was setting me up, and I scanned the walls for hidden cameras. Then, with her deposit left on one of the paving stones, she walked across to the table where I had placed all my brushes and equipment. She calmly tore off a square of my kitchen roll and, after wiping her backside on it, left it on the table next to my brushes. She then pulled up her old clothes and walked back into the pub. Jo Barrett came running out from behind the bar. She looked down and was almost sick. 'I actually needed a bit of brown to do this bit of shading,' I pointed to the pile on the floor. 'But that's a bit too light.'

With her hand over her mouth, Jo went running back into the pub. Unbelievably, ten minutes later 'Charlie Drake' came out again and attempted to repeat her performance. Thankfully, this time Mally, who works at the pub, intervened, sent her packing and cleaned away her first deposit.

I was once working on a job at a new 12-bedroom house in Collingham on the Leeds-to-Wetherby road. It was a very grand establishment, and working alongside me was Stevie Priestley. Stevie is one of life's real characters, as well as being a Leeds fan, of course. One afternoon, I was working in the lounge of the house, and I called Stevie through from another room. Knowing his sense of humour, I gestured with my head for him to look at the main feature wall above the ornate fireplace. On the newly plastered wall, using my roller and brush, I had painted three pictures. They were cartoons of a girl and a man, a girl and two men, and a girl with a dog, all in what can only be described as compromising positions.

Stevie laughed out loud and, not to be outdone, added a couple of 'accessories'. We left the masterpiece for a couple of hours, and then I began to paint the walls properly. After three coats of emulsion, the cartoons were still showing through, and it took another three coats to completely obliterate the offending 'artwork'.

About a week later, the whole house was complete, and I was showing the new owners, an elderly couple, round to inspect the work we had done. They were very impressed, and I chuckled to myself as they checked out the lounge walls. 'That's a nice shade, I like that,' the man said. 'You would if you saw what was underneath,' I thought to myself. About another week later, the whole place had been carpeted and the couple moved into the their luxurious home.

At 8.30 p.m. the following Monday my phone rang. It was the man from Collingham, asking if I could go to see him as soon as possible? 'Is there a problem?' I asked.

'Just get here as quickly as possible,' was his curt response. I told him I'd come over immediately.

When I arrived, half an hour later, I met the man at the door. I slipped off my shoes, and my feet sank into four inches of lush new carpet. 'Come into the lounge, please,' he said. His wife was sitting on a large leather sofa with a large gin and tonic in her hand. She had a rather stony-faced expression. It was then that I noticed a large cotton bed sheet pinned to the wall over the fireplace. My heart skipped a beat as, not unlike the Queen unveiling a plaque, the man pulled down the sheet. I noticed the woman take a large gulp of her drink as all three of us stared at the wall. My artistic doodles had once again bled through the emulsion, and there, before our very eyes, was a rather explicit orgy. I swear the dog's tail was wagging. I have to admit, it did look quite impressive against a pale violet background, but now wasn't the time to start blowing my own trumpet. Instead, I told him that it must have been one of the labourers messing about when we weren't there. I apologised and assured him I'd rectify it first thing in the morning. After helping him replace the bed sheet for the night, I bade them goodnight.

I returned as promised, and, after a coat of expensive stain block, I repainted the wall.

I assume everything was OK after that as they did not ring me again. But who knows, the masterpiece may have come back, and they decided to keep it as a feature.

My immense dislike of red has kept me on my toes, and never more so than in September 2003. BBC's *Look North* had asked me to go into the studio for a chat about the current situation at Leeds United. The night before, Leeds were at home to Southampton, and Collar, who sits directly in front of me in the Revie Stand, pointed at my nose. He knew of my TV appearance the following night and said, 'You're gonna look lovely if that comes through.' I had felt a slight twinge on my nose all day and was fearful that a spot was beginning to emerge. Apparently, it had already started and was gaining momentum. On the morning of my television appearance, I was confronted in the mirror by a huge boil right on the end of my conk. And it was red! I stormed out of the bathroom, cursing and swearing. Wub was lying in bed reading, and, when she saw it, she broke into fits of giggling. 'Yeah, go on, laugh,' I said. 'I'm gonna look a right twat!' She suggested putting foundation on the hideous manifestation; I replied with an icy stare.

Cheekily, Wub asked if she could tag along and watch the interview from behind the cameras. For some strange reason, I told her she could come. As we entered the BBC's building in Leeds, we were met by the director of the programme who introduced us to a girl with a camera and her assistant. I was conscious of my boil, and all eyes in the reception were focused on it. 'We'd like a few shots of you outside in the gardens first, Gary, if that's OK?' said the girl. I agreed, and we went outside. Most of the shots were taken with me in the shade, and I was convinced that it was done that way to hide the boil, but she never referred to it, except for a couple of stray glances and one or two stifled smiles. Once we were back inside the building, we were shown to a drinks lounge. I was told that the presenters Harry Gration and Christa Ackroyd would be ready for me shortly. A few minutes later, a girl came in and asked, 'Gary, could you follow me to through to make-up?' As I walked with her along the corridor, she noticed my boil but, politely, never mentioned it. Once inside the make-up room, I sat beside Christa Ackroyd, and, without once mentioning my boil, we chatted for a few minutes. She then left to take her place on the set.

Meanwhile, my make-up girl began work on my boil . . . er, face. I broke the silence.

'Is there 'owt you can do with that, love?', indicating my nose in the mirror.

'Oh yes,' she replied instantly. 'No problem. You should have seen Jimmy Saville before I got my hands on him.'

She was right. Fifteen minutes later, my boil was totally invisible, and I was led through into the studio. Wub stood quietly behind the camera as Harry introduced me.

During our conversation, in which Christa called me mad on more than one occasion, I was asked about my Leeds United match-day programme collection. I'd been asked to bring it with me, and many fine examples were laid out on the table in front of us. I was asked if there was a Bradford City programme among them. I fished one out and handed it to Harry. He asked if I would leave my programmes with them, and they would forward them to my home later. I had an idea what it was for. My interview had been pre-recorded in the afternoon, and, as I watched that evening, the magic of television emerged. My interview was shown so that it actually looked as though it was being done live. Immediately after the interview, the camera moved onto Paul Hudson, the weatherman. Paul is about three and a half feet high and, allegedly, once received a thumping from Ken after he was seen dating Barbie. Oh, and he is a Bradford City fan. He was holding the match programme I'd given to Harry Gration that afternoon. Cleverly, the programme gave the impression that I was still in the studio but without actually cutting back to me. After Paul had fired a few insults at Leeds he did his weather report, and then the programme ended. Within minutes, my mobile phone rang. I then received a couple of texts. They were all basically asking the same thing: 'Why didn't you smack the little Bradford git?' I had one hell of a job explaining that it was done in two parts, and, when the final programme was shown, I was watching it at home like the rest of them. I've met Paul on the odd occasion since, and, apart from his Bradford allergy, he's not a bad bloke really.

Some weeks later, I met with Harry Gration again. A handful of Leeds fans had been invited to take part in a television programme. *Leeds United on Trial* was a BBC documentary analysing United's recent fall from grace. The television studio had been set out like a mock courtroom. Harry was the judge presiding over the rights and wrongs of the club's demise. To be truthful, it was all a bit bizarre. Taking part were Martin Kelner, from Radio Leeds, Bill Gerrard, Professor of Sport Management and Finance at Leeds University Business School and dedicated Leeds fan, and, among many others, a journalist from the *Sunday Telegraph* whose name escapes me.

While the programme makers got things set up, which took a couple of hours, we were looked after in the hospitality area with food, hot drinks and beer. One table was covered by dozens and dozens of cans of lager and bitter. The lager was disappearing at top speed, whilst the bitter remained totally untouched. Puzzled by this, the producer enquired why there was a serious lack of interest in the bitter. John Moran gave him his answer: 'It's Boddington's, mate. It's from manchester, we can't be supping that, old mate.' The lads echoed his sentiments, as the last of the lager disappeared. The producer was gobsmacked. 'Man, you boys are keen,' he said, as he returned to his duties.

Minutes later, we were all sitting in the audience. The format was that we would hear the arguments for and against the club, and that would be followed by a question and answer section involving the audience and the 'actors'. We had all been given these stupid cards, a bit like on *Ready Steady Cook*: one was red and one was yellow. We were to hold the relevant colour up as a way of showing which way we voted on each subject. Whatever the question was, I held up my yellow card at all times; my red one had been slyly pushed under my seat. The whole thing went on and on, for over two and a half hours. Despite sterling efforts by the judge, prosecution and defence, the whole concept of the programme just didn't work. I honestly can't even remember what the verdict was.

Before the programme, Stuart Hayward from Kippax, who was, as he put it, 'shitting it about going on telly', had already got his questions ready and when the time came he delivered them perfectly, in spite of his nerves.

Danny 'Willie' Waite was also anxious about broadcasting. A week earlier, Willie was part of a group of Leeds fans invited to take part in a live radio show on BBC Radio Five Live. The panel also included me, Ralph Benson, Simon Jose from the Leeds United Independent Fans' Association, and some members of the Maverick Whites, an unofficial Leeds supporters club and one of the most loyal groups of fans in the country. The *Yorkshire Evening Post* reporter, and Sports Writer of the Year, Paul Dews made up the posse. As we sat round the table at Woodie's pub in Headingley in Leeds, the microphone was passed around so that we could all have our say.

Willie was visibly nervous at the prospect of speaking, and, when the microphone was thrust under his chin, he babbled, live on air, 'Oh, I can't fuckin' do this.'

One morning a parcel arrived at my home. It was from a mate of mine, Billy Burton. Bill is presently serving time in a jail in Manila in the Philippines. He was arrested, and subsequently jailed, for carrying hashish through Customs. I say, 'through Customs', but, in fact, he never reached Customs. He was stopped and searched before he even reached that point. Bill is a survivor of thalidomide, which makes it even more strange. Despite the fact that Bill is one of my very best friends, I firmly believe that others, whom he never saw again, used him as a decoy. I'm not for one minute condoning what Bill did, and, more importantly, neither is he. No one realises more than Billy that what he did was wrong and foolish, but he has now been in jail since 1992.

I opened my parcel: it contained a T-shirt. A very brightly coloured T-shirt. Dare I say, it was almost red! It wasn't quite red, but it was a very bright orange. I began reading the letter that accompanied the shirt. It was as if Bill had read my thoughts. It began, 'Here's a T-shirt for you, Snake, it's a genuine prison issue, and no, it's not red!' I held it up. On the front it said, 'Maximum Inmate' and on the back, 'Bureau of Corrections. NBP'. I liked it, despite its dazzling orange colour. I carried on reading the letter:

> Today is Boxing Day. It's ten years to the day since I got nicked. Life's much the same here and yesterday, Xmas Day, it kicked off. Two gangs had a shoot-out (not penalties) and three blokes were killed. It went off at midday when the place was full of visitors. When order was restored all the visitors had to leave early. Tell you what, Snake, it's not like in the movies, when they're shot they don't jump around for five minutes, they go down like a sack of shit. Today no visitors were allowed in and they won't be until the guns are handed in. Both sides deny having weapons but there are three corpses in the hospital with fatal bullet wounds . . .

The letter went on for another five pages. It was clear that, despite his incarceration, Bill still hadn't lost his sense of humour. To mark the Millennium, the King of Thailand pardoned many rapists, muggers, murderers, paedophiles and arsonists. There was no such similar reprieve for anyone connected with drugs in any way in the Philippines. Back in 1992, we had hoped that Billy would do, possibly, just a few months of a sentence – or, at the most, a couple of years. But there is, as yet, no sign of parole, and there are fears that he may have to do his full sentence of 20 years. John Wade, a good friend of Billy's, went to visit him during Christmas 2003 and has campaigned tirelessly to secure Bill's release for the past 13 years: maybe one day he will succeed.

Another letter from Bill was quite astonishing. In it he wrote about a gang member who wanted to join the Leeds United Supporters Club. It went like this:

> I think I told you before that this place is run by about nine gangs. The largest is called Sigue Sigue Sputnik and the commander is called Amado Ateinza. The authorities don't make any changes without first consulting him. He's very powerful, dangerous, loyal and insane. Luckily I've become a firm friend of his and after telling him all about my travels watching Leeds United, he wants to affiliate his gang with LUSC. I've been to his place (cell) and after a smoking session have watched him play Russian Roulette with a .22 Magnum Revolver. This bloke has killed 15 people while he's been in here and apparently he drinks the blood of his victims. He's got a Polaroid camera so I'll get him to send you a photo of his armoury.

I've still to send in Mr Ateinza's application to the Supporters Club. Somehow, I can't see Sigue Sigue Sputnik, with their vast armoury of weapons and booze, blending in with the Fullerton Park or Griffin Branches.

Quite frankly, I don't even think the prison guards themselves would gain club membership. In another letter, Bill wrote:

> I recently bought a bottle of gin off one of the guards and me and him and two other prisoners drank it one night in my cell. The style of drinking here is that you have a shot of gin

> followed by a shot of water and you continue around the table until the bottle is empty. By the time we were three-quarters down our bottle, the guard was shit faced, stripped to the waist and he gave me his gun because he didn't trust himself.

No, I think I'll hang onto those membership applications a while longer.

Strangely enough, hating red as I do has actually resulted in me saving a few bob. One Monday night we were away at West Ham. Four hours after a resounding 3–0 defeat, Stewart 'Webby' Webb and I walked into my house. As he was working with me the next morning, he slept at my house. I wanted to go to bed, as it was around 2 a.m. Webby declined the offer to sleep in the spare room and, instead, opted to kip on the settee downstairs. I went straight upstairs. 'I'll just watch a bit of telly,' Webby said, opening a can of lager. I got into bed next to our lass, but, after about 20 minutes, I began coughing really badly. Thirty years of being in the painting and decorating business means that I have to use inhalers now and again. After using them I wasn't much better, so I went into one of the other bedrooms to let Wub get some sleep. I was just about drifting off when I heard Webby come running up the stairs. 'Snake! Snake!' he shouted.

'In here,' I told him.

He came in and shouted, 'The Leeds plane has crashed, Snake – with all the players on it!' I jumped up with my mouth open, but I couldn't speak. I began to asphyxiate really badly. I was gasping for air. I wanted to ask him if the players were dead, but I couldn't speak. I couldn't breathe. 'What's up with you?' asked Webby.

I scrambled for my inhaler and took a gulp of air, but it didn't make any difference. 'Get our lass,' I managed to squeak.

She came in and put a pillow up behind me. All the while, Webby stood in the doorway staring at me. I was getting worse when the emergency doctor arrived. He immediately gave me two steroid tablets and offered me a big, green inhaler, which eased my breathing considerably. All I could think about was the Leeds players.

'The Leeds United team have been in a plane crash, haven't they?' I asked the doctor.

'I couldn't tell you sir, I was in bed,' he said, writing a prescription.

I apologised for dragging him out, and then, seeing I was much better, he left some tablets on the bedside table and said, 'Take two of these if it starts again before morning. Good night.'

As soon as he'd left the house, I shouted Webby up. 'Well?' I said, 'What's happened? Are they all dead?'

'Oh no,' he said calmly, 'they didn't actually crash, well they did, well not really . . .'

'Fuckin' 'ell, Webby!' I shouted, starting to cough again. 'What happened?'

He proceeded to tell me all about what he'd seen on the late news and explained that everyone was all right.

Apparently, the pilot, Captain John Hackett, had performed heroics by bringing the stricken plane down safely after one of its engines caught fire. The right engine of the Emerald Airways British Aerospace 748 exploded 150 ft up, and Captain Hackett crash-landed the plane, leaving its nose digging into the runway. Speaking to reporters afterwards, Captain Hackett said, 'This was not just an engine fire. There was an explosion with the real possibility the wing could catch fire.' He added, 'My heart went out to Leeds. They have my support for the future.' Captain Hackett singled out Leeds assistant manager David O'Leary for helping with the evacuation, along with his crew, Gary Lucas, Helen Dutton and Nicola Mee. The club showed its gratitude, a couple of weeks later, by presenting an award to the captain in front of a packed and very grateful Leeds crowd.

The very next day I phoned Peter Houghton, known to Leeds fans as 'Pete the Badgeman'. He was the big fat bloke who always used to sell badges, T-shirts and scarves out of the back of his Volvo in The Peacock car park. Sadly, Pete died in January 2005 after a massive heart attack.

'It's Gary from the Kippax, Pete. I want some T-shirts doing,' I told him.

'OK, mate, write down what you want, and bring it to the next home game,' he replied.

Next time I saw him, I handed him my piece of paper. 'I want 50 T-shirts with this on, please, old mate.' The piece of paper said, 'SAS – Stansted Air Survivors. God Bless Leeds United. SAS Elite'.

'No problem, mate,' said Pete. 'Ring me next week.'

The following week, I had to meet Pete to pick up the T-shirts. I met at him at his 'office', the Florence Nightingale pub across from Jimmy's (St James's) hospital in Leeds. He handed me a bin liner stuffed with white T-shirts. I took one of them out to look at it. It was brilliant. I had a pint with him, paid him and left.

Over the next week the T-shirts were distributed among the lads; they were all impressed. A week later Wub and me set off for a few days in Southport. Whilst there, we decided to spend a day in Liverpool. At lunchtime, we went into a pub for something to eat. I had my SAS shirt on, and, after we'd sat down, Wub asked, 'Have you seen your T-shirt?'

I looked down. 'Yeah, good, innit?' I said proudly.

'It's spelt wrong,' she said.

I looked again. 'What's wrong with it?' I said.

'How do you spell survivors?' she asked, smugly.

I looked again. There was only one 'v'. It read, 'Stansted Air Surviors'. I was absolutely gutted. Without eating in the pub we returned swiftly to our hotel. It was trivial, but I did feel really gutted. I rang 'Big' John Martin back in Leeds. 'John, it's me. Have you seen your SAS T-shirt?' I asked.

'Not half,' he replied proudly. 'I'm looking at it right now out of the kitchen window: it's on the washing line. This is one of your better ideas, Edwards,' he added.

'John, it's spelt wrong.' Silence. 'Hello John?' Silence. Over the phone I heard a muffling sound. John had picked up again.

'Where? I can't see it,' he said. He had the T-shirt in his hand. Before I could tell him, he said, 'Surviors?' He was really pissed off. 'I've been all over the place wearing it, and nobody's even noticed. Including me!'

'Leave it with me,' I said. 'I'll ring Pete. See you later.'

This is where the reference to red comes in. Thanks for staying with it. 'You're joking!' said Pete, when I told him over the phone.

'Sorry Pete, it's spelt wrong. I must admit though, I didn't spot it.'

'It can't be, Gary,' Pete went on. 'I did it from that paper you gave me, I've got it here somewhere, hang on.' I heard a rustling of paper. 'Yes, here it is, it's in your writing, mate – red writing.' What Pete said sank into our respective brains simultaneously. He was first with a response. 'Bollocks!' he said, realising his mistake. 'I'll have you a new batch on Monday.' God bless you Pete, we'll miss you, pal.

Her Majesty the Queen does not seem to have the same dislike of red as I do. I'm still a massive fan of hers, but when she gave Alex Ferguson a knighthood, a few years back, my huge painting of her was banished to the cupboard. I felt sure that she would never be as stupid again. How wrong can one be? She'd only been out of the cupboard for five minutes when she gave David Beckham an OBE. I was cross beyond belief. It was obvious that she just hadn't learned her lesson. There was nothing more for it; I had to put pen to paper. I told her, in no uncertain terms, how terribly disappointed I was in her. A week later, a letter from Buckingham Palace dropped through my front door. It read, 'Dear Mr Edwards, I have been instructed by Her Majesty the Queen to thank you for your letter regarding Mr Beckham. Such decisions however are made at Downing Street . . .' I couldn't believe it. She was passing the buck. The letter ended by informing me that my letter had been passed on to Tony Blair. About another week later, a letter duly arrived from Downing Street. In it Tony Blair defended his ludicrous action by insisting, 'I feel that to award David Beckham with the OBE was the correct decision at this time.' I thought about what he had written: 'correct decision at this time'. I wondered if that meant that it could be taken away from him at any time. I live in hope.

Anyway, as if any further proof were needed that all things red are inferior: who is Captain Scarlet's boss? Answer: Colonel White. 'Nuff said.

4

Up, Up and A-Wahey!

> Often, when I'm watching the safety routine by the cabin crew, I imagine that we've crash landed in the sea and that the whistle I hear is that of the referee, Ray Tinkler. I am then able to suitably 'thank him' for robbing Leeds United against West Brom in 1971.

I've been on one or two dodgy flights in my time. The first time I ever flew to watch Leeds play, in Dublin back in 1988, remains fresh in my memory. The gale force winds did not make it a pleasurable flight, but it was only a taste of things to come.

Ten years later, Leeds played a pre-season friendly against German side Wolfsburg. We had decided to make Hannover our base and all gathered in the 'Yorkshireman Bar' at Leeds Airport. I remember not really being happy about where our luggage seemed to be going, but I thought to myself, 'They know what they're doing; go and have a beer, it'll be OK.' When the time came to board our aircraft, everyone was in high spirits, and we settled down for the relatively short flight to Germany. I was sat near the front with our lass, Lesley, and Jeff. We noticed that a lot of the cabin crew seemed particularly anxious, and about half an hour later we still hadn't moved. Eventually, the plane made its way to the runway for take-off. It just didn't seem right as we hurtled down the runway at what couldn't have been more than 50 or 60 mph. Then the plane slowed down even more and began heading back towards the terminal. The captain assured us that everything was OK, but a further check on one of the plane's engines was required. You could actually hear arses nipping. We parked up, the door opened and a couple of mechanics with spanners got on board. We then sat there in disbelief, as a bloke climbed on board with a sweeping brush. The cockpit door was open, and everyone at the front of the aircraft watched as, one by one, the mechanics and the bloke with the brush all offered their opinion as to what was the problem. Our lass almost fainted as the bloke with the brush leant on it, pointed towards the dashboard and simply said, 'What about that button there, do we know what that is?' One of the spanner men told him what it was, so the brush man said, 'Well what about that one, then, have you tried that one?' A cleaner then joined them. I say 'cleaner' because he still had yellow rubber gloves on. It looked as though he had been called away just when he was halfway through cleaning the toilets. He stared for a while at the controls before offering his theory. This fiasco went on for about 15 minutes. Then came the captain's voice again: 'Sorry for the delay, ladies and gentlemen, we don't think it's anything too serious; we're going to have another go. Please make sure your tables are up and your seat belt is securely fastened.'

Now call me an old sceptic, but when you can clearly see sweat dripping from the foreheads of the cabin crew it is time to worry.

The spanner men and the brush man got off, waved at us and then the door closed.

I likened the silence that followed to that at Hampden Park in 1970 when Billy Bremner scored that tremendous equaliser against Celtic in the European Cup semi-final.

I held Wub's hand. 'Well, it's been a good laugh,' I said. 'See you on the other side.' The plane was making exactly the same noises as it had done before, as we again made our way down the runway. Fortunately, readers, we headed back to the terminal once more. This time we were told to disembark. We were given a free breakfast and a couple of beers, and then we boarded a different plane and took off without any problem. Apart from our luggage. That went on a quick trip around Europe before being delivered to our hotel, in Hannover, at about midnight.

We had quite a pleasant stay in Hannover: the last time we had been there was in 1969, and a lot had changed since then. On match day, we had to travel by train to Wolfsburg. Wub decided to have a stroll around the shops in Hannover, as opposed to going to the game. As we all converged on the railway station, I had a quick word with Jeff Verrill. He had been learning to speak German, and this was his big chance to make an impact. He spent 15 minutes asking the girl behind the counter which train we needed to be on. He may as well have been speaking Swahili. Eventually, amidst fits of laughter from everyone, the girl told us, in perfect English, which train to board.

As we arrived at the stadium, in glorious sunshine, we made our way to the nearest bar. Little Mick Hewitt told us that some of the lads were getting in free with their Leeds United membership cards. Apparently, the stewards thought we were all officials with the club, and a quick glance at the cards resulted in easy access to the ground. Typically, I had left my card in the hotel room. All was not lost, however, and, after a few more beers, I got in free using my Garforth Liberal Club card.

Inside the ground it was still really hot, and a gorgeous German girl stood chatting with us. She was wearing a Wolfsburg shirt, but not for long. Suddenly, she whipped it off over her head to reveal a rather fetching leather bra. Lunge's eyes nearly popped out of his head. Within seconds, he had had taken off his shirt, and the happy couple exchanged shirts. The girl definitely got the best out of the deal. The Wolfsburg shirt was a sickly lime-green colour and really brought the best out of Lunge's complexion.

The worst thing that can happen to an aeroplane is for it to be struck by lightning – or so they say. During a flight to Portugal – for the Inter-Cities Fairs Cup game against Vitoria Setubal, just before Christmas in 1973 – I was sitting between Mick Collins and John Walker when our plane was struck by lightning. The aircraft swung violently from side to side, and the lights flickered on and off. The plane then dropped what seemed like hundreds of feet. Mick looked at me and simply said, 'I don't like this, mate.' I don't think I answered him. John also sat there in silence. Eventually the plane began climbing and everything seemed to be fine. We were then hit again, but it was nowhere near as bad as the previous time. I think it was just a warning from the 'Man upstairs' that lightning can strike twice.

A similar thing happened on a flight to Zurich for a pre-season friendly in 1979. A flash of lightning struck the side of the aircraft, and the plane swung briefly out of control. A constant travelling companion at the time, Brod, said, 'I wonder if it's too late to order another large whisky?' A sudden drop in cabin pressure prompted me to order the same.

Recently, I was returning home from my favourite haunt: Key West in Florida. While there, we'd had a few drinks with a big Leeds fan who has lived in Key West for nearly 25 years. Perry Ferguson, originally from north Leeds, still follows Leeds whenever he can. In fact, during that distant memory of Champions League football in 2002, he managed to get to every game in Europe.

We spent our final night of the holiday in Kissimmee, to be near the airport for our departure. There were four of us, and we ended up in a sports bar. Spoon and Ste were playing pool, as Wub and I sat sharing a large pitcher of beer. 'It's been another good trip, Wub,' I said, as we raised our glasses. Just then a girl came in with her boyfriend. They were English, and she immediately noticed the Leeds shirts that Ste and I were wearing. She'd had a fair amount to drink and began singing, 'Leeds fans here! Leeds fans there! Leeds fans every fuc . . .' Her boyfriend slapped his hands over her mouth, and she slumped to the nearest chair. The two of them were Leeds fans from Wakefield. She then said, 'Have you seen the scum bastard?' Ste came over. We both instantly knew who she was talking about. Only a month earlier, Alan Smith had committed the cardinal sin of signing for manchester united. But surely he wasn't here? In America? In Kissimmee?

'He fuckin' is!' she slurred. 'We saw him earlier in a hotel bar, he was signing autographs for some scumbags.' She looked at her chap. 'He was, wont 'e?'

He nodded. 'Aye he's here, alright, the little shit.'

Ste and I spent the rest of the evening looking for him, but the main drag in Kissimmee is ten miles long, and the chances of bumping into him were remote. We never saw him, and I'm kind of glad we didn't, really.

About 15 years ago, I remember watching a programme on television about young footballers at the Lilleshaw Academy. One of the youngsters was Alan Smith. He was a trainee at Leeds, and, as they interviewed him in his room, he was crying. He was homesick and wanted to go home. He was also wearing a white football shirt. A white Liverpool shirt, that is. I'd never forgotten that moment, and, throughout his career at Elland Road, I'd always had a deep mistrust of him. Don't get me wrong: I, too, had been carried away with the euphoria of our home-grown hero. I remember chanting his name for about four hours in a bar in Munich, after he'd just scored our winner against 1860 Munich. Now I feel so dirty.

We'd forgotten all about Smith as we pulled up at the airport the next day. I just couldn't believe the thunderstorms that greeted our arrival. I have never witnessed lightning, both fork and sheet, like it, and the crashing thunder was like something out of a Hollywood movie. The flight was delayed for about an hour, after which it was deemed safe enough to 'have a crack at it'. I kissed the Leeds United badge on my shirt, and we took off with lightning going off all around us. A dull thud was followed by a loud crash on the left of the aircraft, and then, on the right, we were treated to a massively bright illumination that lit up the whole plane. The cabin lights flickered off and on at random. After about half an hour or so, the captain informed us that we had 'got over the worst of the storm' and that things should be OK from now onwards. Fortunately, things were OK but only after he informed us that we had taken a 200-mile detour to avoid the worst of the bad weather. He also told us that, the very second we took off, we were hit smack on the nose by a massive bolt of lightning – that was the thud we had heard – and that we were escorted for 100 miles by constant thunder and lightning. Interestingly, the captain told us that lightning itself doesn't pose such a major problem. I think the blood trickling from my hand where Wub had been squeezing it told a different story.

Russian aircraft aren't particularly famous for their safety record, and I can certainly undertand why. I've travelled with Aeroflot, Russia's flagship carrier, and to describe them as basic is a massive understatement. To be fair, I never felt in any danger – apart from the clouds trying to sneak in through a crack in the ceiling – but the whole experience was, let's just say, 'economical'. There was no in-flight entertainment whatsoever and very little cabin service.

Not long after we'd been to Japan with them, an Aeroflot flight crashed, killing everyone on board. It was later discovered that the pilot had allowed a young boy to take the controls. The plane immediately nose-dived, and, despite frantic efforts, it could not be brought back under control. Many of the passengers may well have been dead before impact. Dead from either starvation or boredom.

In the 2002 UEFA Cup, Leeds met FC Mertalurh from the Ukraine. It was here that I was to have yet another dramatic flying experience. Our flight from the UK was from Gatwick to Kiev, and, originally, our organiser, big Mick Hewitt, had planned for us to travel by train from Kiev to Dnepr overnight, and then by coach to Zaporizhzhya, where the game was to be played. Overall, this journey would have taken something like 18 hours – one way. It was decided that the best way to reach our destination was by air. So we chartered a flight to take us, instead of enduring the gruelling trip overland.

The Ukraine was nothing like I expected, and the Western style of their culture was a real eye opener. Kiev is a beautiful city, and we spent two nights there before our plane trip. As you'd expect, 'ladies of the night' were prominent, and it didn't take some of our lads too long before they became acquainted. An absolute stunner approached Robbie in the hotel bar, and, within minutes, the two of them disappeared upstairs. Half an hour later they both returned, and, as his girlfriend moved towards another client, Robbie gave us all the details. 'She was something else!' he said. 'She will do anything. We were doing "doggy fashion" when all of a sudden she poured a glass of water down her back and onto my manhood. It was heaven!' Danny 'Willie' Waite was listening intently. I noticed him glance over at the girl, and, within seconds, he had moved in, and they too had disappeared upstairs. Half an hour later they returned.

The girl once again began mingling with potential clients and, as with Robbie, Willie sat down to tell us all about his 'exercise'. However, he wasn't nearly as enthusiastic as Robbie. In fact, he was a little pissed off. 'What's up?' asked Jeff. 'Wasn't she any good?'

Willie still seemed a bit upset, 'Yeah, she was alright.'

Robbie interrupted, 'Did she do the glass of water thing?'

Willie replied, 'Oh yeah, she did that, well nearly.' We hung onto his every word. 'I asked her to wear my new Leeds shirt, the white one.' So far, so good.

'Go on then!' he was urged.

'Well, we were doing the doggy and she poured a glass all down the back of my shirt, but it wasn't water: it was bleedin' Coca-Cola! It's fuckin' ruined. Bitch!' We were still laughing about it when we reached the airport the next day to fly to Zaporizhzhya.

I must say, though, I use the term 'airport' very loosely indeed. It was a very small airfield with a small building for Customs and a small bar to purchase a large bottle of the local brew. As we passed through a small X-ray device, which seemed to be home-made, the alarm, predictably, sounded. I was carrying my large glass bottle of beer through, so I apologised, and placed it on the table at the side. The attendant said, 'No, no.' He came over and pointed to my belt. I removed my belt and put it on the table. He put the beer back in my hand, and I passed through safely. Then, we all walked outside and immediately came face to face with our 'transport'. It was a very small aircraft, and the outside of it was covered in small repairs. One of the propellers seemed to be fastened on with industrial string. The small steps creaked as we all nervously boarded 'Budgie', so named, by one of the lads, after Sarah Ferguson's children's character: only this Budgie sported several large bandages and plasters. A man, in old overalls, casually pumped up one of the tyres with what seemed to be an ordinary bicycle pump, whilst smoking a large cigarette.

It all seemed quite unreal, as we sat in our seats. The whole of the inside had an unpleasant odour: it was as if it had been parked up, unused, for 50 years. There was no staff around. No pilot. No stewards. The walls were covered in an old anaglypta-type wallpaper (about £1 a roll back home) and painted in a light shade of blue. Grubby net curtains hung over the small round windows. More worrying was a dirty brown carpet that lay in the aisle. It wasn't fastened down at all, and it was almost threadbare. I took a drink of beer, as did many of the others. I had never seen anything like it in my life. Just then the pilots arrived: they walked the very short journey to the front and locked themselves in the cockpit. A stewardess then arrived and sat down at the back without saying a word.

At this point, the engine started. It was an eerie, loud whining noise that gradually turned into a deafening growl. Then that was it; we were in the air. No safety talks, no information, no nothing. Only a couple of the seats had seat belts and even fewer had a table. I just had two rusty hinges in front of me indicating where a table had once been mounted – many years previously. About half an hour into the flight, we heard a loud squeaking noise. The drinks trolley had arrived. The stewardess struggled to push it over the brown carpet, which constantly rode up as she trundled down the aisle. Occasionally, she asked one of the lads to put their foot onto the carpet, so she could push the trolley more easily. The 'drink' consisted of a large silver flask containing coffee. No milk. No sugar. No tea. No food. No smile. However, to be honest, when we came down three hours later, it was one of the smoothest landings I had ever encountered.

Once inside the stadium, we had a weird experience. Leeds fans, many still clutching large bottles of beer, were in high spirits under the watchful eye of the very large and serious-looking police contingent. At half-time, I was standing chatting to Chris 'Poison' Archer and Ralph Benson, when Willie arrived bawling his eyes out: he really wasn't having the best of trips. It was reminiscent of the advert where Gazza is shooting out large tears, because that big-eared git Gary Lineker has nicked his crisps.

'What's up, mate?' I asked. He was inconsolable.

'I've just been for a piss, Snake, and these coppers came in after me.' He was still crying.

'What did they do?' Ralph asked. 'Have they hit you?'

'Worse than that: they were going to shag me!'

'What?' I shouted. 'What happened?'

'They just came in; there was only me and four of them.'

'I've told you before, Willie, never go near the law on your own,' I said to him.

'They had me up against the wall and told me what they were gonna do,' he continued, 'when a group of Leeds fans walked in, and the coppers went out of the other door.'

'Bastards!' said Poison. And then, in typical Poison fashion, he joked, 'Are you alright to sit down?'

'The bastards didn't do owt,' sniffed Willie. I gave him a swig of my beer, and he soon calmed down. Another lesson learned, I suppose.

Willie is currently working his way around Australia for a few months, and I was recently talking to his dad Paul in The Viaduct. I asked him how Willie was getting on. 'Oh, he's alright,' his dad said.

'The other night we were woken up at around four in the morning. "G'day, mate!" this Aussie voice shouted. "I'm a chef, and I've got your boy, Willie, here. I'm ringing to ask you how to make Yorkshire puddings."' Willie's dad handed his mam the receiver and she gave the recipe down the phone to a stranger, in the middle of the night, thousands of miles away.

Willie is also an admirer of the Queen, and this almost got him arrested recently. He had taken a taxi back to his hostel, and, on hearing Willie's English accent, the Aussie taxi driver began insulting Her Majesty. Willie listened intently, and, when he arrived at his destination, he produced a $5 note to pay his fare. On the note is a picture of the Queen, and Willie seized the driver and forced him to kiss her face before he would release him. The concierge had to intervene, and the taxi sped off into the night.

One time, we were all sat on quite a small plane waiting to fly to Sofia for Leeds' UEFA Cup game against Spartak Moscow. There was a slight delay before we began taxiing down the runway. Suddenly, Nick Marsh jumped up and began shouting for the cabin crew to let him off. Nick has flown all over the world with us, but, on this occasion, he became very claustrophobic and had to get off the aircraft. Half an hour later they removed his bag, and we left without him.

Usually, cabin crews are up for a bit of banter. We've had some great laughs over the years, and, as long as you know when to toe the line, things tend to run pretty smoothly. That's not to say there haven't been incidents that have got slightly out of hand. Once, on the return flight from a UEFA Cup game in Eindhoven, one of our party thought he'd liven things up. I was chatting away to Jeff about why his mother had packed him two pairs of shorts for the short trip to Holland, when, suddenly, we heard a hissing sound. I looked round just in time to see a large, inflated yellow life jacket take up the entire row behind us, knocking drinks and food from the tables. The cabin crew weren't amused, and the culprit was taken away and lectured. Big Mick moved in to defuse the situation, and the lad was allowed to return to his seat. But, when we landed at Stansted airport, nobody was allowed to leave, as the police boarded the aircraft. The culprit was led away by four armed officers. Luckily, after explaining the situation, our man was released without charge, but not before spending a night at Her Majesty's pleasure.

5

Five Go Mad in Norfolk

> Cinderella was from Great Yarmouth, so I always thought that the Norfolk Broads were Cinderella's ugly sisters.

In 1987, under the guidance of manager Billy Bremner, Leeds just missed out on promotion from the old Second Division, losing to Charlton in the promotion play-off final at Birmingham. John Sheridan had put Leeds in front in the second half of extra time, but Lady Luck conspired against Leeds once again, and Charlton scored twice in the dying minutes. To add to the disappointment, Leeds were also beaten in the semi-final of the FA Cup after extra time, losing 3–2 to Coventry City at Hillsborough.

Feeling deflated, I thought it best to whisk the family away on holiday. We invited Stuart, Wub's eleven-year-old brother, along as company for Spoon and headed for the exotic Norfolk Broads, armed with four dozen cans of Skol Special Strength and ten demijohns full of home-made strawberry wine.

I remember making my very first home-brew. It was whilst I was still living at home, and I had stored about 20 bottles of beer in the downstairs toilet. Every time I used that toilet I would look at all the bottles that had, previously, been filled with Dandelion & Burdock. I would smile proudly, like a new father, as the bottles of fermenting beer all bubbled away happily. One day, I came home from work to find all the bottles had gone. Almost catching my snake in my zip, I rushed out. 'Ma! Ma!' I cried. 'Where's all me beer?'

'Oh,' she said, casually drying her hands near the sink, 'I threw them out with the bin-men this morning. They've been there ages; I didn't think you still wanted them.'

I fell to my knees, with my head in my hands.

That painful memory was well out of mind as I returned to my boat duties. The last time I had been in that neck of the woods was almost a year before. Leeds had been thumped 4–0 by Norwich City at Carrow Road – I was looking for a better result on my holiday. As Wub finished packing, I laid my Leeds United flag neatly over the clothes. She tutted and zipped up the case. 'That flag will look great on the mast,' I assured her. She seemed to ignore the fact that this, the specially made Kippax Branch Leeds flag, was a very cherished item and that each member had to swear to defend it with his last breath. To this day that flag travels all over the world and Europe. This is because Collar left it on the plane in Barcelona in 1992.

We also took our dog Cybil, who was only ten months old, and, just to break the journey up, she pissed on Stuart as she sat on his knee in the back. When we eventually arrived at the Broads, an old fisherman-type character showed us round our 'home' for the next week. Pointing to a lever at the side of the boat, he told me, 'Push it this way for forward and this way for reverse.' Simple. I almost pushed the old chap over the side as I said, 'Right, got it. Thank you, goodbye.' Two hours into our adventure, and with the rest of my crew downstairs watching *Neighbours*, I decided to see what the baby could do. With my trusty old flag flying high, and with my Leeds hat firmly on my head, I cracked open a can of Skol Special and opened the throttle. This was great. 'Slow down,' Wub shouted.

'Shut up! I'm the captain,' I retorted.

Two minutes later, I was flanked by a police boat. 'Slow down, sir,' an officer ordered through his loudhailer. I hate it when she's right.

'Sorry, mate,' I shouted back. He noticed my Leeds flag flying from the mast.

'Bad luck on Leeds this season,' he acknowledged.

'Yes,' I replied. 'We'll get there.'

'Yes, I'm sure you will too, as long as you slow down.'

The officer then spun his boat and went off in the other direction. Cybil, who was on deck fastened to a long piece of rope, barked at him as he disappeared out of sight.

There's nowt to this boat-driving lark, I thought to myself, as I continued up river.

About 15 minutes later I spied a small craft coming towards me. It didn't seem to be making any attempt to get out of my way. In fact, a man in it was waving his arms and shouting something at me. I was bigger than him so I gestured back with an arm signal to tell him to 'get out of the fuckin' way'. Within seconds I hit him and smashed him into the river. As I sailed past him, he was bobbing up and down in the water. It was then that I realised what he had been shouting at me: 'Give way to sail'. Apparently, motor boats must give way to non-powered crafts such as the one I had just trashed. I pulled my Leeds hat down and sailed away from the crime scene. Wub came up and asked what all the fuss was about. 'Oh, some tosser on the wrong side of the road,' I said. She arrived just in time to see the irate figure, waving his fists in the air, disappear over the horizon. As she began to descend the stairs back to her TV, she looked up and said, 'Oh, Gary, look.' I followed the line of her outstretched finger and saw Cybil at what we seafarers call the 'Pointed End'. The excitement had been all too much for our little pooch. She was squatting down and having a shit.

I was beginning to get a bit bored going in, more or less, a straight line and was therefore happy to see a sign that said, 'Wroxham 2 miles'. I shouted downstairs that we would be stopping soon for lunch. As we approached the centre of Wroxham, I noticed a bridge up ahead. Wub and the rest of my crew came up. Wub had already seen the bridge. 'Be careful, that looks a bit tight,' she warned.

'That little old thing is no match for Captain Birds Eye here,' I said smugly. However, as I looked around, I saw quite a number of other boats in the same area. 'This could be a bit tricky,' I said to myself, as my crew disappeared back below deck with Stuart muttering, 'I don't want to see this.'

I slowed down as best I could using my throttle, but the arse end of the boat began to spin around. 'Fasten yourselves in!' I shouted. 'This could get messy.' The harder I tried to slow down, the faster the boat spun. It was now going round in huge circles, as a crowd began to gather on the bridge. As they pointed and laughed at this mad Leeds fan, the boat spun so fast it threw Cybil straight into the water. Her little legs were paddling like hell as, still attached to the rope, she tried desperately to keep up. I was getting fairly angry by now: even more so when two chaps pulled alongside me. They were your posh types. Leather elbows and corduroys. One of them, with hands cupped around his mouth, shouted, in a frightfully posh voice, 'Your dog's fallen in the water.' That was it: I exploded.

'I fuckin' know, you daft twat!' I shouted back at him. They left the scene promptly, and I spied a gap near the bank. 'That's it,' I muttered, 'I'm parking up.'

I tied the boat up as my crew, trying not to laugh, disembarked, and we retired to the nearest pub. The next morning at 6 a.m., with my crew still in bed and no audience on the bridge, I sailed straight under it, no problem. It was a glorious day, as I sailed peacefully into the early sun. Spoon was the first to rise and brought me a nice cup of tea. The day before, we had stocked up with food to cook a breakfast, so I was on the lookout for a nice little picnic spot. As Wub basked on the pointed end (we'd cleaned Cybil's little deposit up), with her nose in a book, I spied a perfect spot to park up. Stuart was driving, and, as he steered the boat towards some bushes at the riverbank, we both realised he was going a tad fast. Seconds later, the front of the boat and Wub disappeared under a large bush. She surfaced seconds later with her hair looking like she'd put her fingers into a light socket. Branches and twigs slowly fell from her shoulders, as she stood up. I noticed a leaf still tucked behind her ear, as we tucked into our bacon and eggs. Thinking it best not to mention it, I looked at the map to plan the day's events. 'This Rockingham place sounds nice; it's got a riverside pub that does Sunday lunch,' I suggested, and no one argued. It looked really idyllic as we pulled alongside the banking and headed into the pub for lunch.

A couple of hours later, we were lounging on the boat, basking in the mid-afternoon sun. Wub and Stuart were playing cards at the back of the boat, and Spoon was stretched out on the roof. I was lying down at the pointed end reading the Sunday paper, with a cup of tea, and listening to radio commentary of Yorkshire v. Northants in the cricket final at Lord's. Yorkshire won the final, and I was feeling good. Then, the serenity was abruptly interrupted by a large splash.

Spoon had fallen into a deep sleep and rolled over, straight off the boat into the river. I was helpless with laughter, as I fished her soaked body out of the water. 'That's two of you that's been in the drink now,' I said, as Cybil wagged her tail.

On our final day we had planned to sail into Great Yarmouth. People we had spoken to had said it was possible, but it did require a fair bit of skill to undertake the strong current. After due consideration, and a check on my mariner's skills, we decided to go by car. It was our last day on the boat, and I was very sad when I lowered the Leeds flag and folded it into the case.

As we sat in a pub in Yarmouth, some lads noticed my Leeds shirt. They came over, and, just as I was preparing for a smack in the face, they told me that they were Leeds fans. They were from Norwich and had been at the play-off game in Birmingham. As we chatted, we convinced each other that Leeds would soon return to the top-flight. The following season Billy Bremner parted company with the club. It was an amicable decision and Billy left, characteristically, saying, 'My only ambition after playing for Leeds United was to manage this great club. I've now done that and can die a happy man.' That same season Leeds entered a new era, with Howard Wilkinson at the helm. He would be much better at steering the Leeds ship than I had been at steering mine.

6

Stars and Gripes

> I'm sure that, in the not too distant future, Malcolm Glazer, an American, will be knighted for all his sterling efforts in ensuring manchester united's future.

One Friday in May 1997 I arrived home from work. I was feeling good. Wub and I were flying to America on the Monday for the first of two Leeds United end-of-season games. But as I walked through the front door, Wub was sitting at the bottom of the stairs. She'd been crying. 'What's up?' I asked.

She sniffed, 'Does our insurance cover cancellation for the America trip?'

I was baffled. 'What are you talking about? What's the matter?'

'I've been to the doctors this afternoon, and I've been diagnosed as diabetic.' She started crying again. I felt numb. I have to admit, the thought of the America trip was hovering in the back of my mind. This could mean missing the Leeds games. But Wub had to be the priority here, didn't she?

'What does that mean? How do they know? You're going to be all right, aren't you?' As she sniffed and wiped her tears away, I sat beside her.

'I can't go to America on Monday.' I was silent for a few seconds.

'Don't be daft,' I said. 'They can't stop you.' She told me that it was too early for her medication to have any effect on such a long trip. I heard myself say, 'Well I won't go, then.' Cybil, our dog, came and sat with us. I swear she looked at me as if to say, 'Yeah, right.'

'You'll have to go,' Wub said. 'Don't be silly, we'll lose all our money if you don't go.' I was stunned.

'I'll ring Mick Hewitt and see what the chances are with the insurance. Are you sure they won't let you travel?' Mick confirmed that she would receive all her money back – and me too if I wanted. 'Whoa, steady Mick, she's told me that I have to go,' I told him. 'In fact,' I added, 'she's insisted.' I was trying to convince myself, as well as Mick.

The day before we set off, Leeds condemned Middlesbrough to relegation with a 1–1 draw at Elland Road. In the bar after the game, Big John Martin couldn't wait to tell me that he had taken Wub's place, and he would be sharing a room with me instead of her. Naturally I was delighted. Who wouldn't want a 20-st. man sharing a room with you instead of your doting wife?

Ironically, John was also a diabetic: he had been diagnosed a few months earlier. Diabetes does put certain restrictions on a person's lifestyle. One such restriction is level of alcohol intake allowed. John was coping very well with diabetes, and, on the coach down to Heathrow, he'd knocked the top off his third bottle of beer by the time we passed Denby Dale, barely ten miles down the M1. We touched down in New York, about fifteen hours and five crates of beer later.

We had to catch an internal flight on to Columbus in Ohio. It was a relatively small American Eagle aircraft and, although the weather was perfect, it was a very bumpy flight. Columbus was a cracking place, and our hotel was conveniently located in the German Village area of the city. It was full of bars, restaurants and great nightlife. However, before sampling all that, I had a very important phone call to make. It was 11 p.m. back in England, and Wub picked up the phone at the side of the bed. 'How are you?' I asked.

'Alright,' she said. 'They've rung from the hospital. I've got to go see them tomorrow to sort out medication and discuss what happens next.' I still felt very guilty and extremely sorry for her. I looked across the street at a bar where the rest of the lads were holed up.

'It's not that good here, anyway,' I lied. She managed a little laugh. She knew I was lying. We'd been to the States together on numerous occasions, and she knew full well that everywhere we'd visited had been fantastic. I asked how Cybil was, and she told me that they were curled up together on the bed. With that cosy image, I said goodnight and said I'd call her the next day.

Back in the bar, I forced one or two beers down, and, then, a few of us headed for some supper. Later, the taxi dropped me and John at our hotel, and we were chatting away as we walked to the reception area. The taxi driver came running after us. We both looked at each other. We'd paid, hadn't we? He ran up to John. 'Here you go, man, you dropped this in the back of my cab,' he said as he handed John his wallet. In it was all his money for the entire trip and his credit cards – and, more importantly, his two match tickets. Well, as they say, 'Only in America'.

The following day we boarded a coach and headed for the Columbus Crew Stadium. Football (or 'soccer') is not huge in the States, but the Crew's stadium was impressive and the Crew fans, many with painted faces, were expecting big things from 'Leeds United from the Premiership in England'. They were going to be very disappointed indeed.

It was raining hard as we drank in a bar near the stadium, and there was a growing fear that the game would be postponed. Luckily, it eased up enough for the game to go ahead. I say 'luckily' for the fans, but we got the distinct impression that the Leeds team just didn't want to be there. Admittedly, they had just finished a long, gruelling season, but a very lacklustre performance saw Leeds beaten 2–1. Brad Friedel, the Crew keeper, even said on TV afterwards that he had been 'slightly disappointed' with Leeds United. Friedel later went on to play for Liverpool and Blackburn Rovers.

Afterwards, back in the bar next to the stadium, some Americans were ranting about how 'Leeds' performance was an insult' and how they thought Leeds United were 'a goddamn Premiership team'. Right on cue, some of the Leeds players walked into the bar. There was no trouble, but, after a quick drink, the players left. However, not before a loud Yankee voice shouted, 'You really should have kicked our ass!'

Later that evening, Kev Morgan and two of the other Lancaster Whites, Pete and Clarkey, came across some of the Leeds players in a hotel bar. Kev said to them that he was a bit disappointed that, earlier at the match, the team hadn't acknowledged the Leeds fans.

Rod Wallace and Brian Deane didn't seem to care less. Tony Dorigo nodded in agreement with Kev and said they would make it right in Washington. Clarkey told him that all they wanted was a bit of recognition for forking out £600 and flying across the Atlantic to watch the team.

The next morning, I was watching cartoons on television. It was only about 6.30 a.m., and I could hear John in the bathroom. 'This is marvellous!' I heard him say. Apparently, he had to piss on a piece of litmus paper each morning to check his sugar level. The results were encouraging for John, who, despite being told to watch his alcohol intake, wasn't exactly easing off the gas in the bars. 'This is great,' he said, bringing me the soggy, piss-stained piece of paper. 'It's well in the safe zone,' he beamed.

I looked at his cheery face, and the limp litmus paper, and said, 'Yeah, great, John,' and returned to *Daffy Duck.* Later, it transpired that John was doing his tests wrong, and he spent a fortnight in hospital when we returned to Leeds.

The breakfasts in America are always amazing, and this trip was no exception. We would all line our stomachs before seriously attacking our livers with a day in the 'Village' bars. My favourite tipple of Jägermeister is readily available on draught in the States, but it was a little early to hit them yet, so I made do with one or two beers instead.

It's not every day you see David Wetherall, the Leeds player, walking down the street. Or a robot, for that matter. But we encountered both as we strolled between bars. After stopping and chatting with Wetherall, the metal monster greeted us. A life-sized robot with flashing lights and a fondness for John came 'walking' out of a doorway. 'Howdy, guys! How you doin'?' it said. John had a T-shirt with Cape Cod emblazoned on the front. 'Hey, fella,' said his metal friend, 'are you from Cape Cod?'

'A bit further afield than that, old cock,' John quipped, in his best Yorkshire accent. This confused the robot, and, while we were trying to work out who was operating it, it disappeared up the street, whistling. We couldn't see signs of anyone working it, prompting Jason Hirst to say, 'Probably it's a real one.' We maintained a silence that dignified his last remark, until we hit the next bar.

Later that afternoon, I slipped out and rang home. I asked Wub how things had gone at the hospital. The one thing she was dreading was being put on a course of insulin injections, but she had fairly good news: she had been put on a course of tablets instead. I could hear the relief in her voice as she told me. After 20 minutes chatting, I said I was thinking about her and would ring her again soon.

Later that day, as we were having a bite to eat, Lee Sharpe walked into the bar. The week before we flew to the States, Leeds had been down at Chelsea. Kev Morgan and Clarkey had been sitting near to me and had been taunting Lee Sharpe, who was on the Leeds bench. We had been sitting quite near the front and Kev had plucked a five-dollar bill out of his wallet. He had waved it at Sharpe and shouted, 'Here, get your bleedin' hair cut in America next week!' To the amusement of the crowd, Sharpe stood up and took the five dollars. He waved it back at Kev and shouted, 'I don't think I'll bother, but cheers, anyway.' This prompted about 50 Leeds fans to begin imitating scissors with their fingers – it was very comical. Meanwhile, in America, we noticed that Sharpe still had a full head of hair. Clarkey wasted no time in approaching him. 'How come you've still got your hair long?' he said.

Sharpe was nonchalant and replied, 'Oh, I've decided to keep it this way.' Clarkey wasn't having this.

'You can fuck off, yer manc bastard,' he laughed. 'Get it cut or we'll pin you down and give you the skinhead.' The next time we saw him, Sharpe was sporting a nicely trimmed barnet.

After a few more days in Ohio, we flew on to Washington. Leeds' next opponents were to be DC United, who share the RFK Stadium with the famous Washington Redskins gridiron team. DC United had just finished a fairly successful season in Major League Soccer (MLS), and we hoped they would bring out a better performance from Leeds. However, we had a few days yet before the game so we embarked on a spot of sightseeing. After a few poses on Capitol Hill, and the obligatory photo in front of the White House (with our Leeds flags hung on the railings), we headed downtown to the Hard Rock Cafe for lunch.

I like the atmosphere in these restaurants, and wherever I am in the world I try to seek out a Hard Rock. I was once in such a place in Tijuana, Mexico. The bartender serving me recognised my Leeds shirt. Mexicans, unlike the majority of Americans, are pretty well up on football and he told me that, 'Leeds are a very good team, but . . .' Leeds fans seem to have a sixth sense when dealing with the 'enemy', and I knew full well where this 'but' was heading. '. . . manchester united are my team.'

'Oh,' I replied, 'I've not heard of them, do you mean Man City?'

He was a bit surprised by my response and blurted out, 'No, manchester united. They won the English league . . . didn't they?' The doubt in his mind was now evident, and I continued to turn the screw.

'No, a team called Charlton Athletic won it.' He was totally confused, and, after stuffing a slice of lime in the bottleneck of my Corona, he walked away, shaking his head and muttering to himself.

Meanwhile, back at the Washington Hard Rock Cafe, John, Ralph Ingelby, Jeff Verrill and I ordered massive roast pork sandwiches. As we all gazed around at the huge collection of rock memorabilia adorning the walls, I noticed a poster of Bill Haley. It reminded me of a little fella back in Kippax. Gordon, now in his 60s, is a well-known character in the village and can often be seen running errands for people, to earn himself a few quid, ranging from putting on bets to getting people's shopping. A few years back, Gordon had got a nice little part-time job at the local church. He was responsible for putting on cassettes and records requested by the wedding and funeral congregations. Gordon loves his music, and the vicar had given him permission to listen to any of his own music when he was in between weddings etc. as long as it didn't 'interfere with the service'. Gordon would usually be hidden away in a small room at the back of the church, and one particular morning, when things were a little slow, he was heavily engrossed in listening to some music. So engrossed, in fact, that he forgot about the 11.30 a.m. service. As the huge doors of the church opened, in walked a sombre funeral party to be met with a resounding 'Rock Around the Clock' blasting, full volume, from the large speakers. Gordon was soon running back up and down the high street clutching betting slips and bags of shopping.

We left the Washington Hard Rock and headed for a bar that we had been told had a great 'happy hour'. However, on our arrival, we found out that happy hour didn't start for another 20 minutes. We noticed that next door to the bar was the house that Abraham

Lincoln had died in, after being shot at a nearby theatre. So, we extended our sightseeing a bit longer. The house was now a museum and shrine to Lincoln, but it was very small: it would be just the thing to kill – if you'll pardon the pun – 20 minutes. As we stood in the actual bedroom where Lincoln had died, John looked at his watch and said, 'Right, that happy hour should have started now, let's go.' Unfortunately, an American tourist heard him and wasn't at all impressed with our brief visit. He was still mouthing at us as we made our way down the stairs.

The following day was football day, and we were all pretty impressed with the RFK Stadium. Whitby John, as was the norm, had gone on a little trip around the ground hunting for any souvenirs. He came back like a dog with two knobs. 'Follow me, Snake,' he said excitedly. We arrived at some private boxes that were unlocked and, more to the point, unoccupied. Amazingly, we watched the whole game uninterrupted, in superb comfort. The game, again, was a slight disappointment and ended in a 1–1 draw.

After the game, Tony Dorigo and the team were true to their word to Kev and went over and acknowledged the travelling Leeds fans. It sounds crap to anyone outside of football, but this small gesture means so much to travelling fans. The Leeds contingent had been boosted by a large number of USA-based Whites supporters. We'd been chatting with these fans before the game, as they all scoffed their picnics and swigged beer in their cars. Very quaint indeed.

We left the stadium and headed for the subway. Again, we found that the Americans weren't very complimentary about Leeds' performance. As we stood waiting for our train, a huge American started chatting with Ralph. Ralph is only about 5 ft tall, and he peered up at the American. 'Are you some sort of Marine?' Ralph asked, somewhat cheekily.

'I sure am, buddy,' replied the 7 ft one. 'Say, you guys must be purdy embarrassed at your team's performance tonight, huh?'

Ralph answered in an instant, 'Not as embarrassed as you fuckin' Yanks were at the Alamo.' To avoid Ralph being placed on the tracks, we moved further down the platform.

The Leeds team and supporters had been invited to nearby Senators Bar for 'complimentary food and drink'. We arrived to discover that the team wasn't coming. Apparently, according to our travel organiser Mick Hewitt, some of the Leeds players were unhappy at some of the comments levelled at them during the trip. It didn't help the PR situation, but it left more grub and beer for the rest of us. Later in the evening, the DC United players arrived, and the tone was set for a really good evening. One of the lads, Jim Unsworth, is a bookmaker in his native Lancaster. He was there with his son Jamie and had news of a very good 'win' back home. So, when the complimentary beers ran out, he bought the others. I had a really good feel for the place. We mingled freely with the Americans (both DC and Leeds fans), and, a few beers down the line, Collar and I got up on stage and gave them our full rendition of 'Ilkla Moor Baht' 'At', that good old Yorkshire hymn. To say our hosts were taken aback by our little song is a major understatement. We went down a storm and were cheered and clapped off the stage. Then came the tricky bit: the Americans wanted to know what the song meant. In particular, they were intrigued by the lines, 'Then 'ducks'll cum 'n eyt up t'worms', and 'Then we shall all av eyten thee'. After our explanations, most of them just nodded politely, but I was certain that they didn't have a clue what we were talking about.

Before I lost my voice completely, I slipped out and phoned home for an update on Wub's condition. Everything was going OK and she seemed cheered up when I told her we were coming home the day after next.

The following day Collar, Whitby John and Russ Townend flew on to New York for a couple of days. That night, the rest of us headed for Downtown Washington. It was Nibber's birthday, and it would have been rude not to help him celebrate. We descended on a large downstairs bar that advertised 'All you can drink for $10'. After being searched for firearms, we gathered at the end of the very long bar. As the bartender placed my beer on the bar, I noticed a brass plaque: 'Tom Cruise sat here', it proclaimed. I looked at the stool next to me, and, quite honestly, I couldn't see Tom Cruise being tall enough to reach the bar from it, let alone climb onto the stool in the first place. There was a great atmosphere in the place, apart from one rather snooty barmaid. She seemed to resent us having more than three drinks for our $10 and had a very annoying habit of disappearing whenever one of us approached the bar. We didn't cause a fuss and, instead, used a bartender who was obviously well into his 60s. He was a smashing fella, and we tipped him regularly to ensure a steady, uninterrupted supply of cold beers. A few hours later, Nibber was well on his way to oblivion, but the bouncers were great and stood chatting with us. However, 'Little Miss Miserable Arse' was still trying to avoid serving us. On one occasion, when our usual bartender was unavailable, I tried to catch her eye. True to form she ignored me, and I should have just waited for our regular server. But her behaviour was really getting to me. I watched her make her way right down to the other end of the bar, where she had been most of the night chatting with people who were obviously her friends. With empty glass in hand, I made my way towards her. She was leaning on the bar, chatting away; I popped up from in the middle of her friends, and, in my best English accent, I shouted, 'Excuse me, my dear. Could I possibly have one of your finest ales please?' I put my glass on the bar. 'Thanks awfully!' She was really angry and embarrassed, and when she slammed my beer back on the bar there wasn't too much left in it. However, I picked it up and left saying, 'Thank you so much. Good evening to you.' I looked across at the bouncers: I thought I may have gone a bit too far, but they were helpless with laughter. At closing time, we returned to our motel for our final night's kip.

The next morning, we boarded another small American Eagle to New York's JFK airport. As we waited for our next flight, on to London, in walked the Leeds squad. George Graham had chosen not to take part in the trip, and his assistant David O'Leary was in charge. The team looked smart in their matching blazers, and it seemed that they were happy to be going home. A little chat with David Wetherall revealed that, overall, the players would rather have done the trip pre-season, as opposed to straight after the last game of the season just finished. I noticed Kev and Clarkey chatting and joking with Lee Sharpe. He did look smart with his new hairdo.

A couple of months prior to that trip, Leeds had played at White Hart Lane. The infamous incident between George Graham and Tony Yeboah occurred that day. Graham had substituted Yeboah, and, on leaving the pitch, the player threw his shirt at at his manager on the bench. He then stormed straight down the tunnel to the dressing-room. Outside the ground afterwards, Kev waited for the team to board their bus. As soon as he saw Yeboah, he raced over, took off his Leeds shirt and threw it at the bemused player. The moral to this little story is a clear warning to Leeds players: 'Don't upset Kev!'

It was this very same Kev, who, only a few years later in 1999, voiced his concern regarding Peter Ridsdale. Our chairman was basking in glory, as Leeds United looked to be on the brink of taking the football world by storm. Kev lives a couple of miles away from Ridsdale on the west coast of Lancashire, and he regularly confronted the chairman to air his displeasure at some of his policies. As Leeds' European adventure went from strength to strength, Kev's protests were snuffed out (he often received verbal and physical threats from Leeds fans during this time) and, consequently, he received a restriction order from Leeds United banning him from attending Leeds games for four years. Kev immediately launched an appeal, and his ban was increased to eight years. As the horrible turn of events unfolded at Elland Road during the following three seasons, Kev's reservations seemed to be vindicated. Kev is one of the top Leeds fans in the country, and his passion for the team is so great that at times it can give people the wrong impression of him.

Once reunited with Wub on my return, I told her that as soon as we could, we would go for our own trip to America. It made me feel better about abandoning her; I was determined to make it up to her. It also meant that I could return to America, but, of course, that was just a bonus.

At the end of another season of football – in the summer of 1998 – Wub and I made that trip to America. We touched down at LAX airport in Los Angeles. We were met by Wub's sister, Gina, who lived a little further south in San Diego. She told us that we had to rush and drop our bags off at the hotel: she had a surprise for us, but we had to hurry. After a quick pitstop at the San Diego Marriott, where Gina worked, we were off again, on foot, to a nearby theatre. On the way there, Gina told us that we were going to a stage production paying tribute to the music of the Doors. Knowing that Wub and I were fanatical about Jim Morrison and the Doors, she had bought us tickets for this, the last night of a sell-out tour. As we hurried through the streets of San Diego, I was still wearing the Leeds United shirt in which I had arrived. How could this get any better? We arrived at the San Diego Repertory Theatre, and the three of us had just enough time for a quick drink at the bar. I looked at my programme for the evening: 'The most anticipated and ambitious world premiere in San Diego REP's 24-year history', it proudly announced. International film star Jeff Meek was to play the leading role of 'the Stranger' (Jim Morrison).

Now, I must admit that I'm not the most ardent of theatre goers, but the show wasn't the best interpretation of the Doors I had seen, although it did have its highlights.

'I'll go order our drinks for half-time,' I whispered in Wub's ear. 'OK,' she whispered back, 'but it's the "interval" not "half-time"!'

The foyer was almost empty as I stood at the bar. Suddenly, two men walked past me. I almost choked on my beer: one of them was Ray Manzarek, the keyboard player from the Doors and co-founder of the band with Jim Morrison back in 1965. As he disappeared down a corridor, I rushed back in to tell Wub. She thought I was seeing things but returned to the foyer with me, and brought the camera with her. As the audience began to converge on the bar, I noticed him going into the toilet. His appearance had altered over the years, and hardly anyone else appeared to recognise him. Gingerly, I approached the toilet door waiting for Manzarek to come out. Wub stood behind me, with camera at the ready. As he walked out I said to him (like any star-struck fan would), 'Hi, Ray, have you washed your hands?' Obviously, he was taken slightly aback.

'Er . . . sure, man,' he replied.

'Great. Can I have a photo, please?' Shaking hands, we both smiled into the camera. 'Take a couple,' I urged Wub. Just as well. The second one, without the lens cap, was a much better picture.

We chatted for a few minutes, and, as he signed his autograph on my ticket, he said, looking at my shirt, 'English soccer, huh?'

I nodded. 'Yes, Leeds United.'

He seemed politely interested. 'Yeah, are they good?'

I looked back at him. 'Yes, the Champions of England,' I lied.

'That's cool, man, great!'

As we left him to the hordes of American fans, who by now had recognised him, Wub said, 'Champions?'

'Well, he won't know, will he?' I said. 'He's a Yank. And anyway, we were Champions in 1992.'

Later, as the show came to a finale, the audience was told that Ray

Manzarek was in the theatre that evening. To deafening applause, he took to the stage to play keyboards, and the hair stood up on the back of my neck as he belted out the intro to the classic Doors song 'Light My Fire'.

Twenty minutes later the show finished. I kissed Gina. It had been out of this world. It was going to be hard to enjoy the next two weeks in the Californian sunshine, but I'd give it my best shot. I owed that to Wub.

Whilst I'm playing the villain of the piece, I may as well share a couple of other occasions when I have let my better half down. In the 1998–99 UEFA Cup, having squeezed past Maritimo, Leeds were paired with Roma. The first leg was in Rome on 20 October. As usual, I booked on with Mick Hewitt's party for a few days in the Italian capital.

The game was to be played on a Thursday evening, and we were scheduled to arrive on the Tuesday morning of that week. One evening, about three weeks before the trip to Italy, Wub and I were watching TV. 'When do you go to Rome?' she asked. When I told her she said, 'Oh, OK.' I asked her why and she just replied, 'Nothing, it's all right.' After playing cat and mouse with her, she told me that she had to go into hospital that same week. She had to have an operation on her neck and would be in for about three or four days. I didn't quite know what to say. 'I'll be able to come and see you before I leave,' I offered.

'My operation is on the Wednesday; you're flying out the day before.' She was right, of course.

'Well, I won't go then,' I said. We'd been here before, and this was going to be tricky. 'I'll lose my money,' I said, after a long pause.

'No, you've got to go. I don't want you there if you don't want to be there.' She was going for the jugular. My mind was doing overtime to find a way out of this situation. Then it hit me: there was a day trip arranged from Elland Road on the day of the game. That way I could go to see Wub after her operation, on the Wednesday night, and be on a plane to Rome the next day. I'd also be able to go to see her on the Friday. She seemed half OK with this idea, although I think she was still a bit upset that I was going to the game. The other drawback was that it would cost me twice as much because I wouldn't be able to get a refund from Mick, but this was the best way to do it.

She seemed fine when I arrived at Jimmy's hospital in Leeds on Wednesday evening. Everything had gone OK with the operation. She also told me that she didn't mind me going to the game and thanked me for coming to see her.

The following day at 4 a.m., I boarded a coach with Richard Watson bound for the airport. After a creditable performance, Leeds lost 1–0 due to a rare mistake by Lucas Radebe. We arrived back at Elland Road at 3 a.m. on the Friday, and, after a few hours' sleep, I went to see Wub. When I arrived, she was dressed and sitting on the bed. 'Right,' she said, 'let's go home.'

On the way home, I played my usual trump card and told Wub that I would take her to Rome for a break at the first opportunity. That opportunity came the very next season, in March 2000, when Leeds were again drawn out of the hat with Roma: this time in the Champions League. We travelled, as usual, with Mick Hewitt, and I took Wub and Dave Green took Debbie, his wife at the time. The day after the game, a 0–0 draw, the four of us went sightseeing. Dave is known as Dr Doom, because you hardly, if ever, see him smile. There certainly wasn't going to be any smiling that day. Against the better judgement of Dr Doom and me, we were heading for the Vatican. Now, I'm not a particularly religious man; I firmly believe that if there had been a God, Leeds would have won the 1975 European Cup in Paris, but that's another story. We arrived at the Vatican and were greeted by the longest queue I'd seen since I queued all night at Elland Road for my FA Cup final ticket in 1970. Three hours later, we entered the famous building. I have to admit that the first couple of painted ceilings were very impressive, but I'm a decorator (and a wall muralist), and, believe me, once you've seen one painted ceiling you've seen them all.

About an hour into our visit, I decided that a serious plan of action was needed to get us out of there. Whilst the others gazed at some obscure artefacts that were all described in full detail on the adjoining plaques – in Latin – I sneaked away and discovered a staircase at the back of the building. I investigated further and returned to the other three. I told them I'd found a way down to the next level without becoming embroiled with hundreds of other visitors, and we could even get ahead of everyone else. I must have been very convincing because minutes later we were halfway down the staircase.

'Are you sure we aren't missing anything out?' asked Debbie.

'No,' I said, with as much honesty as I could muster, 'we just need to go down to the next level and we can carry on with our visit.'

Half an hour later, we came, thankfully, to the exit. As we left the building, the two girls were very quiet. 'Are you sure we didn't miss anything out?' Wub asked.

'No, I'm sure. Come on. Let's go get something to eat,' I replied. My evil plan had been successful. We had missed out four floors.

Once outside, we walked past the large queue still waiting to go inside. I noticed Keith Gaunt and his travelling companion, Mel. They were standing near a board that said, 'Waiting time from here – 6 hours'. As we left, and headed for a nearby bar for lunch, I felt so, so sorry for them.

As we relaxed on the flight home, I was happy that I'd gone someway towards making up for going to Rome for the game two years earlier. However, another obstacle was just around the corner.

In the 2002 UEFA Cup campaign, Leeds were drawn against Israel's Hapoel Tel Aviv. Because of the troubles in Israel, the game was switched to Florence, Wub's favourite city in Italy. Now, my lady is a very intelligent person, and, as well as being called Mrs Lesley Anne Edwards, B.Sc, she was awarded by her employers, Carlsberg/Tetley Brewery, in 2002 for 25 years' loyal service with a special invite to the Thistle Tower Bridge Hotel in London. There, she and her spouse would attend an exclusive awards ceremony and dinner and would be provided with a night's accommodation. Thrown in were two first-class return train tickets from Leeds. Of course, it was too good to be true: it was on the same night Leeds were to play Hapoel in Florence. This was to be the straw that broke the camel's back. A desperate attempt by me to get Tetley's to change the date proved fruitless, and so I spent two weeks of sleepless nights trying to find a solution to my latest problem. Nothing was forthcoming, and four days before the game I rang Mick Hewitt and cancelled my place on the trip to Florence. He was surprised to say the least but said, 'Well, it's her big day, mate, you've got to be there, I suppose.' His last two words didn't help. The following day, as we had lunch in The Aire of the Dog in Leeds, I told Wub about my phone call to Mick. She was as surprised as he was but said, 'If you're sure, thank you.' I honestly didn't intend it, but, without warning, plan B came into operation almost immediately: I sulked. I sulked so much that as soon as we got home she rang Mick and booked me back on the trip, although she didn't tell me until the day after.

A few days later I was in Florence, and although we won 4–1, thanks to a goal flurry from ex-Yorkshireman Alan Smith, my thoughts were definitely with Wub back in London. After the game, I spoke to her on the phone: she said it had been a great night and that she and Spoon, who'd gone in my place, were having a ball.

It has to be said that my not going to London caused serious problems between us, and she even told me that the 'Hemsley Curse' (Hemsley was her maiden name) had been put on my club and me. We were relegated two seasons later, and I'm now in the process of arranging a luxury trip on the Orient Express to appease her. And hopefully get us promoted.

7

Flares, Floodlights and the Flip of a Disc

> Aye, Aye, Aye, Aye, Gary [Sprake] is better than Yashin [Lev], Albert [Johanneson] is better than Eusébio and Chelsea are in for a thrashing.
>
> Leeds song from the '60s

It was 10 p.m. on a Wednesday night, and my head was stuck down the toilet. Nothing new there, I hear you cry. Only this was in 1968. I was 12 years old, and I was in the downstairs toilet of our semi-detached Coal Board house. 'You're going to have to stop taking this so seriously, you know,' Dad shouted through the door.

I had just returned home with Dad from Elland Road, after having witnessed Leeds United get beaten in an European Fairs Cup game. I wasn't used to seeing my team get beaten, and I was physically sick whenever they did. However, the team that night had been something special. Leeds, holders of the Fairs Cup, came up against quite simply the best opponents I have ever seen. Ujpest Dozsa from Hungary were absolutely devastating. I offered a feeble excuse back through the toilet door: 'It was because they played in our kit,' I said.

For some reason, many European sides from that era travelled without a change strip, and, just as the Belgian team Standard Liege had done in the first round of that same competition, Ujpest arrived at Elland road with only one kit. On that previous occasion, Standard Liege ran out wearing all white, obviously clashing with the all white of Leeds. A long discussion ensued, and Leeds reluctantly agreed to change. It was thought at the time that Leeds could have actually claimed the tie, but they decided to do the honourable thing and play the Belgian team. The first leg in Belgium had finished 0–0, and when Leeds found themselves 2–0 down at Elland Road they must have been regretting their decision to change into an all-blue kit with white socks. It turned out to be the most memorable game I've ever seen, and Leeds ran out 3–2 winners in the dying seconds.

Meanwhile, Ujpest Dozsa One Strip had turned out, rather cheekily, in Leeds' very own white shirts, sporting the famous owl badge. Leeds, once again, courteously reverted to their blue shirts and shorts with white socks. This time, however, it was no fairy-tale ending. A perfect performance by Ferenc Bene, a goal from Antal Dunai and a superb penalty save from Antal Szentmihalyi rounded off a torrid evening for Leeds United.

I was still stunned early the next day, as I boarded the pea-bus. It was, as always, a damp and foggy morning. To fund my early forages into Europe, I used to go with Ma and other mothers into the surrounding country fields, during the summer holidays, to pull up peas and potatoes. Local farmers would provide a bus or tractor and a trailer and would pay us handsomely at the end of a hard day pulling. The pea and potato picking, working at Dad's place, Stembridges, on Sundays and chopping firewood to sell on our Coal Board estate meant that I had money coming out of my ears!

I sat next to Andy Robinson on the bus that day. He had been to Elland Road with me the previous evening. 'They were a cracking side, them, mate,' he said. 'We've no chance over there.' He was right, of course, and two weeks later I was leaving Budapest after a 2–0 defeat with Leeds losing 3–0 on aggregate.

My regular guardian, John Hamilton, couldn't make that trip, so I was allowed to travel with Mick Collins and his dad. As was usual in those days, we flew there and back in the same day, and so it seemed like hardly any time at all before I was sitting in the back of Mr Collins's car, clutching my souvenir pennant from the trip and heading home to Kippax. I had gone to the first round of the competition in Belgium versus Standard Liege with Mr Hamilton but had travelled with Mick and his dad to the next two rounds. To compensate for our disappointment at being knocked out, we began reminiscing about the trips to Italy and East Germany. I had collected pennants from these games too, and the one from Italy still sends a little shiver down my spine. It read: 'Napoli versus Leeds Utd. 7th Novembre 1968. Sao Paulo Stadion'. Big Jack Charlton had scored both goals in a 2–0 win over Napoli in the first leg at Elland Road, and there seemed no danger of Leeds losing the tie. The Italians must have thought so too as only about 15,000 people turned up at the 85,000-capacity ground.

Two years prior to the Leeds game, Burnley had played Napoli in Naples and had to be escorted from the stadium under armed escort. The Leeds game was to be no different. A permanent 8-ft-wide moat surrounded the pitch, and large metal fences prevented a really good view of the game. Rockets whizzed across the pitch from the very first minute, and although the referee had to duck to avoid one of the missiles, the game was never going to be abandoned. Leeds keeper Gary Sprake was hit by a bottle and had to receive stitches before playing on. Riot police surrounded our small band of supporters, but Mr Collins led Mick and me away: it was safer to blend in with the Italians than to remain a sitting target. One Leeds fan was taken away with blood pouring from his face. Leeds doctor Ian Adams tended to the injured fan and then, seconds later, had to turn his attention to Peter Lorimer, who had been left almost unconscious from a vicious attack by a Napoli defender. With play being allowed to continue, Lorimer had to be dragged from the pitch before he could receive treatment.

Minutes later, Paul Madeley lay motionless in the middle of the park. After three or four minutes had passed and the ball had gone dead, Dr Adams, deputising for the absent Les Cocker, was allowed on to attend to Madeley. Not surprisingly, Napoli pulled a goal back and then, with only five minutes remaining, Charlton was adjudged to have fouled an Italian in the penalty area. Despite Jack being at least a foot away and outside the box, the attacker performed a dive that would have put Francis Lee or, indeed, Harry Kewell to shame. At 2–2 on aggregate, Leeds battled bravely through extra time, all the time ducking the constant barrage of missiles hurled from the psychotic home fans as well as the lunging challenges from the Napoli players. Amazingly, only three Italians were booked and, laughably, right-back Dino Nardin was booked twice and remained on the park. Near to the end of the encounter, Napoli goalkeeper Dino Zoff thwarted Mike O'Grady, but, quite frankly, nobody in the stadium would have expected the goal to have been given anyway.

Don Revie, foreseeing the potential danger of the tie, had asked for two members of the Inter-Cities Fairs Cup committee to be present. After the explosive two hours, one of them said, 'The output of fireworks, bonfires, boos and hisses were only about normal.'

With the game tied and the penalty shoot-out not yet introduced, the outcome of the tie was left to the toss of a huge red and blue disc. For once, the colour red was very welcome as Billy Bremner called correctly. As he and the other Leeds players danced around the park, the desperate pleas of 'best out of three' from the Napoli team fell on deaf ears. Mick and I laughed as Mr Collins said, 'Keeping you two quiet leaving that ground was quite an ordeal.'

Thankfully, the game against Hannover 96 at the National Stadium was much more pleasant. To be honest, with Leeds leading the tie 5–1, no one expected anything other than a Leeds victory. Despite Terry Cooper receiving his marching orders, Leeds gave a fully professional display and won through 7–2 on aggregate. The team received a standing ovation from the home crowd, the Leeds fans and the large contingent of British squaddies who had chanted for the Whites throughout the game.

On the flight home, I sat opposite a lad whom I still see occasionally at Elland Road. It's fair to say that the poor chap isn't blessed with the greatest of looks, but he is a Leeds fanatic and I like him. He said something to me about the game, but, to be honest, I was just staring at his grossly uneven teeth. His mouth looked like an exploding graveyard. Behind him was the bloke who used to be known as the Leeds United ambassador. He used to wear a large top hat and tails covered with Leeds badges. He always had a cigar in his mouth and wore a distinctive moustache. Everywhere he went he would carry a large Leeds pennant mounted on a stick. In the days when a lot of fans from all clubs used to hide their scarves, this human mascot would parade proudly around away grounds without a care in the world. I noticed on the plane that he was reading a book that I recognised. It was a special football book given out in return for about eight million discarded Park Drive cigarette packets. To make conversation, I mentioned to him that I had the same book at home. 'Not like this one, son,' he proclaimed. He then proudly turned to the opening page and handed it to me. On the page was a huge scribble. I must have looked puzzled as he took the book back and smiled. 'That's Danny Blanchflower's autograph,' he said. Blanchflower was known to Tottenham fans as a great footballer. At Leeds he was known as a crap commentator for ITV's *Sunday Soccer*. I remember him commentating on Leeds games, claiming 'It's a chance! It's a chance!', in his broad Northern Irish accent, every time a team would approach the opposition's penalty area.

Of course, European nights at Elland Road in the '60s were also special. A lasting memory involving Gary Sprake springs to mind. On reflection, there are quite a few Sprake memories that spring to mind, not all for the right reason. During the 1960s, BBC 2 appeared on our television screens. During a home tie against Standard Liege, while Leeds were defending a corner, Sprake made an error that resulted in the Belgian team scoring. The keeper's excuse was remarkable. Apparently, BBC 2 had positioned a camera on the roof of the West Stand, and a bright light placed above the camera had distracted Sprake as he jumped for the ball. I never realised at the time, but those BBC 2 cameras must have followed Sprake to matches up and down the country, including those played during daylight. Actually, Sprake did have his good moments. I was at Highbury in 1969, when, after a mid-air tussle with Arsenal's Bobby Gould, Sprake let fly with an amazing left hook that knocked Gould unconscious.

Around this time, my dad was studying for his Football Association Coaching Badge, and he told me that they had been shown a few slides of Sprake in action. They revealed quite clearly how he used to clear the ball upfield. He would invite the forward onto his right foot, and as he kicked the ball he would always follow through with his boot giving the player an almighty, undetected kick.

I also remember BBC 2 for another reason. We were one of the first people on our estate to receive the channel and our next-door neighbour Mr Dickinson would come round every Monday night at 8 p.m. to watch *The High Chaparral*.

Another thing I remember about my first trips abroad with Leeds was the 'foreign' smell. In cafés and bars there was always a strong, somewhat alien smell of tobacco and beer: an aroma that was never evident at home. Whether it's because my sense of smell deteriorated or that I just became accustomed to it, I don't know, but it seemed to disappear as we progressed into the '70s.

8

Long Hair, Short Hauls and Tall Tales

> In my opinion, Roy Ellam was better than Rio Ferdinand and Jonathan Woodgate put together.

Following the slight skirmish after the 1975 European Cup final in Paris, Leeds were banned from European competition. This signalled an increase in pre-season activity in Europe, which led to many memorable forays into West Germany, Holland and Belgium.

On our last venture to Belgium, before the ban in 1975, four of us – Gaz Noble, John Walker, Dave Wilson and I – had arrived at Brussels railway station at 5 a.m. We were there for the quarter-final clash against Anderlecht in the European Cup. It had taken us around 14 hours travelling by train and ferry, and we were greeted by a massive snowstorm. We were cold, hungry and out of supplies. The first sign we saw was the famous Jupiler beer sign: one with which we were to have a close relationship over the next 30-odd years. Wind and snow swirled around our heads as we trudged around looking for a cheap hotel or at least a café bar that was open. After half an hour, we found both side by side. Luckily there was one room left at the inn, and whilst they prepared our room for four we warmed up next door at the small café. As the day progressed, the snow turned to sleet and then rain. Leeds supporters were everywhere, and we soon converged on a bar near the train station that had been engulfed by damp Leeds fans. By the time we made our way to the ground, the rain was seriously threatening postponement of the game. The pitch was like a mud bath, and, once again, a Billy Bremner goal was enough to give Leeds a 1–0 victory and an aggregate of 4–0. Although there was a roof over the Leeds end, the wind and rain attacked the fans from both unsheltered sides of the stand. Dozens of Leeds fans left their flags as they were too wet and heavy to carry. Just as we were leaving the stadium, I noticed a large, sodden pile near the exit. It was a Union Jack flag, and, judging by the size of the cross on it, it was massive. So massive, in fact, that we had to carry it back to the hotel in pairs. Once we had washed it in the sink in the room, the flag was as good as new, but we'd made a right mess of the sink, leaving what seemed to be tons of dirt, grit and sand. That very same flag was taken back to England, and, after it had acquired the letters of 'Leeds United', it travelled with us to Barcelona for the semi-final and then on to the final in Paris.

Our very first European trip that left from The Viaduct took us back to Belgium in 1977 for the pre-season game with RWD Molenbeek – formerly known as Racing White and these days called FC Brussels. The trip, arranged by Tony Frith, was a laugh from start to finish. Inside the stadium, the home fans heckled the four hundred or so Leeds fans. The bulk of us were behind the goal, and the locals were situated on the halfway line. They appeared to have a small brass band in the middle of them. This band accompanied their every song, and the atmosphere seemed to be good. However, things began to turn ugly as a few Leeds fans near the Belgians began to chant Leeds songs. Some of the Belgians attacked the singing fans, and all hell broke loose, as Leeds fans behind the goal broke through the thin line of police and joined those near to the Belgians. Eventually, police reinforcements arrived, but instead of stopping more Leeds fans moving down the side of the stadium, they formed a line between those two groups already there. This meant that, before long, all the Leeds fans were standing next to the Belgians separated by a relatively thin line of police. Luckily, things didn't really turn violent: instead, they became more comical than nasty.

Lenny from Aberford had removed his false teeth, in readiness for what seemed to lie ahead. He was also very drunk. He began shouting at the police near him, and two of them grabbed his arms. Lenny had a large woollen V-necked jumper on, and, within a flash, his right arm appeared out of the V-neck and punched the copper, who was left holding an empty sleeve, right in the nose. Lenny was about 15 stone and not too light on his feet, and therefore he was quickly overpowered. As he was led out by about half-a-dozen officers, he was cheered by the Leeds lads. Things began to calm down, and the two sets of fans continued with mainly friendly banter. The band accompanied both sets of fans and I think the game ended 2–2. As we walked out, Vince Donnelly and Howard Wilson said that they'd seen Gaz Noble get nicked earlier and that he hadn't returned. He didn't return to us at all during that trip. He was eventually deported and warned that if he ever set foot in Belgium again he would be locked up. He needn't have worried. We weren't to return to Belgium for many years.

I was always impressed with how clean West Germany was, and, of course, it has some of the best beer in the world. It was no different when we travelled, between 1977 and 1981, to places such as Leverkusen, Stuttgart, Hamburg and Cologne, as well as Nijmegen and Roda Kerkrade in Holland in 1978.

On 29 July 1979 Leeds were invited to play Schalke 04 in Marburg. It was a delightful little town and very picturesque. We pitched our tent by the side of a lake and went into town. At the top of a very large hill in the town, surrounded by dozens of trees, was an intriguing building that was all lit up. It was half castle, half mansion like. We were in the town for three nights and every evening Brod, Dave Fry, Mally King, Dave Burrows and I would set off to see what it was. Each evening we would take a different route up the winding pathways and narrow lanes. And each evening the castle would remain the same distance away: we never did get to see it up close.

However, at the game itself, we did come up close to the Schalke supporters. Very large Schalke supporters! After a few beers we mingled with these huge Germans and had a few photos taken with our hosts. The original Kippax Branch flag made its first appearance in one of those photographs. In the town afterwards, we trawled the bars with our giant German friends, and they then joined us later for a beer and barbecue party round the campfire, back at our tent. There was a small Hell's Angels chapter called 'Bones' pitched up close to us, and it wasn't very long before they too joined the party. 'Where's Dave?' Brod asked. Everyone shrugged their shoulders, and at that moment we heard a squeaking and clanging come towards us from the dark night. The bikers roared with laughter as drunken Dave came hurtling past us all on a beat-up old bicycle and went straight into the lake, where he slept for the rest of the night.

It was a hectic little tour, and the very next day the five of us set off in our little white hire car up the autobahn to Bremen. The usual faces were to be seen in town, and, before too long, we were hooked up in our first bar, enjoying a cold one with Collar, Frank 'Jock' Rounding and his buddies. 'Mad' Andy Holmes was once again present. He was on army leave, and it was amazing how every summer he would just appear in the country where Leeds happened to be playing. He was, and still is, a nutter but is a thoroughly decent chap, all the same.

It was Yorkshire Day (1 August) in 1979 when we played SV Werder Bremen. Dave Watson had just moved to Werder from Man City; he had also played for Sunderland before that. A few of us had gone to Bremen's stadium to get tickets for the game that evening when Brod spied Watson. He was standing chatting to a club official. One of our lads called over to him, and he looked round and immediately noticed our Leeds shirts. Unbelievably, he uttered something about Sunderland and the 1973 FA Cup final. The abuse that was hurled at him instantly forced him to disappear inside the building to safety.

After the game that night, we were drinking in a bar in the city centre when dozens of riot police stormed in. They immediately descended on Silvers from Bradford, who was drinking with Collar and me at the bar. Dave Fry noticed that outside the police had surrounded the place. With the police was a small local woman who was placed in front of Silvers. She muttered something in German, and, despite our protests, Silvers was led away. The remaining police stayed and blocked the door, preventing our exit. Two hours later, the police had disappeared and in walked Silvers.

Apparently, there had been a stabbing earlier in a nearby bar, and the locals had said that the culprit was a 'British person'. Silvers had been in that bar earlier with his mates but had not seen anything. Evidently, the woman had pointed out Silvers as the guilty one. However, what the police didn't know was that Silvers could speak German: he knew that the woman had told the police that Silvers wasn't the man she saw involved in the stabbing. This did not matter one jot to the police, and they hauled him away anyway. It was only in the car that Silvers spoke in perfect German and told them, word for word, what the woman had said in the bar. To save face, the police detained Silvers for a couple of hours before releasing him.

The next day we left for Düsseldorf. The next game was to be in the Rheinstadion against Fortuna Düsseldorf. A much larger city than Marburg and Bremen, Düsseldorf oozed with nightlife, and the local tipple of Jägermeister stood no chance as we quaffed what seemed to be every drop in town. We only had one night there, so we made the best of it. The next day, we slipped across the border into Holland to play a game against Eindhoven that night, which, of course, meant two games in two nights. After the game at the PSV Stadion, the five of us found ourselves in a local disco bar on the outskirts of the city. Things were going pretty well, although there was a slight tension around the place: a handful of British squaddies were getting louder and louder and were attracting attention from a lot of the local boys. They were jostling with the local girls and didn't give a hoot about whom they upset. We weren't exactly quiet ourselves, and you could sense it could kick off at any time.

A scuffle between a squaddie and a Dutch lad was quickly stifled by both sides. The squaddies were getting fewer and fewer in numbers, and the Dutch ranks were swelling. 'I reckon we ought to get the hell out of here,' Dave said, as we watched three more squaddies slip out of the back door. We drank our beer, and, as we left, we noticed that there didn't seem to be any squaddies left in the place at all; they seemed to have simply vanished into thin air.

'I reckon we're being followed,' said Brod.

'Just keep walking, and get in the car,' I said. It was my turn to drive, and we all clambered into the tiny car. It was raining, and the windows immediately steamed up. Brod was on my right, and, as he wiped the inside of the windscreen, he said, 'Oh shit!' I peered through the smeared window. About 30 locals were walking towards us. They were armed to the teeth with sticks, baseball bats and what appeared to be truncheons. The engine started, thankfully, first time, and I began to reverse. Because of the steamed-up windows I couldn't see a thing, and the mob was getting closer. I felt a car on my left and, as I looked in the wing mirror, I noticed I was scraping up the side of it. I ground to a halt. There was nothing for it: I was going to have to go straight forward. I revved the engine, and the little white bonnet bounced up and down to the revs. 'OK, here we go,' I said. 'This is the only way out, lads. We'll have to go straight through them.'

Just then, a small man ran up to the car and went to Brod's side. He resembled that little bloke Tattoo (Herve Villechaize) from the programme *Fantasy Island*, famous for his catchphrase, 'De plane! De plane!' He was peering through the car windows and checking us out. It looked as if he was the leader: his henchmen were closing in behind him, with baseball bats at the ready.

Just then, Brod wound his window down, and I had to smile as he said, in some sort of fantasy foreign language, 'What eez de problem?' Tattoo was still looking in the car and turned to his men and said, 'No! No! Not them!' We all breathed a huge sigh of relief. As we were allowed to drive off, Dave Fry said, 'Fuckin' good job 'n' all. We'd have had them. Easy!' We were all laughing, but I actually got the distinct impression that he believed it.

We found out later that one of the squaddies that night was Phil Roberts, who, years later, was to join the Kippax Branch. He told us that he remembered getting into 'a bit of bother with a couple of the locals' and did the dishonourable thing and left by the back door.

Unbelievably, one of the hottest places I've ever been was Zurich. Leeds played the Grasshoppers in a friendly at the end of the '70s, and we were literally baking as we walked around the town. On the outskirts of the city, Leeds fans had pitched tents on some wasteland. The heat was so intense that one of fans had actually been able to sink his tent pegs into the surrounding pavement. However, the sun gradually melted the tarmac and, whilst the lads were out having a beer, their tent sunk into the pavement; they returned to a crumpled black smouldering heap.

Later, we went on a cable-car ride, and to say it was high was an understatement. Every time the car rode over the connections on the overhead cables, we thought it was the end. We were relieved when the car arrived at the mountain top and the sanctuary of a small secluded bar. The car rocked violently as Brod and I stepped off, leaving it unevenly balanced. The slender frame of 'Hong Kong White' was left clinging to the other side of the car for dear life.

I had bought Ma an ornament from Zurich and had put it my hand luggage for the journey home. When we got to the airport, my bag went through the scanner and immediately sparked a commotion. Ma's present was an ornamental lighter in the shape of a gun, mounted on a shiny wooden plinth. Unbelievably, the authorities had mistaken it for a real gun! They questioned me for a few minutes, whilst the 'gun' was taken from its box and whisked away by security. By the time they returned, everyone had retrieved their cases from the conveyor belt and was waiting for me. I asked about my lighter and was told it was still being checked and would be with me shortly. Another half an hour later, Howard Wilson and everyone else fell about laughing as around the corner, on the empty conveyor belt, came my gun-shaped lighter. I was a bit annoyed at having to wait for so long and couldn't resist a parting shot at the authorities. 'I suppose that's a good enough reason for your country remaining neutral during the war,' I said to a guard standing near to the conveyor. 'It really helps if you can distinguish a gun from a lighter.'

9

At Least Until the World Stops Turning Round?

> The International Flat Earth Society is the oldest continuous Society on [*sic*] the world today.
>
> Charles K. Johnson

Luckily, as Leeds United began life in the old Second Division back in 1982, I had other things to keep me sane. I discovered that the earth was flat. I was not alone in my discovery. Some other lads on the coach – notably Gordon Findlay, Pete Dillon and Greg Gater – had also noticed it. We discussed the issue at great length and came up with a number of questions. For example, if the world was round, why didn't all the oceans fall off? And why weren't aeroplanes curved to circumnavigate the earth?

No one could come up with a logical explanation to any of these important posers, so, in May 1982, Gordon and I founded the Kippax Flat Earth Society (KFES).

Our patron was the ancient Greek philosopher Thales of Miletus. As well as the first-ever known philosopher, Thales was a mathematician and a scientist. He was born in, funnily enough, Miletus in 624 BC and he said the earth was flat: that was good enough for us. He believed that the earth floated on water (a bit like Tony Currie) and that all things come to be from water. He also claimed that the earth was a flat disc floating in an infinite ocean. Due largely to the fact that he died in 547 BC, he very rarely attended any

KFES events. (In March 2000 when Leeds played Roma, many KFES members paid homage to the bust of Thales of Miletus, which is housed in the Capitoline Museum in Rome.)

Word quickly spread of our organisation, and people were flocking to join our cause.

Recruitment was particularly easy amongst Leeds United fans, and our membership grew to over a thousand in the first two months. It seemed everyone wanted a KFES membership card to accompany their LUSC one. KFES T-shirts sold out time and time again, as did the much sought-after KFES badges. We published our own magazine called the *Flat Weekly*, which came out every fortnight. It featured articles proving beyond doubt that the earth was flat. A free gift was given away with every issue. One week it was a balloon, which was stapled to the page, forever making it a flat balloon. Another week, we gave everyone a brand new '5 lb' note. One edition was printed entirely in Italian. The free gift on that occasion was a tin of tomatoes: Italian of course. Each Friday evening, copies of the *Flat Weekly* were placed on the bar at The Royal Oak, alongside a large glass bottle. Each copy cost 20p with the proceeds going to a different charity each month. However, on the 'Italian' occasion Gord and I encountered a small difficulty. Most of the lads were dressed for a night on the pull and were reluctant to take their tomatoes along. 'Can't we leave them here and pick them up later?' they would plead. But we were adamant: 'No tomatoes, no *Flat Weekly*.' So, off they would trudge, with a tin protruding awkwardly from the side pocket of their brand-new flared trousers. The next morning, there must have been 50 tins of tomatoes strewn all over the high street. Many had opened on impact, after they had been thrown against a wall. It seemed the tins had cramped the style of our fashion-conscious KFES members.

The KFES would regularly hold talks, many with students who would argue passionately that the earth was indeed round. How misguided can one get? Of course, the strong team of KFES delegates would present them with overwhelming evidence of the earth's flatness. Indisputable facts such as, if the earth was round, all the trees would be leaning towards the sun, instead of growing straight out of the ground. One night, a member of the audience had heard that the KFES was planning a parachute jump. Sarcastically, he said that if the earth was flat, the jump would be impossible, because of the gravity situation. He had, of course, played straight into our hands. As usual, one of our members had the answer. 'Free falling has nothing to do with gravity,' Gord said. 'It's just that we weigh about 14 stone and can't fly.'

Andy Ricketts was totally engrossed in our preparations for the jump. He demonstrated this one evening, when Lesley picked me and him up with Andy Cockx, who had come to Leeds for a game at Elland Road. As we pulled up to Crossgates, Andy opened his door and rolled out of the back and along the pavement. 'Tuck and roll!' he shouted. He was still rolling down the path as we drove off.

Unfortunately, our parachute jump never really got off the ground. So many people bailed out that we couldn't get the required numbers.

On one occasion, the KFES locked horns with Derek Houghton, the chairman of the West Yorkshire Astronomical Society. Mr Houghton produced what he said was photographic evidence that the earth was a sphere. It showed a picture, which was quite clearly a fake, of the earth, supposedly taken from a satellite. I calmly rose to my feet and produced our own photographic evidence. The picture was of several round bales of hay in a field. It was just an ordinary field with no hidden props or gadgets. 'Study this picture closely,' I said. 'Not one of these bales is moving. If the earth was even slightly round, the bales would roll off into the hedges.' Of course, Mr Houghton was left quite speechless and presented no further evidence for his flimsy claim.

Meanwhile, we continued to recruit members from Elland Road and further afield. Our campaign had also attracted attention from the media. We appeared regularly on Peter Levy's show on Radio Aire, and he was always sent his copy of the *Flat Weekly*, which he would read out to listeners on air. We were once asked to take part in a show on Radio Leeds. I had a beaten up old Vauxhall Viva at the time. When we arrived at the station's car park, I had to press the intercom at the side of the closed barrier. 'Hello, could you state your name and your business,' the voice said.

'Good morning, it's Gary Edwards and Gordon Findlay from the Kippax Flat Earth Society,' I replied. The barrier was raised immediately.

Gord laughed. 'Look at that,' he said. Several people were up at the window watching us drive in. You could almost hear them: 'They're here, the Flat Earthers are here!' As I drove in, my Viva backfired, and a huge puff of black smoke emerged from the exhaust. It was just like an entrance by Del Boy and Rodney.

Another talk we did was held in the old Leeds United Supporters Club, situated on Elland Road. The club, now sadly demolished, had hosted many important meetings in the past, such as Howard Wilkinson's first meeting with the Leeds fans. Billy Bremner and Norman Hunter had also once held a very entertaining fans forum there, and now the KFES took centre stage.

Midway through the evening, we were asked what our thoughts were in relation to the earth supposedly spinning at several hundreds of miles an hour. This was an easy one to deal with. One common misconception is that the earth spins at around 1,000 mph. Just think how daft that sounds. If that were true, there would be no need for any mode of transport. You would simply have to stand at a chosen point of departure and jump in the air. As long as you had done your maths correctly, when you landed you would be at your preferred destination. For a trip to, say, Europe, or even further, a stepladder could be used. With motorways mainly redundant, hundreds of people would gather, and the hard shoulders would be full of people bobbing up and down at different levels making their way across the country. Trips to Leeds away games would be particularly interesting. Instead of travelling by coach, you would see 50 lads all jumping simultaneously to exactly the same height to get to the game. If anybody was out with their timing it could result in them arriving at the wrong ground, which, in turn, might mean them ending up with a bop on the nose.

Another time, Gord and I were asked to appear at the prestigious Castleford Civic Hall to deliver a talk to a packed audience. Before we started, I peeked through the curtain and noticed that there were a lot of suits and some very important people in the audience, including the Lord Mayor of Castleford. 'We're gonna go down like a lead balloon here, mate,' I said to Gord. But we needn't have worried: within minutes, we had them rolling in the aisles. We received a standing ovation at the end, and, as the curtain fell, we still couldn't believe that so many people were interested in our campaign, which was gathering momentum by the day.

On 26 June 1986 the KFES met with Rolf Harris in Leeds. He congratulated us on bringing the issue to the attention of the public and told us that he was a firm believer in the Flat Earth theory. At the end of our meeting, Neil Malloch, a prominent member of our organisation, stepped forward to receive an autographed cartoon from Mr Harris. It was a sketch of Rolf falling off the end of the earth, addressed to the Kippax Flat Earth Society.

Not long afterwards, at a Leeds United Supporters Dinner, I chatted with Eddie Gray about our conquest. He had no hesitation in putting his name to our cause and signed my KFES membership card. We received several new members that evening: membership cards were given to John Sheridan, Tommy Wright, Dennis Irwin and Scott Sellars. (Irwin's membership was quickly revoked when he signed as a manchester united player. Undesirables were not welcome in our Society.)

In the mid-'80s, we were invited to appear on James Whale's talk show, but, after due consideration, Gord and I thought that he wouldn't take us seriously, so we declined the offer.

In 2005, the KFES was still at the forefront of topical discussion. In January, we appeared on John Boyd's show on Radio Leeds. However, our conversation did drift onto the topic of the recent arrival of Ken Bates at Elland Road, before getting back to the more serious subject of the earth's flatness. Interest in our cause is still marching on and on.

A spokesman for the author Terry Pratchett is about to discuss with the KFES the possibility of a future project on the subject of the flat earth theory, which will interest one of our newest recruits. Dave the Dalek, a fully functional, real-life Dalek, is a huge Leeds fan, as well as being kept very busy due to the recent revival of BBC's *Dr Who*. This is obviously a personal battle for Dave, as it's widely known that Chris Eccleston, the man chosen to be the new Dr Who in the first return series, is a supporter of manchester united. Dave the Dalek is, of course, a loyal member of the KFES. His very structure and the way he operates make it easy to see why Dave is such a big believer in the earth's flatness. Unfortunately, Dave does not attend Elland Road as often as he'd like to. This is due to the fact that he is constantly cautioned for 'persistently standing up'.

I recently spent the afternoon with Dave, and I mentioned my

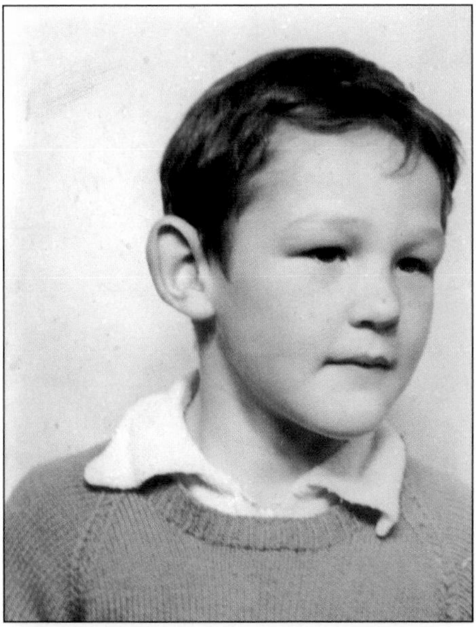

Me in 1961 – Don Revie had just taken over as manager of Leeds.

A Butlins' redcoat eyes me up in 1965.

Team photo in Blackpool's dugout.

Setting off for Paris, 1975.
(Photo courtesy of the *Yorkshire Evening Post*.)

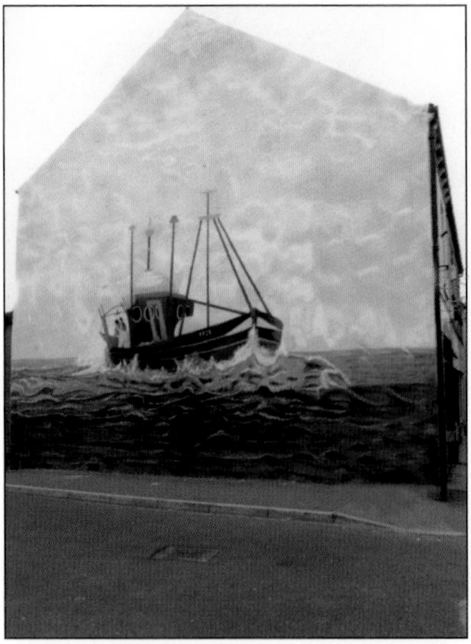

One of my wall murals: a 70 ft trawler on the end wall of the local fish and chip shop.

I met up with Ray Manzarek, keyboard player from the Doors, in San Diego, 2002. I'm on the blue side!

Conclusive evidence of the Earth's flatness – motionless bales of hay.

Me and 'Dave'.

Big Webby puts his foot in it again!

Jimmy Floyd Hasselbaink and I play the tables in Sweden.

Our lads 'marching out together' in Sweden.
It put the fear of God into our opposition.

Inset: Wub and I take the stage on the *Trisha Goddard* show.

Will you marry me, Wub? It'll be all-white!

Braveheart eat your heart out. (Photo courtesy of Varley Picture Agency.)

Wub receives her bachelor of science degree from Baroness Betty Boothroyd.

Some of the lads and I pose with Leeds-supporting actor Ralph Ineson (Finchy from *The Office*).

The family in Blackpool in 1968, just before Ma's wig flew off.

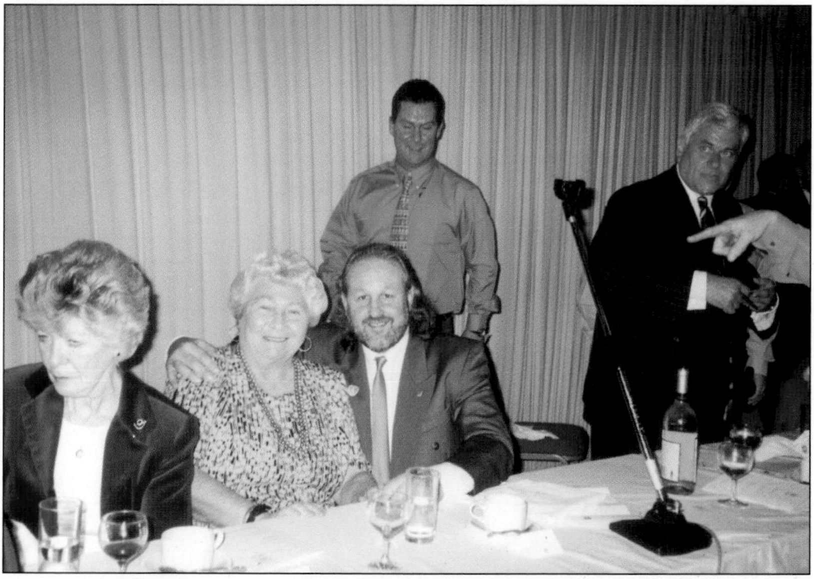

The late Mrs Elsie Revie – God bless.

Leaving The Viaduct for another away jaunt.

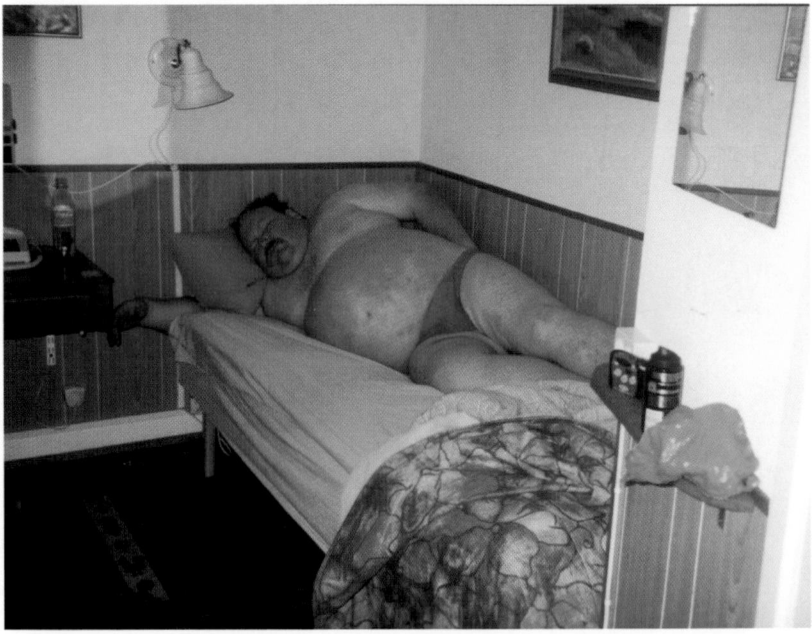

Big Coke rests before another busy day.

concern that we (Leeds United) would never win the FA Cup again, 'as long as I live'. Obviously, having travelled back from the future, Dave would know the outcome. He simply grasped my hand with his sucker thing and winked. Only time will tell what he really meant.

Incidentally, as if to really confuse matters, I once received a newsletter from the President of the International Flat Earth Society in California. In it he explains the 'Flat Earth' theory:

> It began with the Creation of the Creation. First the water . . . the face of the deep . . . without form or limits . . . just Water. Then the Land sitting in and on the Water, the Water then as now being flat and level, as is the very Nature of Water. There are, of course, mountains and valleys on the Land but since most of the World is Water, we say, 'The World is Flat'. Historical accounts and spoken history tell us the Land part may have been square, all in one mass at one time, then as now, the magnetic north being the Center. Vast cataclysmic events and shaking no doubt broke the land apart, divided the Land to be our present continents or islands as they exist today. One thing we know for sure about this world . . . the known inhabited world is Flat, Level, a Plain World.

Well that clears that one up, then.

10

Boys and the Blackstuff

> Recently, a Leeds fan went to buy a copy of my previous book. He walked into Borders bookstore in Waterford and asked for *Paint it White*. The shop assistant directed him to the DIY section. Priceless!

The one thing that our friends across the Irish Sea have never had a problem with is the licensing laws. The British, on the other hand, have taken quite a while to grasp that what is needed is a relaxed arrangement that enables one to have a drink, basically, whenever one chooses.

I can hazily recollect one of the first times I set foot on Irish soil. We had travelled overnight on the ferry from Holyhead and arrived in the early morning darkness at Dún Laoghaire. We had been drinking rather heavily on the crossing and, as we stumbled down the gangway, I jokingly said to the ship steward, 'Is there anywhere we can get a drink round here, mate?'

He looked at his watch and casually said, 'Yes, sir.' He pointed down the street in front of us. 'All those pubs there on the left are open.' It was 6 a.m.

Later, we learned that certain pubs remained open for workers such as dockers, fishermen and other night workers. Our body clocks were thrown into total confusion when these pubs closed, and the usual ones opened at 11 a.m. Gazing through the smoky windows into the glaring midday sun outside, it was hard to grasp the fact that we had consumed possibly a gallon of Guinness already. Our morning's consumption, combined with the constant alcohol intake on the overnight journey, meant it was going to be a long day.

Over the years, we gradually became accustomed to the relaxed Irish lifestyle and found that a hearty breakfast was an ideal way to prepare the body for the onslaught of hospitality that lay ahead. On that first trip, we discovered a small dockside café that provided the usual bacon, egg, sausage and much more. At least that's what we told Stuart Smythe.

We had informed Stuart that the café we were in provided a little extra with the breakfast, and we didn't mean extra mushrooms. Scotty explained to Smythey that if he required a little bit of crumpet in an upstairs bedroom all he had to do was wink at the girl behind the counter and ask for a pot of tea when he ordered his breakfast, and it would be arranged. This he did.

'Certainly, sir,' the girl said. 'Where are you sitting?'

'Over there,' Stuart replied, eagerly pointing to an empty table in the corner. From all over the café we watched as the girl brought Stuart his breakfast.

'Enjoy your meal, sir,' she said, as she set the plate down on the table.

We all giggled as he said to her, 'I ordered a pot of tea, love.' Then he winked again.

'Yes, it's coming,' she said.

'Luvvly Chubly,' he replied, as he rubbed his hands together and gently poured some salt on his sausage. She promptly returned with his pot of tea. She left it on the table and turned to walk away. Stuart took her by the arm: 'Excuse me, love,' he said, winking yet again, 'I ordered a pot of tea.' He nodded down at his silver teapot.

'Yes, sir,' the girl said, confused. 'Is there something wrong?'

Stuart produced a roll of Irish punts and placed it on the table. The girl became very uncomfortable, and we were rolling with laughter, when he said, 'No, love, I just wanted a POT OF TEA,' and he winked again.

'Excuse me, sir, I'll get someone to deal with you,' she said, as she slipped away.

Stuart looked round at us all. 'Now we're getting somewhere,' he announced.

The owner of the café arrived at Stuart's table. 'Is there a problem, sir?' he asked.

'No, mate. I just want a POT OF TEA,' said Stuart and winked at the owner.

'I'm sorry, sir, I don't understand.' Stuart was now winking as if he had some terrible affliction and repeated his request. 'I'm sorry, sir,' said the owner, 'I'll have to ask you to leave.' We were all rolling on the floor with laughter, as Stuart left the café and muttered to us all, 'Bastards!'

In July 1991, Leeds played two games in Ireland. Wub and I had decided to take our big, old American car over, so we could travel around Ireland as we pleased. We almost missed the boat, but, just as the doors were about to close, the police and security guards frantically waved us through. Like something out of *Starsky and Hutch* our big, blue Oldsmobile leapt through the air and landed heavily on the tailgate of the ferry. Our three passengers in the back, Paul 'Lunge' Turnpenny, Paul 'Robbo' Robinson and Bob Dove, sat in horrified silence as, with sparks flying everywhere, we ground to a halt next to the last car on board. Luckily, there was no damage done, and we were able to drive off the ferry after the crossing. It was a short drive into Dublin from the ferry. Once there, the car was immediately put to bed, and we all headed into the city centre for a pint or two of the famous 'Blackstuff'.

The morning after, nursing a few delicate heads, the five of us sat down at our breakfast table in the hotel. There was just enough time for a traditional cooked Irish breakfast before the day's events began in earnest. As usual, Wub opted to pass on the game and, instead, caught up on the latest Stephen King novel in the comfort of the hotel room. The rest of us met up with the Leeds fans already converging on the pubs near to Tolka Park. We had a bit of a shock, as we looked around at the newest additions to the walls in The Ivy House. A framed Leeds United picture was hanging on one wall, and on another wall was a picture of Liverpool FC. However, the offensive item was a framed picture of manchester united. To avoid any major disturbance, a fan placed a Leeds flag over the picture. However, it was too late. Nicholas Jerema (aka 'the Doctor'), whilst drinking in The Cat and Cage 20 yards away, had already heard about the picture and stormed in to investigate. 'Where is it?' he asked. It was obvious what he was referring to, and, within seconds, the smashed picture and frame were lying on the floor in tiny pieces. The landlady wasn't too happy about what had happened, and, as she left the bar to investigate, the Doctor simply said, 'Don't bother banning me, love. I'm off!' With that he returned to his pint in The Cat and Cage. We supped up and followed him.

The day after the game, we set off for Cork in the south of Ireland, and we soon met up with Terry Dooley and some others from the LUSC Cork Branch. Cork is a superb place; I wish Leeds would play there more often. The countless bars always make it easy to settle in. We've been a couple of times since that trip, but it's not nearly enough.

If my memory serves me correctly, I think Wub actually came to the game at Musgrave Park that evening. One thing I definitely remember about that game was Robbo shouting at a lad walking around the pitch. The young chap was wearing a bright yellow Sheffield United shirt. 'What's that horrible shirt you've got on, mate?' Robbo hissed. 'I don't see them playing here.'

We all turned around to look at Robbo. Bob was the first to speak. 'What are you talking about, Robbo?' he asked. 'What about that shirt you've got on?'

Robbo was wearing a Glasgow Rangers shirt, and, realising his mistake, he deflected the attention and asked, 'Anyone fancy a pint?'

Normally, on our trips to Ireland, we like to spend a day at the seaside whenever we can. A 20-minute train ride from Dublin takes you to Bray. It's a great little place with live bands playing on little stages along the sea front. While there, we regularly bump into seasoned Leeds supporter John Farrell and his lad, Adam. John has been going to Leeds games for years. He is from Harrogate, which is a frightfully posh town outside Leeds. If you are unfortunate enough to get beaten up in Harrogate, they will dust you down afterwards and apologise. Now that's posh.

On 22 July 1992, we played Shelbourne at Tolka Park in a game billed as the 'Match of the Champions', due to both teams having won their respective leagues.

Unusually, we arrived in Dublin without a prior hotel booking. We assumed it would be no problem, but we were wrong. There was a game going on at one of the Gaelic football stadiums, and there wasn't a room to be had anywhere. Some Leeds fans had managed to squeeze into backstreet hotels here and there, and Collar and Scottie had found a little bed and breakfast establishment near the city centre. They had quite a few additional guests in their room that night. After leaving a nightclub, six of us made our way back to Collar's 'twin room'. We crept upstairs, bouncing off the walls as quietly as we could. I settled down for the night under a coffee table, with the tablecloth wrapped around me. During the small hours, I went into the bathroom for a tinkle. I was greeted by Collar's motionless body slumped over the toilet. The walls were black, completely black. It looked as if there had been a fire in there and that the walls were charred. It was, of course, about a gallon of Guinness plastered all over the walls. I was genuinely worried, as I tried to waken Collar. He had nothing on but his undercrackers, and eventually he came round. When I awoke next morning the whole place was spotless. Collar must have spent the rest of the night cleaning up.

We sneaked out of the hotel early and made the mistake of calling into McDonald's for breakfast. I just stared at my 'breakfast' with its cardboard egg and left it untouched.

Whenever we're in Dublin, Wub and I try to get to a hotel bar where the resident jazz/blues band are tremendous. On one particular stay, we were at the other side of town and were having difficulty finding it. A local man told us, 'Yes, I know the one you mean. Follow this road straight on, turn left and when you come to a big tree turn right, and it's 100 yards on your left.'

We spent over an hour looking for the tree, and we were going round in circles when Wub pointed up at a building opposite: 'Do you think that could be our "tree"?' she asked. Painted on the building was the number three, about ten foot high and painted in white. That was our 'tree' alright: we'd not accounted for the strong Irish accent of our guide.

In the late '90s, Leeds took part in the Carlsberg Tournament at Lansdowne Road. The other teams involved were Liverpool, St Patrick's FC from Dublin and Italy's Lazio. We were staying in a hotel near to Dún Laoghaire and close to the main train line into the city. Collar had taken his daughter Ruth with him on the trip, and she fell deeply in love with Neil 'Hudsy' Hudson. When Collar, the ever-doting father, noticed this blossoming romance he didn't let Ruth out of his sight, and, when he did, he designated Tracy Mosley to look after her. Collar even came down to breakfast one morning still wearing his pyjamas, in case he missed an early-morning cuddle by the young sweethearts. I kid you not.

Later that day, we all boarded the train into the city centre. It was packed with Leeds fans – both British and Irish – and there was a handful of Liverpool fans dotted around. The train ride was very bumpy, and we all stood holding onto the safety straps overhead. One of our lads fell into a woman passenger standing near the door. She wasn't at all pleased, and, in a stupid attempt to defuse any animosity, I went to the woman and apologised, 'Sorry, love, he didn't mean to do it. It was an accident.'

This seemed to work and she smiled. 'It's OK,' she said, 'no harm done.'

Just then, the train swung violently. I was thrown towards the woman and ended up putting a hand on each of her breasts. Feeling that another apology would be futile, I sheepishly moved away down the train.

In 2005, Leeds fulfilled an outstanding invitation to play Drogheda in a special game to raise funds for a cancer charity backed by Leeds United's Gary Kelly. It was a great cause and a great excuse for us to visit somewhere different on the Emerald Isle. We travelled in a small group organised by big Mick Hewitt. We split into two groups and stayed at two different guest houses, each within walking distance of the town centre. Jeff was with me, as were Ralph and Phil Benson. Our guest house was a quaint little place, delightfully called St Gobnait's. The owners, Mr and Mrs Lucey, welcomed us at the door, with a greeting that is exclusively the reserve of the Irish. However, they did a double take at the Bensons. They are identical twins with the only difference being Ralph's supposed half-inch height superiority. Everyone, I'm sure, has heard of the 'Evil Twin' syndrome, but the Bensons are really quite unique – they both have one!

It wasn't long before we were in a bar with some of Gary Kelly's brothers. And it wasn't long before the Bensons were on stage doing what they do best – singing. Their rendition of Tony Christie's latest revival soon had them rocking in the aisles.

The next day, Leeds fans gathered for an early Sunday-morning drink near the ground, hours before a noon kick-off. Of course, the Mavericks were out in force, as were the Oxford lads (although this time in civvy clothes and not the fancy dress for which they had become known). The landlord was loving every minute of it and chatted happily at the bar with Mozzer and some of the Tadcaster lads. Kick-off came around all too soon, and we trudged off to the match. Leeds shirts were in evidence all around the ground, as Leeds played out a 1–1 draw, before allowing us all to return to the pub.

We were drinking with the Kellys in a pub when some of the other Leeds players walked in; the atmosphere was great. We then met up with Paul Butler, Clarke Carlisle, Danny Pugh and others. Also with us were Kev and Clarkey from Lancaster. New Leeds boy Nicky Gray told us not to tell his dad (Eddie) that he was out having a drink, so we assured him that we wouldn't. Apart from a slight altercation between Kev and Jermaine Wright, everyone went home happy.

Another journey that is still talked about to this day was a rare visit by Leeds to Northern Ireland in 1982 (the previous one to that being in 1971). On 23 March, our minibus picked me up at Crosshills in Kippax. I was the last pick-up, and, before I'd even sat down, I was invited to help myself to a bottle of beer from one of the many crates in the aisle. Collar had organised the trip, and included in the price of the journey was an endless supply of Theakston's Old Peculier. Before we'd even left Kippax, our driver, who came with the hired minibus, leaned back and, with his arm outstretched, said, 'They look OK, I'll have one of them.' Someone thrust a bottle of beer into his hand, and thus started a pattern that was to continue throughout the journey.

Because of a dock strike at Liverpool, we had to travel all the way to Stranraer to board a ferry to Belfast for the game against Glentoran. Throughout the journey north, the driver had continued to drink beer. When we boarded the ferry, we headed for the bar, thinking that the driver would finally get his head down and sleep for a couple of hours. Not a chance! He came to the bar with us and only left a few minutes before we docked at the other side. As he left the bar he said, 'Hey, that Guinness is alright. I'll have to try a few of them.'

When we arrived at the Oval Grounds, the place was buzzing. As we headed for Glentoran's supporters club, we noticed Jack Charlton holding court with several young fans. We entered the club with our driver still in tow. He was beginning to show signs of fatigue, and, as we were travelling back home straight after the match, we began to get a little worried.

Once we gathered inside the ground, it became apparent that Leeds fans were scattered all around, but our little group in the main stand began to attract attention from the locals. A lot of them were still dressed in their school uniforms, and one stood out from the rest. 'I'm a Leeds fan,' he kept saying. He knew every Leeds player on the pitch and sat with us throughout the entire game. He told us that he came over to Leeds for every game. He was obviously still at school, and we found his claim a little hard to believe. He told us that he hitch-hiked from Belfast each week and would often sleep rough on his long journeys. He pointed to Collar, then me, then to Pete Dillon. 'I've seen you lot,' he said. 'You're the Kippax lot.' We were shell shocked. How did he know?

It turned out that his name was Mark Cosgrove, and his claims were, in fact, true. From then on, he would stay at my home every time he travelled to Leeds. His new name was now 'Belfast Bill': a name that has stayed with him to this day. Bill has done very well for himself and is now the director of a major haulage firm in Northern Ireland. Ironic to think that he used to catch a lift with those very lorries when he was a youngster. Nice one, Bill.

After the game – a 5–2 victory to Leeds – we waited on the dockside for our minibus and driver to pick us up. We'd only been there a few minutes when Ray Clowes and I were cautioned by a policeman for having a piss up against a wall. It was really funny: I just zipped up and moved along, but 'Old Ray', a veteran if ever there was one, told the policeman how old he was and that a police officer that young couldn't tell him how to behave. Luckily, the bus arrived just in time to whisk him off.

Old Ray is a right character. In the coach park at Villa Park one year we 'kidnapped' him and got him onto our bus instead of his usual one. We passed the journey by sharing a few cans of light ale. As we pulled into the city centre, our bus took a corner rather fast, and an unopened can of cola fell from the luggage rack and onto

Ray's head, cutting it open. A couple of the lads had to go with him to hospital. We explained to him, before he left the coach that had it been a beer can there wouldn't have been a problem, as it would have been empty.

Another time, I travelled with Old Ray to a testimonial game in Swansea in the early '80s. Along with Brod, we made our way down in Dick Fenwick's trusty old white Morris Marina. Watching the game that night were one or two non-payers: overlooking the stadium was Swansea Prison, and the prisoners were peering through the windows, enjoying a free show. Local legend had it that petty crime soared in the area when a home game was coming up.

Immediately after the incident with Ray and the policeman, our luck continued because one look at our driver (we never did get his name) told us that he hadn't stayed off the booze while we were at the game: he had literally matched us pint-for-pint since picking me up at 7.30 that morning. With the copper watching us, we all held our breath and prayed, as our driver, totally oblivious to the policeman watching him, slowly drove away.

The homeward journey from Stranraer was an experience I'll never forget. We swayed from side to side along the dark, endless country lanes leading back into England. Pete Dillon and I sat directly behind the driver and, on more than one occasion, we had to slap him hard, as he began to fall asleep. We even had to take the wheel from time to time, as we would veer off into an open field, startling sheep who had settled down for the night. Lucky sheep: Pete and I didn't get any sleep that night.

To pass the time, I opened another beer and read my match programme. Inside it was a message from the match sponsors, Leeds Permanent Building Society. It read, 'Take this programme to any of our branches and receive a free gift.' When we eventually arrived home safely, and I'd grabbed an hour in the cot, I went with my programme to the Leeds Society branch in Castleford. They didn't have a clue what I was talking about (I didn't think they would) but, eventually, I walked out with my free gift: one of those plastic towers that you collect coins in. That'll come in handy, I thought, as I drove back to Kippax.

11

Norf and Sarf

> Players can kiss the badge all they like, but, by and large, the only loyalty comes from the fans.

The man primarily responsible for the idea for this and the first book is Alan Osborne. I'd like to take a bit of time out here and describe this unique character. Alan is a dedicated West Ham United fan and was born within yards of Upton Park. His dad Cyril took him to his first game in 1956. Ironically, it was against Blackpool. Exactly ten years later, I would go to my first Leeds United game – against Blackpool.

Rather cheekily, Alan told me that West Ham's League Cup tie against Leeds United, two days after bonfire night in 1966, was one of their best-ever victories. The result that evening escapes me, but I think it was something like 7–0 to West Ham. However, Alan was quick to spring to the defence of Leeds: 'Don Revie said afterwards that that would never happen again while ever he was manager, and he predicted that they would go all the following season [1967–68] without a defeat.' It didn't quite work out like that, but during the 1968–69 league season Leeds were beaten only twice and gained a record number of 67 points (a record that still stands under the two points for a win system).

Alan has lived life to the full, and as a youngster he joined the ground staff at his beloved West Ham United. He later moved on and went to play for Leyton Orient, before becoming their general manager. During that period, he would regularly rub shoulders with George Graham as well as with some real characters of the game from those days, such as

Rodney Marsh and Jimmy Greaves. It was whilst he was at Orient that he first met his idol, Bobby Moore. Leeds fans consider Norman Hunter to be unlucky for not gaining more caps for England, but there is no doubt that Bobby Moore was an outstanding footballer of his time.

Years later Alan was in his office at Orient when his phone rang. It was Carol Stokes, who was the only female secretary of any club in the country at that time. 'Alan,' she said, 'it's Bobby Moore on the phone.'

'Is that you, Bob?' Alan said.

'Hello, Alan,' said Moore. 'Look, as you know, I've just taken over at Southend as commercial manager. We're from the same neck of the woods, so you scratch my back and I'll scratch yours. Know what I mean?'

'Sure, Bob,' Alan replied.

Alan was a boozer – a big boozer – but he admits that he couldn't lace Bobby's boots. 'I'd be drinking with him in the club bar,' says Alan, 'and Bobby would put away about 75,000 pints of beer and walk out as fresh as a daisy.'

It was whilst they were in a Chinese restaurant that Bobby told Alan that he had cancer. He told Alan at the time that he'd beaten it, but, sadly, he died shortly afterwards. The funeral was a private, family affair, but Alan attended a service at Westminster Abbey where many spoke of Bobby, including Jimmy Tarbuck.

Alan was eventually released by Orient and, subsequently, met and married Denise, a lass from Kippax who had lived in my street when I was a kid. Alan moved up to Leeds and remained there for 20 years. It was in Kippax that we became firm friends. I had seen Alan a few times in The Moorgate pub; he was always impeccably dressed and was always holding court with a group of lads from the taproom. No one had a bad word for Alan, and we soon discovered that we had a mutual affection for the beautiful game. We were both passionate about our respective clubs, and, of course, we both immensely disliked manchester united (and France).

Alan came along to a few of the European glory nights at Elland Road in 2000. He soon became a regular, as we would trawl the bars in the city centre and then head down for some top European action. He would often tell me afterwards that the hair on the back of his neck had stood up, as the atmosphere rose to fever pitch. He did, of course, always remain loyal to West Ham.

NORF AND SARF

Alan used to run a business in Hull (he was also a non-executive director at Hull City Football Club) and once, when I got a job there, it gave us the ideal opportunity to meet up for drinks. Some days we would travel across in Alan's car, other days we would take mine or Webby's. One morning, we were travelling along the M62 towards Hull. Alan still has vivid memories of that day: 'It was a crisp sunny morning, and life was wonderful. There we were: the three of us sat in a car, Eddie Stevens [my dad] blasting away on the cassette player, sharing hot, milky coffee from a flask. We were all giddy, as it was "Christmas Eve" [It was a Friday, and we used to call Fridays Christmas Eve because it was the day before match day]. Gary and Webby would be going to Elland Road the day after to watch Leeds play Everton; I would be catching the 7.30 a.m. train from Leeds to London for the Hammers game against Tottenham.'

Webby and I quite liked the odd drink, but Alan and his business partner John were professionals. We were working on a refurbishment at a pub close to Alan's office, and every lunchtime the four of us would go for a drink. The only problem was that the 'lunch-hour' would invariably last for three hours, sometimes four.

Another regular customer of that pub was the rugby league legend Johnny Ward. Johnny had heard that Alan was after a large fridge-freezer. Alan was in his office the following day when he got a phone call from a very irate Denise. She had arrived back home and was unable to put the car in the drive because 'somebody' had left a fridge-freezer the size of a Ford Transit on it. He had to go home and move it.

It wasn't long before I had to put the brakes on our lunchtime get-togethers: we were beginning to fall behind with the job and were in danger of not hitting the deadline. At first, to compensate for our extended lunchtimes, Webby and I began arriving at the job at around 6 a.m. to get a good few hours' work in before the shiny business shoes of Alan and his partner would come tapping up the alley into the pub. One day, I told Webby that when they came for us we'd tell them that we'd see them later and just not go: instead, we'd carry on at work. The next day we heard the familiar tapping of shoes coming up the alley. 'Hallo boys, you ready?' said Alan cheerfully.

'Not quite, Al,' I said. 'We've just got this wall to finish. We'll see you in the pub later.'

'OK mate, no problem,' replied Alan.

Then it went quiet. I looked around and the two of them were sat down in their business suits on our dust sheets draped across the seats.

'What's up, Al?' I asked. 'We'll see you there, mate.'

'It's all right, Snake,' said Alan, opening a newspaper, 'we'll wait for you.' It was an impossible situation, but quite funny looking back on it.

Unfortunately, Alan's heavy drinking caught up with him, and, after the breakdown of his marriage, he realised he had to do something about it. He eventually moved back down to London and took the brave step of checking into a clinic in Weymouth called Clouds to deal with his drinking. It was no ordinary clinic: many stars had been treated there. When he first arrived at the clinic with his dad, Alan was understandably nervous and not sure about what he was about to do. Realising his apprehension, the staff told him to go to the pub and have a good drink. This he did and, a couple of hours later, he walked in and never looked back.

While he was in the clinic, two of the lads from The Moorgate pub – Kev Higgins and Sean Plows – went down to spend a few days with him and to enjoy a couple of days by the sea. One evening, they were in the clinic's television room with Alan and some of the other patients. Kev was chatting away to some of them. 'How are you doing?' he asked one who was sitting on the edge of the sofa.

'Oh fine, it's alright here,' he replied.

Kev sat beside him. 'Do you get to go out often?' he asked.

'Oh yes,' he said, 'every night. I'm the chef.'

Nowadays, we often meet up when the opportunity arises and our two teams play one another. For the games in London we meet up with West Ham fans known to Alan at The Mamby Arms in Stratford. One morning, a poor Arsenal fan walked in expecting a quiet morning with his newspaper: instead, he came across 150 Leeds and West Ham fans singing their hearts out. On one such occasion, the landlord Lenny took almost a thousand pounds in just two hours.

Alan's life has now completely turned around. He's off the booze, and, thanks to evening classes, he has discovered a talent he never knew he had. His artwork and paintings are absolutely brilliant. He has been awarded a diploma for his efforts and has recently been accepted into the University of East London.

Alan continues to watch West Ham, but he celebrated the Hammers' recent return to the Premiership with a glass of Coke. I rang

Alan to congratulate him on his team's achievement, and he told me that he had just been round to his local newsagent and won a prize with everyone's favourite newspaper (not!), the *Daily Mirror.* He'd scratched off a 'winning formula' scratch card and quickly inspected the result. Among the prize possibilities were a £1,000,000 cash prize, a two-week cruise or even a brand-new car. Alan's daydreaming was interrupted by the shopkeeper telling him that he had won a two-day trip to visit the set of *Emmerdale.* He couldn't believe it and slowly began to return home. He looked at his prize and despaired. He was determined to win a top prize so stormed back to the shop and grabbed another card. This time he won . . . another trip to *Emmerdale.*

Meanwhile, life back at Alan's old haunt The Moorgate has been dealt a few testing blows. We would regularly follow a day's sport via the Teletext system. Well, I'm afraid to say, things have deteriorated. The owners of the brewery have refused to pay an increase in the entertainment licence, and so the jukeboxes and televisions have been removed from all their pubs. The former landlord, Steve, who used to work as the famous laughing clown at Blackpool's Pleasure Beach has made way for new hosts, Neil and Lorraine. Neil, although of southern descent, is an avid Liverpool fan; Lorraine is a Geordie and, quite predictably, supports Newcastle. In the face of the obstacles placed in front of them, the regulars still file into the famous Moorgate taproom.

Recently, there was a refurbishment to the pub and we went on a little 'pub-crawl' for a few nights, using the lounge area of the pub instead of the usual taproom. Although part of the same pub, the lounge and the taproom at The Moorgate have their own distinct styles and the clientele of each tends to stick with one or the other. Of course, we all know each other and often catch up with the gossip in the shared toilets.

In the corner of the room, on top of the television stand upon a redundant digital box, there now rests a green cardboard 'television', complete with long-distance antenna. The screen is, conveniently, A4 size, to allow customers to bring in their own movies at night. The other evening, we all settled down to watch 'Titanic 2'. Another advantage is that we can produce our own football results. In Kippax, Leeds actually won the Premiership last season.

12

Webby and the Vikings

Around 1,200 years after the Vikings invaded Britain, Leeds fans took revenge and began invading Scandinavia. We won many friends and have been going back ever since. And we still haven't seen a longboat.

Stewart Webb is not your average Leeds fan. He weighs around 18 st. and is about 6 ft 5 in. in height; he is also covered in tattoos and sports a skinhead. Needless to say, he is an intimidating figure. Originally from the Pontefract area, he now lives in Swinton in South Yorkshire. He has a tidy little flat that he shares with his parrot called Snake. Every wall is covered with very impressive framed Leeds United autographed shirts and pictures.

After a particularly boozy night out with local entrepreneur and massive Leeds fan Ray Beverley, they both returned to Webby's flat. (When I say massive Leeds fan I mean massive in every sense of the word.) Armed with a Chinese supper, they both slithered up the back stairway. 'I'll get some plates and some beer,' Webby said. 'You take the snap into the living room.' All of a sudden, Webby heard a crash. Rushing in, he discovered Ray flat out on the floor. Spare ribs, curry, rice and chips were scattered all over the floor. 'Soz, pal,' slurred Ray. 'I tripped.'

Closer inspection revealed a parrot completely covered in spicy noodles. Snake was not impressed, and, as he shook his head, noodles fell from his beak onto the floor of his cage. Undeterred, the two drunken pals scooped up their food and put on a video. They then proceeded to scoff their meal of chips and carpet fur. An hour later, with the duo snoring their heads off, Snake finished off the last of his 'amazing coat of many noodles'.

Webby used to have a part-time job as a doorman at the pub just over the road from his flat. One Sunday afternoon, he was enjoying a bit of exercise in his bedroom with a lady friend. When Webby was stark naked, the handcuffs came out. He giggled as she fastened his hands to the head of the bed with the cuffs. It was about 4 p.m. She had her wicked way with him, and then, at about 6 p.m., she just got up and left the room. Half an hour later, she had not returned. Webby pleaded, 'Come on, love, I'm working at seven. Undo the cuffs, sweetheart.' Her response was immediate: 'You're going nowhere, darling.' At 10 p.m., she telephoned the pub to tell them why he wasn't at work. You can imagine his mates' responses, when red-faced Webby next returned to the pub.

Webby worked for my decorating firm for a few years, and, during that time, we were never short of incident. One day, we were working on a job in Kippax. The owner was a regular customer, and she was going away for a few days. 'Right, Gary, here's the key, and help yourself to anything [i.e. tea and coffee]. I'll see you when I get back. Cheerio.'

Leeds were playing at Elland Road that evening, and, as I left to go to another job, I said to Webby, 'I'll be back around four, mate, and we'll go through to Leeds for the game.'

'OK, mate,' Webby replied cheerfully, as he began putting the dust sheets down.

Later that day I returned to pick him up. As I entered the house I noticed that he had done well: the job appeared to be complete. Everything had been tidied up and was ready to be loaded into the van. But where was Webby? Just then, he called down from upstairs. I thought it was a bit strange: there was nothing to do upstairs.

I began to climb the stairs. 'Where are you, mate?' I shouted.

'In here, pal,' he replied from the bathroom.

Gingerly, I opened the door. There, in all his glory, was Webby, covered in soapsuds, enjoying a nice hot bath. I stared in amazement. A nice hot cup of tea was perched handily on the side of the bath. Unperturbed, he continued to bathe with a huge soapy sponge. 'Kettle's just boiled, mate. Mek yersen' a cuppa,' he said calmly.

'What the bleedin' 'ell are you doin'?' I managed to say finally.

'She said, "help yourself",' he replied. 'I got finished early, so I thought I'd have a nice relaxing bath before the match.' I was speechless. I walked back downstairs, still stunned by what I'd just witnessed. Half an hour later, a very shiny Webby and I went to Elland Road.

Nothing seemed to faze Webby. I once returned to a job in Garforth where Webby had been working up some ladders. As I turned the corner, I noticed the ladders were tilted at an unusual angle. His paint brush and tin were lying on the ground. Then I noticed a yellow piece of paper attached to the ladders, flapping in the wind. The paper read, 'Snake, fallen off ladders, gone to hospital.'

At least he'd spelt it right. Webby is not renowned for his spelling. One morning we were having a cup of tea, and Webby was doing the sports crossword. He'd answered any questions on Leeds United immediately and most of the football ones, but, as usual, everything was spelt wrong: he didn't have a hope in hell of completing it. Frustrated, he threw the newspaper to the floor. I picked it up. As I looked at the unfinished crossword, I noticed four blank squares. I looked at the clue, 'Probably the most famous footballer of all time. Brazilian No 10'.

'You must know that one,' I said, reading it out.

'Not enough squares,' he replied, smugly.

I was confused. 'What do you mean?' I asked.

'I'm not thick, Snake. I know it's Pelé, but it doesn't fit.' He went on, 'P-E-L-L-Y, see – not enough squares.' Again, I was lost for words.

It has to be said that Webby is a great worker: he just gets on with the job. However, sometimes I have to 'guide' him. One time, we were working on a rather quaint country pub. The job was almost complete, and three-quarters of the pub was full with pensioners enjoying their lunch. I was working in another room, and Webby was finishing off the skirting boards in a part of the pub near to the scoffing pensioners. When I had finished, I went in to see how Webby was getting on. I was horrified by what I saw. About 4 ft away from a pensioner tucking into her fish and chips was Webby. He was kneeling down, displaying about a yard of his arse over the top of his tracksuit bottoms. I gently manoeuvred his huge, bulky frame so that the pensioner could pick her jaw up from the floor and continue with her meal.

On another pub job, this time in Hull, Webby once again demonstrated his unique ability to get into mischief. The job was almost complete, and the place was swarming with officials from the brewery and building firms. The clerk of works was mooching around with his clipboard. Now, as I've already said, Webby is a good worker, but he has a tendency to 'stand out from the crowd'. To be on the safe side, I had put him out of the way to finish the toilets upstairs. I was downstairs in the main lounge putting the finishing touches to the decor. Whilst the officials were gathered in another room, I heard a loud whisper: 'Snake!' I looked round. It sounded like Webby and indeed it was. He was calling me through the half-closed door leading to the toilets.

'Snake, here, come here quick!' he hissed. I made my way to the door, looking round to make sure the officials were nowhere in sight. I opened the door, and there was Webby looking at me with puppy dog eyes. He gestured for me to look down. His foot was lodged firmly in a gallon tin of white emulsion. He started to explain: 'I was coming down the steps backwards . . .'

I interrupted him and told him to stay where he was. I got some large shears: we prised his foot out of the tin and cleaned it up. Quickly. However, before releasing his foot, I took a photograph of the great clown. It was at times like those that I thought of calling my firm 'Laurel and Hardy'.

There is never a dull moment when Webby is around, and his antics continue throughout the football season. Like the time when we were on our way to a Leeds game at Crystal Palace. We were at a pub near Selhurst Park, and an intense game of three-card brag was in full swing. Webby was out of the game and had gone to the toilet. With the card game reaching its climax, Webby returned and leant over the table. In the middle of it he placed a 10-in. turd. 'I couldn't flush that baby away without showing you it,' he boasted. The commotion that followed meant that the game finished with the cards all over the floor and no winner.

When the football season finally draws to a close, Webby and I pursue our love of Yorkshire County Cricket Club. During one particular summer, Yorkshire were doing well in the league and cup competitions. Attendances were huge and a bumper crowd was expected for the forthcoming C&G Cup game with Essex at Headingley. Four of us managed to get tickets for the Western Terrace. Normally, alcohol restrictions are quite relaxed, but on this occasion none was permitted through the turnstiles. This didn't please Webby at all. 'They can go bollocks,' was his response. 'I'm taking beer in!'

I explained that we would have to utilise the cunning plan that we had used previously on similar occasions. We would take a couple of cans up to the turnstile in our carrier bags. Underneath the exposed cans, we would wrap four more in paper and silver foil, to disguise them as sandwiches. The steward would inspect our bags, see the cans and say that we would have to drink them there and then before we could go in. He would then ask about the silver packages, which we would tell him were sandwiches. We would drink our cans within sight of 'our' steward before going through 'his' turnstile with our silver package. This plan had worked every time, without exception. 'So,' I repeated to Webby the night before, 'disguise your beers as sandwiches.' He put the phone down, still grumbling.

The next day John Stowe, Big John Martin and I were waiting for Webby at Headingley train station. As the next train pulled in, hundreds of Yorkshire fans charged off. The last to get off the train was Webby. He was dragging a cooler that was the size of a small family car. 'Christ, Webby!' I said. 'You'll never get in with that!' He just mumbled and headed for the ground, dragging his box behind him.

The two Johns and I were chatting to other Leeds fans about the season that had just finished, and so we didn't notice Webby disappear out of sight. When we arrived at the turnstile our plan worked a treat, and we were soon in the ground, but there was no sign of Webby as we began sharing our cans round.

'He's there,' said Big John, pointing towards the Kirkstall Lane End. Webby was coming round from the other side of the ground. Eventually he plonked down by the side of us with his wares. He had talked his way in at another turnstile. I gave him one of my cans and afterwards said, 'Come on then, Webby, let's have one of your beers.'

He opened his cooler and handed me an object wrapped in silver foil. I stared at it and asked, 'What's this?'

'You said "wrap them up in silver foil",' he replied. Webby had surpassed himself, yet again. He had sat up the night before and wrapped 48 bottles of Budweiser, individually, in silver foil.

Webby then tried to divert attention from himself. During a lull in proceedings on the pitch, Webby noticed Chris Silverwood, the Yorkshire and England ace bowler. Webby had spent the night before with Chris's sister and thought it would be a good idea to shout and tell him about it in front of a packed crowd. Characteristically, Chris laughed it off. 'Silvers' is from Kippax, and I recently had the pleasure of removing all traces of red paint in his home. I enjoyed that.

Webby's antics are not just confined to these shores. The Scandinavians have sampled his delightful presence on many occasions, a pre-season game against Gallastad in Sweden in 1998 being a good example. As is usual on this type of trip, the game was played in the middle of nowhere. We were in a small picturesque town with a population of around 5,000, all of whom, it seemed, had turned out to watch Leeds United. It was during the regime of manager George Graham, and, to be honest, things weren't going particularly well. It was a good hour before the kick-off and I was enjoying the sunshine with a beer to hand. I was outside the specially erected beer tent with Webby, Big Mick Hewitt, Ian 'Coke' Cockayne, from Wellingborough, and Geir Jensen, from Norway. The Leeds players were out on the pitch loosening up and doing some stretches. Everyone was in a relaxed mood, and the Leeds fans present were attracting a fair bit of attention from the local media. A couple of journalists spied us at the beer tent, and one of them said, in perfect English, 'Excuse me. The Lord Mayor of this town has asked if someone from Leeds would come and speak about the Leeds team.' We all picked up our beers and pretended we hadn't heard him properly: except Webby, of course.

'Here, mate, I'll do it, no problem,' he said loudly, because that's how he speaks – loudly. 'Come on, mate,' he continued, 'where do you want me?' He walked off with the rather bemused media man and his colleagues. He was escorted to a gazebo situated on the halfway line. It was adorned with ribbons and rosettes. It was all very grand indeed. Webby was then introduced to the Mayor and other distinguished guests.

'Welcome, sir,' the Mayor began. 'What is your name?'

'Er . . . Stewart, your worshipness,' Webby shouted down the microphone. The sound system let out a loud screech, and the crew moved to turn the sound down a little. I looked at Mick and we began to snigger.

'Welcome to Sweden, Stewart, and welcome to all players and supporters of Leeds United!' the Mayor continued. There was a big cheer all around the ground, and in the beer tent the people around us raised their glasses to us.

The Leeds players and manager George Graham were now sitting relaxing on the pitch: Stewart had their undivided attention. 'Now, Stewart, how do you think Leeds will play in your Premiership this season?' the Mayor asked.

Webby took the microphone back off the Mayor and blew into it and tapped it, almost blowing the headphones off of the crew. 'This lot?' he asked, pointing towards the pitch. 'No chance!' Sherry glasses fell to floor, as Webby's words echoed all around the ground. Webby then pointed to the manager and continued, 'Until that twat there gets his hand in his pocket, we'll win fuck all!'

The Mayor slumped into his chair and was being wafted with a large white napkin. Two stewards tried to discreetly remove the microphone from Webby's hand, but he was now in full flight. He pointed to poor David Hopkin and said, 'And him there, he's the worst footballer I've ever seen in my life!'

The Leeds players didn't know where to look. For the benefit of the few people in the ground who didn't speak English, each word was being translated to them. 'I've spent more on beer today than Hopkin's worth, and I'll tell you another thing . . .'

Five or six stewards finally wrestled the microphone from Webby, and he returned to our table. Tears were streaming down my face, and I could hardly speak. My stomach was hurting like hell from all the laughing. Coke and Mick were leaning on each other and roaring with laughter, too. As if to reinforce our mirth, Geir said to Webby, in Scandinavian English, 'Yeah, well, you might be right, you know.' Half an hour later a hurt and a subdued Leeds team kicked off.

Later that evening, we bumped into Nigel Martyn and David Wetherall in a bar. 'Where's your mate?' Nigel said to me. 'That big fella: the guest speaker before the game.' I told him that he was in another bar.

David Wetherall spoke next: 'He's set Hopkin back again – he was just coming out of his shell, and now he won't speak to anyone.'

Apparently, Hopkin, who had been receiving some stick from certain sections of the Leeds fans, had just regained his confidence, and, around that time, he had certainly started playing better. In one swipe, Webby had knocked him for six. Later, when we saw Webby and told him of our talk with the players, he just shrugged his shoulders and said, 'He's shit.'

The next day, possibly in an attempt to remove Webby from any further contact with any other Leeds players, we decided to have a day at the local theme park. It was a pretty impressive set-up called Liseberg, not too far from where we were staying.

Webby, Jeff and I spent an hour whizzing round at 100 mph on various rollercoasters, and then we spied a huge tower. As we arrived at the huge 80-ft structure all three of us looked up at the twelve seats that encircled it. Its function was to shoot a dozen victims high into the sky at devastating speed, and when it came back down the shaken and screaming occupants would be launched into the air once again. That process would be repeated about four or five times: it was the ride for us. After queuing for 20 minutes, with mainly 15-year-old Swedish girls, we boarded the ride.

We eagerly strapped ourselves in. Jeff and I struggled with our fasteners, but eventually squeezed our bellies in enough for them to click shut. No such luck for poor old Webby. He was struggling and cursing, as the giggling young girls watched him frantically wrestle with the fastener. A young female operative came to help. My sides were splitting as she bounced up and down on Webby's large beer belly, in a vain attempt to fasten the buckle. Eventually, with everyone around us howling with laughter, she said, 'I'm sorry. You're too fat to ride this.' Sulking, Webby got out of his seat and walked slowly away, still cursing. We were still laughing when we heard a small hiss beneath our seats and then – WHOOSH! We were propelled skywards at what seemed like warp speed. It certainly was a good job that Webby hadn't been allowed to ride without his seat belt fastened. At the top, the ride stopped, but the passenger carried on with the momentum that had been generated and was lifted right out of their seat until the belt and barrier prevented the body going any further. If Webby had ridden without his belt he could quite easily have ended up in northern Russia.

Webby was still cursing and swearing when we reached the next ride. It was a long carriage with two large mechanical arms at either end. Once on board, everyone was shaken about vigorously. At one stage, we were all turned upside down with only the metal bar across our bellies, including Webby's this time, preventing us from plummeting to certain death. Then, the sadistic operator turned up the pressure. Once again, we were shaken about, but this time it was much harder and we were hanging upside down. Everything from loose change to false teeth fell into the huge ditch below. Jeff had just bought three packets of cigarettes, and he watched as they too plummeted towards the ditch, never to be seen again. We left the park soon afterwards, windswept and full of ice cream.

Webby is not the only oddball that chose Leeds United as his team. One of the most colourful characters amongst the Leeds faithful is Nicholas Jerema. He's known to some as 'Heil', after his German mother, but more people know him as the Doctor. His long, thick flowing locks and sharp facial features bear an uncanny resemblance to our favourite time traveller Dr Who (the one played by Tom Baker). The Doctor is amongst the elite of the regular Leeds fans and appears at every game: home, away and abroad. Some years ago, I was watching a dreary reserve team match at Elland Road. It was cold, raining and the wind was blowing around the half-full West Stand. Ten minutes into the game, I was joined by none other than the Doctor, who was carrying a crash helmet. Despite the atrocious weather, he had travelled to the game on his scooter – all the way from his home in Scunthorpe!

The Scandinavians have also sampled the delights of the Doctor's presence. In 1997 Leeds were in Sweden and the first game on the agenda was against Ostersund. It was a nice little town and, as with almost everywhere in Scandinavia, was spotlessly clean. Ideal for Wub. We were to be there for a few days, and on the first day we became acquainted with the local taverns. We were in our first bar, and it wasn't too long before some of the Leeds players were spotted mingling freely with the English and Scandinavian fans. Jimmy Floyd Hasselbaink, who had just signed for Leeds, headed straight for the roulette table in the corner of the pub. Gary Kelly was at the bar surrounded by two dozen Swedish Leeds fans. He was having a great time! David Wetherall came over to our table with Robert Molenaar: they bought Jeff, Pencil and me a beer, which was very welcome at nearly four pound a pint.

Pencil was another of Leeds' top supporters, travelling to every single game. It was that night in Sweden that he announced to us that he was 'retiring' and that he was buying a pub in Pattaya in Thailand. He and Ralph Ingelby had talked about it for quite some time, and the two of them had decided that the time was right to move on. Ralph is a self-confessed pervert, and his decision to move to Thailand surprised nobody, but with Pencil it was a different matter. At first we dismissed it as a pipe dream, but Pencil was determined and moved to Thailand a few months later – with Ralph in tow.

As day turned into night, we moved to another bar, and then another. Ralph, Whitby John Hartley and the Doctor had now joined us. The Leeds players had, by that time, disappeared, and the atmosphere had stepped up a gear. The Swedes were loving it, and so too were the bar owners. They told us that they had seen nothing like it before. It was midweek and, normally, Scandinavians do not venture out at all during the week, preferring to party at the weekends only. At around 3 a.m., a group of us were walking back to our hotel when we came across a Swedish Leeds fan who'd been drinking with us all day. He was standing outside his house throwing little stones up at the bedroom window. 'What y' doin', mate?' asked the Doctor.

He looked round at us and replied, in fairly good English, 'My wife will not open the door. She says I drink too much.'

The Doctor moved him aside and pulled off a large piece of white fencing that was fastened to the wall beneath the downstairs window. 'You don't want to be throwing little stones like that, mate,' he said and threw the piece of fencing straight through the bedroom window. 'There, old cock,' he said, 'she'll come now.'

We left the Swede behind: his mouth was opening and closing but no words were coming out. As I looked back, I noticed the bedroom light come on: the Doctor was right. The window was boarded up for the rest of our week-long stay, and we never saw that particular Swede again.

The game against Ostersund was a pretty low-key affair and was overshadowed, not for the first time, by the Doctor. After the game, we sat on a grassy bank, near the team coach, talking to some locals. The Leeds players were on the bus, and the Doctor decided to hop on board and get Gary Kelly's autograph.

George Graham leapt to his feet and began shouting at the Doctor to get off the bus. The Doctor walked up to Graham and began prodding him in the chest. We heard the Doctor shout, 'Hey up, you Scottish git! I only want his autograph, sit down!' Graham sat down, and the Doctor got his autograph. He then left the coach, with all the players stifling giggles and Graham staring straight down at the floor.

The next day, Ralph, John and I were in the post office in the town, changing some money. Nigel Martyn and Robert Molenaar came in and joined the queue behind us. We were chatting to them about the team when Ralph interrupted: 'Well, I wouldn't pay them out in washers!' he said defiantly. 'They're not bothered.'

Martyn just smiled and Molenaar said, 'Say what you feel, mate, won't you?'

Ralph responded, 'I will, mate. They are shite!' With that he left to go to the counter. John looked at me and then said to Molenaar, 'Take no notice, pal; he's a bit loopy, know what I mean?'

They both smiled back and Martyn said, 'It's OK, don't worry about it.'

When the three of us had changed our money, we said goodbye to the two players and left. Once outside, John said to Ralph, 'What are you playing at?' Ralph didn't have a clue what John was talking about. 'What did you lay into them two for?' asked John.

Ralph still didn't get it. 'Why,' he said, 'did you know them?' We laughed, and, after John had told him who they were, Ralph just replied, not unlike Webby, 'Oh, was it? Anyway, they are shite.'

Before we had set off for Sweden, Big Mick Hewitt had told us to bring a spare Leeds shirt, some shorts and some socks. We had been challenged to a football match in a remote part of the country called Sveg. When the day arrived, we boarded our chartered coach with our boots. We were to stay the night in Sveg in log cabins. When we arrived, they were more like garden sheds but cosy nonetheless. Wub immediately went to the local store and stocked our fridge with ice for the drinks later that evening. The ground we were to play at was close to our cabins, and we set about erecting our Leeds flags on the poles outside the clubhouse. The dressing-rooms were in the clubhouse, and, shortly before kick-off, we emerged to the tune of 'Marching on Together' bellowing out of the loudspeakers around the pitch. The game had attracted quite a lot of attention, and a crowd of about 2,500 applauded us, as we stepped onto the lush green turf. The media were also present, and cameras clicked away, as some of our players gave interviews. The crowd were obviously bemused by the many different shapes and sizes of the players in our team: I was in goal; 6 ft 5 in. Mick Hewitt was up front; 18 st. Mark Belshaw was the midfield anchor man; 4-ft-high Ralph, the pervert, was on the right wing; and big Coke, at 20 st., was our midfield dynamo. A free midfield role was given to Mick Garner, assisted by Leicester's very own Nigel Bland. The two Jeffs, Verill and Proud, were my reliable full-backs, with dependable sweeper Simon Featherstone holding things together in defence. Up front, Keith Gaunt and Kirk Emery were our secret weapons. Nigel 'Nibber' Bray was our very own 'Allan Clarke'. Making up our outfit were two Swedish Leeds fans, Bo Johanesson and Stefan Sjostrom, who, along with Bo's wife Annika, had arranged everything for the day. We expected big things from our two Swedish guest players. A few miles from Sveg was a small village called Ytterhogdal, and it was there that England's assistant manager Tord Gripp lived. He had coached both Bo and Stefan in their junior years. We had a large squad, and looking at the blue skies and sunshine above, combined with the blistering heat, we knew we would need every man. Our opponents came out next. They looked smart and fit in their Celtic strip. In fact, they looked too fit.

Unbelievably, we scored within a few minutes of the kick-off. After Nibber had rounded the keeper and slotted the ball home, I thought, 'God, that'll make 'em angry.' But, to everyone's surprise – including ours – we held our own and went in at half-time with the score standing at a creditable 1–1. During the interval, some of the media began to mingle with our players. They asked Ralph, 'You are doing very well, do you think you can win?'

Ralph, puffing and blowing, emptied his left nostril and just missed the shoe of the reporter. 'Yeah, easy,' he said. 'If we can hold onto our lead, we've got 'em.' The reporter pointed out that the score was, in fact, level. 'Oh is it?' Ralph said. 'I didn't see them get one. It must have been when I nipped for a piss in them bushes.'

The second half couldn't come quick enough for the media. Again, we took the lead. After they equalised, we dug in, and the game finished 2–2. We could have won, but Nibber missed a late penalty.

After the match, we all tucked into a barbecue and loads of beer, all compliments of our hosts. The crowd mingled with the stars, and we all listened to the entertaining singing guitarist, ably assisted, now and again, by Coke. I was lucky enough to be awarded man of the match and was given a big bottle of bubbly, which lasted about three minutes.

When the party was in full swing, Whitby John and the Doctor joined us. They had travelled up with us to Sveg but had decided to go bear hunting, instead of watching the game. Not surprisingly, they had returned empty handed.

As dusk fell, the midges were out in force, and many of us received large bites. Jeff Verill even had to go to hospital, when one of his bites swelled to the size of a golf ball. He had to have an injection and a course of tablets to combat it. After an extremely humid night in our cabins, we returned to Ostersund for the final two days of the trip.

This turned out to be George Graham's last tour with Leeds United. The following season, Graham left to go to Tottenham. Many felt, with some justification, that he had used Leeds to get back into football, after he had been kicked out over allegations of bungs and money scandals.

His final game in charge of Leeds was an absolute farce – it was, conveniently, against Tottenham at White Hart Lane. On the morning of the game, a few of us were in the Leeds railway station when in walked Peter Ridsdale, the then chairman of Leeds. There had been much speculation that Graham was about to move to Spurs. 'Peter,' I asked, 'who is our manager today?'

He smiled and replied, 'Your guess is as good as mine. I'll tell you one thing, though: about a week ago we [Leeds] tried to sign David Batty back and George [Graham] pulled out of the deal. Draw your own conclusions.' When he finally did go to Tottenham, one of George Graham's first moves was to try and sign David Batty.

During the game, Leeds were winning 3–1, with less than 15

minutes to go, when Graham made several bizarre changes, including taking Tony Yeboah out of the attack. The game finished 3–3.

To my mind, Graham never liked Yeboah. He saw him as a 'problem player', along with Tomas Brolin. At the time of Graham's arrival at Leeds, both players had been in dispute with the club. It was very rare for Graham to play Yeboah, but on one occasion at Sunderland, he was forced to put him on as a substitute. Within a minute, the ball fell to Yeboah on the halfway line. Instinctively, Yeboah looked up and, seeing the keeper off his line, had a shot at goal. With the keeper completely beaten, the ball crashed against the crossbar and, luckily for Sunderland, was scrambled to safety. When asked about that particular incident on television afterwards, Graham replied smugly, 'Oh, I was fastening my shoelace at the time. I didn't see it.'

David O'Leary was in charge of Leeds for our next venture to Sweden. One of Leeds' opponents was a team called Byske. It was only a small team with a small ground, but, on 14 July 1999, 2,049 people witnessed Leeds United's highest ever victory: 15–0. As the score suggests, it was a bit of a stroll, with Leeds fielding almost a different side in each half. After the match, I did my nerdy bit and had my match ticket signed by the whole squad. David Batty, an old friend, had returned to the club, and I asked him if he would take a shirt and get it signed by the players: I would then see him later in town. For the record, the Leeds goals that day were scored by Smith, with four, Hasselbaink, with three, Kelly, with two, and one each from McPhail, Hopkin, Haaland, Jones (Mathew), Kewell and Bowyer.

Byske was a little town with a few small bars and wooden houses with gingerbread-style fencing: it was all very picturesque and atmospheric. Our hotel was one of those wooden establishments that are typical in Sweden. It was more like a large house, with about a dozen rooms, and the polished wooden floors creaked under every footstep. Bookcases lined the walls in the reception and lounge area, and large, comfortable leather chairs were in abundance everywhere. Big Mick had arranged our accommodation in advance, which proved to be a very good decision. Ours turned out to be the only hotel in town, and many of the other lads were finding it very difficult to find a bed for the night. In our hotel's large garden was an old caravan. Having been turned away from the hotel, the Lancaster Whites – aka Kev Morgan, Pete Varley and Clarke Richardson – spied the caravan. Sneaking round the back with their bags, they tried the caravan door. 'It's open, lads. Come on, we're in,' said Kev. They were a tad too late: the caravan was already occupied by Mick Garner and some of the Scunthorpe Whites. 'Bollocks!' said Clarkey, and they resumed their search around the town.

Fortunately, at the game, the lads got chatting to Byske's secretary. The secretary's friend owned a large house just on the outskirts of town, and, luckily, he was away on holiday. The Lancaster lads were handed free lodgings and were later joined by Whitby John and the Doctor.

We were situated about a mile inland, and, after the game and a quick shower, a dozen of us made our way to the coast. It was holiday season, and this was a holiday hot spot for the Swedish. We quickly found ourselves in a large bar, inside a type of holiday camp. We had a great night, and, as things began to wind down at the bar, we were invited to a party in one of the holiday chalets situated on site. At around 6 a.m. – once again, it had been daylight all night – we made our way back to the hotel and grabbed a few hours' kip, before our breakfast of cold ham, cheese and boiled eggs.

Later that day, we met up with the players at one of the few bars in the town. Bats came over with my signed Leeds shirt from the day before. The players were all having a meal in the adjoining restaurant, and we were just enjoying a beer before going somewhere else to eat. I was chatting at the bar with Dave Ricketts, one of the Shropshire Whites, when Jimmy Hasselbaink came over and helped himself to a glass of water from a free machine positioned next to us on the bar. He gulped it down and promptly helped himself to another one and then a third. Jokingly, I said, 'Greedy bastard.'

I'd obviously hit a nerve and he retorted, fairly angrily, 'I am not a greedy bastard!' He had obviously mistaken my comment for something entirely different because he then said, 'I'm prepared to stay at Leeds, it's not up to me.' Dave and I looked at each other, puzzled. I pointed out that I was referring to his third glass of water. Realising his mistake, he quickly retreated to the restaurant.

It soon came to light that these were to be his last few games for

Leeds. O'Leary and the club had refused his extortionate new wage demand. Apparently, he wanted to be Leeds' highest-paid player, to receive a bonus for playing and a bonus for scoring. Within weeks he had been sold to Spanish club Atletico Madrid for £12 million. Atletico were relegated after Hasselbaink's first season. Because of a chance meeting at a free drinks machine, Dave and I had almost gained a world exclusive.

Our next game on that particular tour was across the border in Finland. It was my first venture to that country, and I had always perceived it be the dearest and dullest of the Scandinavian countries. How wrong I was.

The opponents were Tervarit RY from Oulu. The first night we were there – the night before the game – we all gathered at a local restaurant. I'm not a vegetarian by any means, but, after glancing at the menu, I could quite easily have become one. Bear, antelope, reindeer and buffalo were readily available. A large moose's head protruding from the wall above us persuaded me to opt for the seafood.

I was quickly becoming aware that Finland, or at least this part, wasn't dear at all, and it was very lively. I was drinking with Geir, from Norway, and Jeff, and the town was our oyster. We made our way down to the harbour area. It was Friday night, and the place was bouncing. The atmosphere was brilliant, and, in almost every bar, live bands played well into the night and beyond. It never gets dark at that time of the year, and so all track of time simply disappears. In one bar, we began chatting with a bloke who told us he was the head of security for the next day's game. His name was Ville Rosedahl, and he said he would arrange for a couple of passes for us to go into the VIP tent for a drink or two after the game. We arranged to meet him the next morning.

Meanwhile, we were continuing to sample the delights of the busy nightlife. It was still daylight, of course, and we had no idea of the time, but things seemed to be slowing down a little. We then noticed a postman on a small moped and decided to return to the hotel for an hour's sleep before 'match day'. Ninety minutes later I was having breakfast with Tim Lee and Nibber. They said that they'd heard that the bars opened at 9.30 a.m. on Saturdays. I gulped my ham and eggs down and went to wake Jeff. He was dead chuffed at the news.

Scandinavians are very patriotic, and the walls in our first bar were all adorned with the blue and white flags of Finland. The locals were huge and most resembled tough bikers. We soon got chatting to them, and we passed a great few hours before we made our way down to the ground. We had arranged to meet Ville at a nearby bar to pick up our VIP passes. He stressed to us that he wasn't supposed to give these passes to us and asked us to remain discreet whenever we were in the tent. We would also have to go into the tent in ones and twos to avoid detection. After the game – a 1–0 win, with Hasselbaink's last goal for the club – I was partnered, unfortunately as it happened, with Geir. He's not the quietest person on the planet when he's had the odd slurp, so I was a tad apprehensive when our turn came to slip into the tent. I mentioned the importance of staying quiet, but I needn't have worried: we walked into the tent no problem, although I had a feeling that they knew we were English, or near enough. Some of the other lads had gained entrance as well, and, as we sipped our beers, David O'Leary arrived to make a small after-match speech. Dozens of cameras and reporters surrounded the table with all the microphones perched on it. There were several Finns in the tent sporting Leeds colours. O'Leary thanked Tervarit RY for the game and for making it such a great occasion. He then began to thank the supporters. Instinctively, I noticed a surge in Geir. O'Leary continued, 'It's particularly pleasing to see so many Leeds fans here . . .' That signalled the end of our stay. Before he had a chance to finish his sentence, Geir was chanting at the top of his voice, 'We are Leeds! We are Leeds! We are Leeds!' Two stewards came to quietly escort him from the tent, and I went with him. O'Leary winked as we walked past his table. Eventually, the rest of the lads joined us in a bar outside the ground.

I had noticed that the stewards had been wearing orange T-shirts with the teams, venue and date printed on the back. I wanted one, and when I mentioned it to Ville later that evening, he told me that most of them wanted to keep them as a souvenir of the day, but he'd try and get me one. True to his word, a week after I returned home, one duly arrived in the post.

Another Swedish town worthy of note is Lysekils. It's a great little seaside town, popular with tourists and Swedes alike. The ground that Lysekils played in is the most unusual I have ever seen. It is situated in one of the many coves on the sea front. Behind one goal is nothing but a small office and the dressing-rooms. The opposite end is a very small standing area, the same as the side facing away from the sea. The remaining side of the ground is a huge sloping rock face that accommodates around 500 people. At the top of this rock face is the club's bar. There one can enjoy a cool light ale, while watching the game from its splendid veranda.

It was on this very ground, a couple of years later, that Mark Viduka made his debut and grabbed his first goal for Leeds. Later that same night, some of the lads were spotted leaving a Boney M concert. It is reputed that Mick Hewitt from the Vine Branch was among them. I finished the evening off with Geir Jensen and some other Norwegian Leeds fans.

On the day of our departure from Lysekils, Mark Naylor emerged from the hotel a little worse for wear. He had spent all of the previous evening drinking the local favourite of pear cider; unfortunately, he overdid it slightly and was rushed to hospital with alcohol poisoning. He left the hospital with the doctor saying, 'It is usually not possible to consume that much alcohol and survive.' He kept repeating, '16 pints of pear cider? It is not possible.' A very delicate Mark sat on the coach, with his head in a large black bin liner, vomiting violently. It reminded me of a scene in *The Young Ones* where the rest of the gang had tied Neil up in a bin liner, as he suffered a severe bout of sneezing.

Nothing could prepare us for one place that we visited on the '99 tour – Boden. It sends shivers down the spine of every Leeds fan who has had the misfortune to visit the town. It is without doubt the most boring place on earth. We checked into our hotel and wandered off looking for our first bar. Nothing. The only place we could find that resembled anything like a bar was a pizza restaurant on what appeared to be the main precinct. The place was deserted, and the girl running the restaurant couldn't believe it when 20 of us walked through the door. 'Leeds United, playing here? In Boden?' she said in response to one of the lads explaining why we were there.

After demolishing a huge pizza, Coke asked her where else there was in town to have a beer. One of the locals at another table laughed. 'Nothing happens in Boden,' he said. 'There is a bar down by the lake, two in fact, but they're unlikely to be open.'

Almost before he'd finished his sentence, we were out of there and heading for the lake. Things were starting to get a bit desperate. On our way, we bumped into a group of Leeds players, and Eddie Gray was with them. 'Great place lads, eh?' he joked. That wasn't going to be the only time that we would come across the players wandering aimlessly through the deserted streets.

We saw a large bar on the banks of the river. As we drew closer, it looked promising.

A huge sign painted on the wall proclaimed, 'Party Night! Great Beer! Great Food!' Was it a mirage – an illusion? Then we saw the sign on the door: 'Closed'! Underneath it was another sign, 'Open Tuesday Night'. It was now Sunday evening and we were leaving town on Tuesday at lunchtime. Little Mick is always one for spotting an obscure bar, and I heard him say, 'Is that a Heineken sign there?' He was pointing just a few blocks down, and he was right. We crept slowly towards it, fully expecting it to disappear in a puff of smoke. It was a pub! And it was open. Eagerly, we clambered up the stairs and into quite a dingy-looking bar, but, hey, who gives a shit? It was kind of like an Irish pub, and the landlord, who looked as though he couldn't give a toss, served us all and then carried on reading his newspaper. Four or five beers later, and we set off on yet another pub-seeking expedition. Twenty minutes later, we were back in the same bar. It was as if the landlord knew we would have to return, and we were now under his power. Eddie Gray and the physio Dave Swift walked in shortly afterwards. 'Thought we might find you here, boys,' said Swift. 'This is the only one in town, I think.'

Further down the street was a small takeaway, selling sandwiches and pizzas. Simon Featherstone and Big Mick had been in. 'It sells cans of beer,' said Simon. I'm not that keen on pizzas, and I wasn't a bit hungry, but Jeff, Matty Hindle, Scott Baxter and I strolled down to it. We walked in, and I ordered the tiniest sandwich I could see and two large cans of cold beer. The other two did the same, and we sat at a table and drank our beer. It was just like a little pub-crawl. 'We'd better be careful with all this beer, otherwise we'll not find our way back to the hotel,' I said. We then returned to the 'nightlife' until the landlord kicked us out at 1 a.m.

The next day, as we headed to the ground, we were all, not surprisingly, bright-eyed and bushy-tailed. What we did next was totally out of character and must go no further than this: we went to watch the team training. We all sat there, drinking coffee and watching the players. They were going through a routine of aiming the ball at the crossbar. Once a player had hit the bar, he could go get showered and changed. Dozens of balls were flying over the bar, and I watched one go under a bush. Unnoticed, I strolled over and pushed the ball further under the bush so that I could collect it later, and we could have a game of football. Once training was over, we collected the ball and were soon having a ten-a-side kick-around. After about thirty seconds, one dozy bastard hit the ball skywards, and it landed right in the middle of the nearby lake. It was back to trudging around town. That night we watched a gripping 1–1 draw and then, thankfully, we left town the following morning.

A couple of weeks later, I was in Glasgow for the game with Celtic. I was in the hotel bar with our lass, Wub, and Geir. Eddie Gray was in the bar with his family and he noticed me. He came across, leant over our table and said, 'It's a wee bit better than Boden here, don't you think?'

On one tour of Scandinavia in 2001, we returned to a place called Jönköping in Sweden. When it's open, it's a lively little town, but when the bars are closed the only option is the world's only Match Museum. These are safety matches and not football matches. Luckily, the ground is only a short bus ride away from the town centre.

Jim Unsworth, the friendly bookmaker from Lancaster, was on the trip with his son Jamie. We had a meal together in town before making our way to the game. As usual, Kev Morgan and Clarke Richardson were also knocking around town. A 6–0 win sent us happily to our next port of call, Kungsbacka.

Once again, we had arrived in a town that resembled something from a classic Western film: there were wooden buildings everywhere, all with balconies, and small bars dotted around the place. It wasn't long before we were mixing in with the Swedish locals, many of whom were Leeds fans. One group we were chatting to came from Norway. Geir Magne Fjellseth was there with his son, John, who were both huge Leeds fans. Soon, another Geir joined us. It seemed that Norwegians were everywhere. Geir Jensen, a big friend of mine, has been a Leeds United fan since the early '70s. Once again, Leeds ran out fairly easy winners, and the curtain was brought down on yet another successful Swedish tour.

The following season's tour to Scandinavia raised more than a few eyebrows. We were situated in the coastal town of Varberg. It was a lovely day and some of us decided to rent bicycles. As we all sped down the hill to the seaside, like a bunch of crazed Hell's Angels without engines, I noticed that my cycle wasn't going as fast as the others. Within minutes, I was walking back up the hill to the rental office, dragging my bike along and carrying the front wheel, which had fallen off. Every cloud has a silver lining, and I came back out of the shop with a brand-new silver, 12-geared, gleaming, streamlined machine. And I had it for another 24 hours. Later that afternoon, I was taking a shower and Jeff was on his bed reading the brochure of the town's activities. 'Hey up!' I heard him shout. 'They've got a nudist beach.'

Half an hour later, the two of us boarded our cycles and went in search of that paradise. A mile or two down the sea front, we arrived at the first of many cordoned-off nudist areas. Swedish females occupied that one. Now, everyone I know has a glamorous image of the female Swede; however, this image was entirely blown away, as we perched on our bikes and peered over the large wooden fence surrounding the enclosure. There didn't seem to be one below 20 st. We looked at each other and gulped. They were quite horrendous! Without wishing to be offensive, the 'Fat Slags' in *Viz* immediately sprang to mind.

Jeff then suggested we move on to the male nudist area. 'What for?' I said, worriedly.

'To get our kit off,' he replied excitedly.

'Just me and you?' I asked. 'Yer can bollocks! We'll look a right pair of twats!' I suggested we come back with the rest of the lads. 'It won't look as bad with a load of us,' I said.

Jeff was disappointed, but he soon perked up that evening, as we put it to the lads over a beer. The early response wasn't too encouraging, but, a few beers later, everyone agreed. However, one absentee would be Emyrs Jones. He is the head teacher at a school in Wales, and his pupils would have had a field day if a photograph of our escapade had fallen into their hands.

The next day, we all cycled down to the beach, led, not surprisingly, by Jeff Verrill. Gingerly, we all shuffled through the gate into the male enclosure. There was a group of men whose average age must have been 80, sitting around a table playing cards, without a stitch on. And I'll tell you what: some of their 'utensils' put some of us relatively young 'uns to shame. Whilst the rest of us scuffed around awkwardly, Jeff could wait no longer and ran down the beach towards the sea, throwing off his clothes like Reginald Perrin!

One by one we discarded our clothes to reveal an assortment of bodies never before seen anywhere in the world, except, possibly, in the female enclosure further up the beach. John Green was beginning to enjoy it, and, before long, he was stretched out over a rock revealing his 50-year-old glory in its entirety. Nibbs strutted about with nothing on but a pair of sunglasses. In the background, Coke fumbled with his attachment to bring it up to some sort of respectability, whilst Mark Smith walked about knacker bare, as if he was one of the coastguards. Dave Ricketts finally took his socks off, and there we all were, showing Scandinavia all we had. Mick Hewitt and Simon Featherstone leant against a rock discussing world affairs, and I walked over to the nude card school and asked one of the sprightly old men to take our group photograph. As he rose to his feet, he slung his knob over his right shoulder and followed me to the rest of the lads. The photo appeared for all to see in the next issue of *Leeds Leeds Leeds*, our embarrassment covered only by a small match poster.

After our little adventure there was the small matter of the Leeds game. Although we were in Varberg, we were playing Gais, who came from Gothenburg, 30 miles up the coast. After yet another Leeds victory, we had a couple of free days to take in the splendid seaside atmosphere, before flying back to good old England.

After a couple of summer tours elsewhere, Leeds once again returned to Sweden in July 2004. Unbelievably, we returned to Boden, but this time forewarned was forearmed, and it was unanimously decided that we visit Boden for the game only and then get the hell out of there! Our first port of call on that trip was Stockholm. Our hotel was a huge moored-up boat. This is normal in Stockholm, and there are several huge boats permanently moored up along the quayside. Ours was a little tatty, it has to be said, with one toilet in the hallway for twenty of us. On our first morning, as usual, I was up and about early. With towel and toothbrush to hand, I made my way to the bathroom. After the three S's – apart from the shave – I went to unlock the door. No chance! It was a huge metal circular handle, but I couldn't turn it. I dried my hands again and tried once more, but it wouldn't budge. I could hear someone outside trying to get in. I looked around at the porthole: my athletic figure wouldn't stand a hope in hell of squeezing through that. After 15 minutes I managed to turn the handle. Keith Gaunt was waiting patiently outside. 'I wouldn't lock it if I was you, mate,' I said and told him of the difficulty I'd had. By the time I got back to my room, I saw Keith was already leaving the bathroom.

I entered the room just in time to see Jeff struggling to get off the top bunk: knacker bare and arse high in the air. I declined to give him a leg down and went out for a walk. When I returned 20 minutes later I was walking back across the gangplank and was just in time to see little Tim Maguire squeezing out of the bathroom window.

I watched as he precariously dangled out of the window, with his legs straddling the gap between the boat and the dock. In between him was a 30-ft drop to the sea. Luckily for old Tim, the only thing to make the plunge was one of his socks.

His little escape meant that no one else could use the bathroom, but by now most of the lads were heading for breakfast.

After breakfast Jeff, little Mick and I were in our room. Coke came in. Unusually for him, he was late for breakfast, but he'd come in to tell us about Tim getting locked in the bathroom. The disturbing thing about that little episode was that I was lying on the bottom bunk when Coke's huge figure entered. He was dressed only in a pair of extremely large Y-fronts, and level with my eyesight were his huge testicles dangling from either side of his pants. I'd seen enough flesh in that last hour to last me a lifetime. Luckily, half an hour later we were on our coach and heading for our next destination. We headed far up to northern Sweden to a coastal town called Lulea. This was to be our base for three nights for the match in Boden.

Strolling around Lulea, we soon came across many of the usual faces. Mark Threlfall and his lovely missus, Freddie, and the kids were there, and other Maverick Whites were dotted around. Then, in our first bar, we met up with *Yorkshire Evening Post* writer, and UK Sports Writer of the Year, Paul Dews and photographer Steve 'Fritz' Riding. The pub was called The Bishops Arms and was just like a piece of merry old England in the far corner of Scandinavia. They were both tucking into traditional roast beef, Yorkshire puddings and vegetables. This was much better than staying in Boden, but, the following day, we had to grip the bit between our teeth and head there for the match. This time, even the Irish bar we frequented before wasn't open. Reluctantly, we trudged up to the only 'bar' we knew would be open – the pizza place! When we got there, it was full, not surprisingly, of Leeds fans. Barry Mortimer and his lass were contentedly consuming cool beers and scoffing pizzas. He said they were going to have a wander around town before the game. We informed them of the hidden treasures of Boden, so well hidden in fact that we'd never found them, and he promptly ordered more beers.

The game itself marked the debut of Michael Ricketts: he capped his appearance with a goal and Brian Deane, the returning prodigal son, grabbed the other in a 2–0 win. A few minutes into the second half, we were soaking up the relaxed atmosphere; the great smell of the barbecue provided for the supporters was wafting through the air. Most of us were enjoying a can of ice-cold beer, when Pete Southam from Oxford came over to stand with us. We were standing near the wall that separated us from the pitch. Pete was slightly inebriated and had a look of worry on his face. 'What's up, Pete?' I asked. 'You look a bit preoccupied.'

'Oh, nothing, mate, I'm OK,' he answered.

Just then two police guards joined us. 'Excuse me, sir,' one of them said to Pete. 'What have you got down your shorts?'

'What are you talking about?' Pete slurred back at them. With that, one of the policemen put his hand down Pete's shorts.

'Hey up, pal,' Jeff quipped. 'What you playing at?' Just then we all stared in amazement as the officer's hand came out of Pete's shorts, carrying a large axe! How the hell had he got that down there and, more to the point, why?

Pete had been for a piss behind one of the club huts and, on his way to stand with us, had apparently seen an axe buried into a huge log: it had been used to chop wood for the barbecue. I shuddered to think what could have happened, but the two guards simply gave Pete a bit of a rollicking and returned the axe to the huge log. When he told his wife, Tina, back at the coach, she didn't seem the slightest bit surprised. 'You idiot,' she said. 'When will you grow up?'

The next day, back in Lulea, some of our party decided to head up to the Arctic Circle, which was just a few miles north of where we were. Feeling slightly less adventurous, Jeff and I met up with Dewsy and Fritz and spent the afternoon testing various lagers and ciders. Pear cider and a lovely concoction of strawberry and citrus cider made a welcome change from the lagers for an hour.

That evening, we decided to go to a local disco, which was held on board a large ship moored in the harbour. Once again, the myth that all Swedish girls are gorgeous reared its ugly head. The only two females interested in us were an over-sized lass, who was the spitting image of Olive from *On the Buses*, and her mate, a right old boiler who looked for all the world like David Bowie, only older! 'Olive' was soon escorted from the ship by two security guards, after she thought it would be a good idea to raise her jumper and treat us all to a long look at her tits. Bowie followed her off, and we continued with our beers.

The following day, we left Lulea for the next game on the agenda in Pitea. As we arrived at Skoogs City Hotel it was hot and sunny, and we were soon out and about exploring the sights. Pitea is another pleasant little coastal town, and, as we played a few games of pool, we were joined by the Oxford lads and Wakey Steve.

Mark 'Macca' Ledgard and Dave 'Procky' Procter are full of surprises and on one trip to Melbourne, for the tour of Australia in 2002, they had us gasping for breath and dying with laughter, when they appeared in a large kangaroo outfit and a grotesque Robin costume. They were muttering excitedly, and I could tell that they had another plan up their sleeve. Even then, I was totally unprepared for what followed. During a bit of lull in the beer drinking, I noticed that Macca and his mates had disappeared. Assuming they had gone for some shut-eye, before coming out for the evening, I told Jeff I was nipping back to the hotel to phone Wub. As I walked up a packed pedestrian precinct, on the way to the hotel, I collapsed on the floor at the sight in front of me. Coming towards me over the horizon were five larger-than-life characters. Amongst them were Skippy and Robin. I, of course, knew who was inside those particular costumes, but, this time, they were also joined by Hedgehopper, who was dressed as Kid Creole, Harry, who was dressed in leather shorts, feathered hat and moustache to complete his German outfit, and Wakey Steve, who was wearing a hilarious ostrich costume *à la* Bernie Clifton. The five of them were walking side by side towards me, and the looks on the faces of the Swedish shoppers were priceless. Once again, they had rendered me helpless with laughter, but it was about to get even funnier. At the game against Pitea, the five of them casually walked onto the pitch and, as the two teams stood in a line, they joined at the Pitea end. They all stood proudly as the national anthem was played, and then, to everyone's amazement, the 'Swedish Anthem' was played. It was Abba singing 'The Winner Takes it All': I kid you not. The Leeds team could not refrain from periodic fits of giggles. Later, they managed to stop laughing long enough for Danny Cadamarteri to secure a 1–0 victory in the second and final game of that tour. It was the first time in eighteen months that Leeds had won two games on the trot and kept clean sheets.

One thing is for sure, the support in Scandinavia will continue for many years to come. For a start, the Leeds United Supporters Club of Scandinavia (LUSCOS) is the biggest LUSC branch anywhere in the world. Originally formed in Norway, by Arild Bekken and Thorbjørn Lerfald, the branch now includes Sweden, Denmark, Finland, Greenland, Iceland and those nice whale lovers, the Faroe Islands. Many Scandinavians move to Leeds to be nearer to their heroes. Norwegians Svend Anders Karlsen-Moum and Trond Kasin are prime examples of this, and Matteaus from Sweden has taken up residency at The Viaduct (you can't get much closer to Leeds United than that) on Briggate in Leeds. Another claim to fame for the Scandinavians was the discovery of the Icelandic international Gylfi Einarsson. Norwegian Leeds fan Vidar Loftaas had spotted him playing for his local team, Lillestrom. Acting on Loftaas's recommendation, Kevin Blackwell and his backroom staff had him watched and bought the player in 2004.

The Icelandic LUSC branch has around 500 members, one of whom has watched Leeds since the early Don Revie days. Thorleifur Leo Ananiasson from Akureyri in Iceland started watching Leeds as they entered the old First Division back in the 1964–65 season. The Olver is a popular sports bar in Reykjavik and is the home of the Icelandic Leeds fan club (LUSCIB). The pub sponsors the Icelandic Whites and on match days changes its name to 'Olland Road'. Each member also has a membership 'credit card' allowing a discount on the free-flowing liquid refreshment. I've yet to visit Iceland, but, when I do, I know where my first port of call will be.

13

European Law and Disorder

When you're the supporter of a football club, your human rights are forfeited.

Before a game in Moscow, a young Leeds fan was locked in the back of a police truck, stripped to his underpants and released by laughing policemen without charge after the game. He was minus £200. Unfortunately, this is not an isolated incident.

The sinister side of almost every competitive game in Europe is the heavy-handed behaviour of the police and, in particular, the riot police. Countless Leeds fans have painful memories of having their skulls smashed in. Broken arms and fingers are commonplace. Some are relieved to escape with cuts and bruises. I have witnessed on many occasions mindless, unprovoked baton charges by over-zealous riot police. Of course, some countries' forces are worse than others but, almost without exception, all have their violent element.

Take Bulgaria, for instance. We were in Sofia for the re-arranged UEFA Cup tie with Spartak Moscow in 1999, and the bar outside the ground was packed with Leeds fans. There was no trouble whatsoever, but, as usual, there was a very heavy police presence outside of the bar. About ten minutes before kick-off, Leeds fans began drinking up and heading for the turnstiles. It was then that the riot police came inside the bar. I was with Jeff and Mick Garner, Big Craig and others from the Scunthorpe Branch. The landlord was shaking hands with Leeds fans as they left: he and his staff were delighted with the bulging tills from the last two hours.

'You must leave now,' said a very serious-looking policeman to our table.

'OK, mate. No problem,' said Steve Powell from Scunthorpe, as he put his glass to his mouth to drink the last drop of his beer.

Another policeman came onto the scene. 'Now!' he shouted, and he smashed his baton onto the table, knocking the remaining empty glasses onto the floor.

'Alright,' said Steve, 'we're going.'

As he put his empty glass on the table the barmy copper brought his baton down heavily onto Steve's shoulder. We all winced as he writhed in agony. The other policemen looked at their colleague worriedly. He had totally flipped. He was literally shaking and, as he raised his baton again, his colleagues intervened. They said something to him as they ushered him away into the corner. As we walked out of the bar, the landlord shook our hands and apologised. He was still shrugging his shoulders as we left. After the game, the brutality continued, as Leeds fans were herded back to the coaches suffering abusive harassment every step of the way.

You become accustomed to the danger signs in these types of situations, and when you see the riot police pull on balaclavas, followed by the lowering of helmet visors, you know that it's time to 'get the hell out of there'. We witnessed this very same ritual at Leeds' UEFA Cup game in Malaga in 2002.

It was all very pleasant when we arrived the day before the game and set up camp in nearby Torremolinos. Hundreds of Leeds fans were scattered all over town, and the atmosphere was brilliant. Malaga has a heavy influx of English supporters: they are all ex-pats and hundreds of them chose Malaga CF as their team and follow them home and away. Dave Redshaw, a Man City fan, has lived out there for 20 years. We met up with him through friends of ours from Kippax, Lord and Lady Harland, better known to friends as Tim and Mary. Regular travellers to that part of the world, Leeds fans Tim and Mary had met Dave several years previously. They couldn't believe it when the two clubs were paired together in a European game.

On the day of the game, Dave invited our lads to drink in a place called Inchy's Bar in Benalmadena, which is a small town very close to Torremolinos: they even share the same time zone. Inchy's is owned by former Birmingham City player Steve Phillips, and he made all the Leeds fans welcome. It was a sports bar decorated with flags and scarves from just about every club in the world. Spanish-based Leeds fans were anxious to get the latest news from back at Elland Road, as television crews from both Spain and Britain mingled with the hordes of fans crammed into the bar. The rain fell heavily outside. It was as if God knew that everyone inside the bar was English and had provided the weather to suit.

I was with Jeff, Ralph Benson and Steve Gibson. Oblivious to the football talk going on all around us, Steve told us about the time when he had suffered a severe bout of constipation. We all listened intently, as he told us that he had tried every remedy without success; in sheer desperation he had resorted to rather unorthodox methods. As Ralph munched on a large pizza, Steve described, in great detail, how he had picked away at his arse with a set of chopsticks for over half an hour, removing the blockage piece by piece. Not surprisingly, Ralph didn't finish his pizza. And we certainly won't be going to Steve's house for Chinese food any time soon.

As fans enjoyed the atmosphere in the bar, outside a massive police presence was building. We learned that, because it was an English club, hundreds of riot police had been drafted in from Madrid. A couple of Leeds fans were messing about with a football, and, without warning, the police charged the hapless footballers and left one of them needing hospital treatment. It was as if they were practising for the main event.

From our part of the resort, the only fans that were heading for the Estadio la Rosaleda were Leeds fans. Spanish-based Leeds fans accompanied them, along with English Malaga fans. The atmosphere was still relaxed, but the police that were stationed all along the route created an air of uncertainty. In a bar near the ground, I had a beer with Neil Jeffries, the editor of *Leeds Leeds Leeds*. Everything was calm, but the menace of the strategically placed riot police remained. The short walk to the stadium was punctuated with sporadic baton attacks on Leeds fans whose only crime was to chant the name of the team they had flown hundreds of miles to see. Inside the stadium, it was quite bizarre. In one section of the ground were the English

Leeds fans. In another section were the ex-pat Leeds fans. English Malaga fans occupied the section next to them, and all three sections were separated from each other by lines of riot police. We had been told on several occasions that the Spanish Malaga hooligans were in awe of their English counterparts, and they spent the entire game watching the performance of the English fans, in preference to the action on the pitch. It's probably fair to say that they were better entertained, as the game ended in a dull 0–0 draw.

Incredibly, all the Leeds fans were kept locked inside the stadium for almost an hour afterwards. As we made our way slowly down the steep steps at the back of the stadium, I saw two policemen pointing at a Leeds fan talking to his mate. He was around 6 ft 4in., and because he had a skinhead – I could see no other reason – one of the policemen attacked him with his baton. People around him rushed to his aid, as his head split open like a leather football before our very eyes. All at once, the Leeds fans noticed the balaclavas being pulled on, and a crazy, pointless fracas ensued, leaving more Leeds fans spilling blood everywhere. Outside, Kev Morgan asked a policeman if he was going the right way to the Leeds' coaches, and a baton crashed down on his outstretched arm with so much force that it swelled badly, and he too needed hospital treatment.

The next day, with the Madrid police gone, the holiday atmosphere returned, and Leeds fans once again mingled with the locals. We just had time for our final taste of fine Spanish cuisine: Jeff, Ralph and I tucked into roast beef and Yorkshire pudding, accompanied by a cool pint of John Smith's.

When Leeds played AC Milan in November 2000, Lee Dyson travelled to Italy with a dozen lads from Barnsley. Around 7,000 other Leeds fans also made the trip. Travelling with his group was Lee's brother-in-law John Bramm, all the way from Canada. As with the vast majority of Leeds fans, they were there to have a good time and sample one or two glasses of the local brew, although in Italy this is sometimes easier said than done.

On the eve of the game, Lee and his troop opted for a meal at a restaurant, before moving onto a few bars. A cock-up by their taxi driver left them nowhere near where they thought they were heading. They were supposed to be going to a bar called Hollywood's, but the taxi had dropped them off well short of their destination. A local directed them towards the bar, and they began walking down a long street. As they passed another bar, a few Italians began blowing kisses at them and waving. As there were only about half a dozen of them, none of the lads were that worried. One of the lads, Kel, however, sensed danger and told the rest of them to stay in the middle of the road and 'keep marching'. As they approached the end of the street, they could see Hollywood's. People were milling about, but things looked OK. Then all hell broke loose. Shouting, bottles breaking and cries of 'Remember Istanbul' could be clearly heard. One of the locals then got out of a car and produced a spike about a foot in length. Lee turned to face them with Kel and the rest of his group. By now there were about 50 locals, and the atmosphere was turning very ugly. Well outnumbered, they made a run for it, but Lee tripped and fell face down. As he tried to get up, he noticed blood coming from his hand caused by the broken bottles on the ground. That was the least of his worries: he then felt a sharp pain in the bottom of his back, as he was stabbed from behind. A further blow from behind hit him in the head, and then he remembers nothing. Eyewitnesses later said that the locals had circled around him like a pack of animals, but there was nothing they could do to help Lee. The rest of Lee's group then had to scatter for their lives. Apart from a few minor injuries, the rest of them escaped unhurt.

Lee then dropped in and out of consciousness, but he does remember being in the ambulance, looking up at the roof and then, later, going into the hospital operating theatre. He also remembers battling, successfully, as someone tried to take off his wedding ring. After that, he had the feeling that he needed to go to the toilet but was told he couldn't. He tried several times to get up but was held down by a number of male nurses. Finally, he tried again and a bearded nurse pushed his thumb into Lee's eye, inflicting immense pain and rendering him unable to move. Lee, however, had not given up his battle and defiantly started to urinate. This immediately burst the stitches in his stomach, and, within seconds, the nurses were covered in a lovely cocktail of blood and piss. Then the morphine kicked in, and Lee was out for the count.

The following morning, he awoke on a coronary ward with five elderly Italian gentlemen. The result of his attack was over a dozen stab wounds – including an incision that went fifteen centimetres into his body, piercing his bladder – a loss of five pints of blood and a resulting blood clot that was a constant concern during the three weeks he was to spend in Milan's Fatebenefratelli Hospital. He was informed that if someone had not called the ambulance when they did, and if the hospital had not been so close, he would almost certainly have died. The doctor also told him that minutes rather than hours was the critical period, due to the loss of blood.

Obviously, Lee's immediate thoughts were of his family and, in particular, his wife, who was five months pregnant with their first child. John Bramms was his first visitor: he told Lee that there was a media scrum downstairs and that one photographer was offering up to £1,000 for a photograph and quotes. Lee shook his head and declined the offer. Money was the last thing on his mind. The police were the next visitors, and, predictably, their main focus was not on the Italians but on how much Lee had had to drink. The police even asked if the attackers could have been non-Italian. When Lee explained that he'd had his watch and wallet stolen, the police seemed more interested in a violent robbery and left, saying that they would return.

Leeds director David Walker was Lee's next visitor, along with a contingent from West Yorkshire Police. At this point a photographer found his way in and began taking pictures. Lee's present guests were more than happy to pose for pictures. As Lee said later, 'It was not a very good one of me. My head bandages made me look more like Tomas Brolin at Crystal Palace!'

The rest of Lee's mates visited him on their way to the game. The match was relayed to him by a fellow patient. Later that evening, a young nurse came to Lee with a newspaper, asking if he was the hooligan in the paper. Typical!

Over the following few days Lee learnt a bit of Italian, read a lot and kept the nurses entertained with the size of his 'meat and two veg'. Weeks later, once the hospital staff were satisfied that the blood clot had disappeared, Lee was allowed home. But not before further questioning by the police, who showed him photographs of his possible attackers. A lengthy stay at the police station almost caused Lee and his dad to miss their flight home, but, after a further delay at the airport in Milan, he touched down on English soil (albeit Gatwick) and his ordeal was finally over.

14

Ellie the Elephant Packed his Trunk

> Whilst we were on stage on the *Trisha Goddard* show, Lesley cried. I *think* they were tears of joy.

At 9.25 a.m. on Friday, 22 April 2005, sandwiched between *Bear in the Big Blue House* and *The Wright Stuff*, was the *Trisha Goddard* show on Five. This was no ordinary show, as far I was concerned. Wub and I were on the stage talking to Trisha. The title of the show was 'Bad Husbands'.

It had all started a few weeks earlier when our branch secretary Ralph Benson told me that Five wanted me to ring them about appearing on the show with our lass. Like any normal human being, I hate daytime television, so, naturally, I refused. Ralph said they desperately wanted me to appear, and they would be ringing me back. They did: six or seven times. I made a few phone calls to Leeds fans who I thought may want to appear instead. Kev Morgan was the first to reply. After initially thinking I was joking, he refused on the grounds that he and his missus would end up wrestling on the stage in front of the audience. 'That's precisely what they want,' I assured him, but he still refused.

My next phone call was also a 'knock-back'. 'I've heard that telly makes you look fat, and I've got to keep looking my best for the ladies,' was the reply from Mark 'Smurf' Smith. 'Besides, our lass would knock my head off!'

Five persisted in ringing me, and I found myself talking to a persuasive researcher called Laura. I told her that it wasn't the type of show I would feel comfortable appearing on, and she told me that Wub had said the very same thing earlier that day. I just didn't fancy being shouted and screamed at by an audience full of crazy women intent on sorting a stranger's life out.

'It's really not that kind of show,' Laura said. 'It's a totally different format to the ITV series. This is much more laid back, and we'd love to tell your story to the whole of Great Britain.'

As a final attempt to get us to travel to their London studio, they said that they would allow some of the crowd from The Viaduct pub to travel down and be in the audience.

A week later, we were on our way to Elstree Film and Television Studios in north London. Les Hince, the landlord of the pub, was driving and also with us were Ralph and the bar manager Jo Barrett.

As we signed in at reception, the nerves were beginning to jangle, and I could see that Wub was apprehensive too. 'What will you do if the audience boo you?' she asked, as Ralph leant over the desk with the final signature.

'It might be you that they boo,' I replied.

The nerves really took hold when they took me away into a room on my own. It was to be another four hours before I saw Wub again.

I was in the room when one of the show's staff, Chris, walked in with another man. 'Gary, this is Brian,' he said, 'and Brian, this is Gary.' We shook hands. With that he left the two of us alone. That was when I really began to wonder what the hell I was doing there. Brian was an Austin Powers lookalike. He actually thought he was Austin Powers. He began practising his lines on me. Not being a huge fan, I didn't have a clue what he was talking about.

'Do you find me horny?' he asked, flashing his huge white teeth at me. I was stunned. Apparently, this is one of Austin Powers' many one-liners, but, not knowing this at the time, I kept my distance. For the next two hours, Brian told me his whole life story. He was a nice chap, really, but, quite honestly, I didn't want to be there. He had just begun telling me about his wife and kids when my heaven-sent angel walked in.

'Will you follow me to make-up, Gary?' said a very attractive lady. As I sat in the chair, she could sense I was a little uncomfortable with the prospect of having make-up put on my face. 'Don't worry,' she said, 'it's only a bit of powder to stop your face shining under the studio lights. Nothing too elaborate.' She turned out to be responsible for the make-up for the Kaiser Chiefs, who had been in the studio the previous week. As the Chiefs were from Leeds, we struck up a nice conversation.

Fully powdered up, I returned to my dressing-room to discover that two more lads had joined us. One was a motorbike fanatic called Phil from Bristol and the other one, from London, was there to ask his wife, a Cher lookalike, to dress up in the wig and long boots in the bedroom. It was all very surreal. The good thing was that both of the new arrivals had brothers who were huge Leeds fans. Austin Powers read a magazine as the three of us swapped Leeds United stories.

Half an hour before I was due on stage, we were visited by the lady herself. Flanked by a large security guard, Trisha walked in and introduced herself. She was much smaller than I expected, and I noticed she was wearing a wig and had very pointy feet. She seemed very relaxed but was a little taken aback when Austin Powers said to her, 'Hi, how about a shag?' Then Austin wet his finger and put it on Trisha's arm, saying, 'Oh dear, we'll have to get you out of those wet clothes.' With that, Trisha hurriedly said her goodbyes and left.

When my turn came to go on, I was led to the back of the stage. I had no idea what was in store for me. With one of the crew waiting to give me my entrance cue, I could hear Wub on the stage telling Trisha and the audience how, 'Sometimes I think that Gary thinks more of 11 men in white shorts than he does of me.'

Then my heart pounded as I heard Trisha announce, 'Well, shall we meet Gary?' The audience whooped and shouted, 'Yes!' With that I was told to go through the door and onto the stage. Strangely, the audience gave me quite a good reception, but this went to the back of my mind, as I noticed Wub. She was wearing a red manchester united shirt!

I had also noticed during an earlier sound check that the seats on the stage were awfully close to being red. I vowed to myself that I would switch the seats when I got on stage, but, because of my disbelief at Wub's attire, I sat on the almost-red chair.

Trisha loved this. 'Your friends here,' she said, pointing to Les, Ralph and Jo on the front row, 'said you wouldn't sit on that seat.'

'It feels very weird,' I replied. 'I'll paint that free of charge,' I then said, pointing to the shirt Wub had on. Wub looked really uncomfortable. She told me afterwards that they 'insisted' she wear it in order to get a reaction from me. The fact that she told them that she hadn't worn red for 27 years didn't make the slightest bit of difference to her tormentors.

After the usual banter about me not painting red and not missing a Leeds game for 37 years, Trisha asked me to look at the screen to my right. It was the Leeds manager Kevin Blackwell. He was live on air from Leeds. I said that I was a fan of his and that, against all odds, he was doing a great job at our football club. Trisha asked Kevin if he had been listening to everything. 'Yes, Gary's the top man,' he said, 'and if it's OK for Gary it's OK for me.'

The mutual admiration was put to the test when Kevin set me a challenge: 'Gary, your loyalty to Leeds is unquestionable, but it's time Lesley received some recognition for her loyalty.' I couldn't have agreed more. Blackwell went on, 'I want you to go on the pitch at our next home game and pledge your undying love to Lesley. Will you do that, mate?' Of course I agreed, and, as the audience and Trisha clapped, I gulped in nervous anticipation.

Deep down, I honestly thought that the programme would not take it any further. The very next day, I received a telephone call from Laura telling me that everything had been arranged and that I would be appearing on the hallowed turf at Elland Road for the very next game, against Ipswich Town.

I admit to being extremely nervous as the day approached. Mr Blackwell had asked me to pledge my 'undying love for Lesley', but I had decided to take it a step further. Everyone thought I was just going to pledge my undying love, but I was about to propose to Wub in front of 30,000 people. We had been together for 28 years but never got round to the marriage thing.

I didn't think it possible, but, on the morning of the game, I became even more nervous, and I began to get really nervous when I started receiving text messages wishing me good luck from some of the people whom I had told of my intentions. One of those texts was from Mark Smith, who lived just around the corner from me in Kippax. Mark has a nine-year-old son who, naturally, is a keen Leeds United fan. The recent defection of Alan Smith to Old Trafford left young Arron with a slight dilemma: his Leeds United shirt had 'SMITH 17' printed on the back. Commendably, he took it in his stride. Every time he goes out with his shirt on, the number 17 is covered over very carefully with masking tape. He proudly tells anyone who enquires that Alan Smith is a traitor, but he can't change his name from Arron Smith.

The proposal had seemed like a good idea, but what if she said no? I went into Beckett's pub for a few pints to loosen up the throat, and the dependable daughter arrived outside in her car, with a huge bunch of flowers ready for me to sign the attached card. Good old Spoon: not a red flower in sight. She left, saying she would see me at the ground in about two hours.

Spoon has never been any trouble to me apart from one unsavoury incident in the mid-'80s. She came to me one day and said, 'I'll always be a Leeds fan, but what would you say if I bought a Liverpool shirt? It's not that I'll support them or anything; it's just fashion.'

I replied, 'Well, if you're thinking of buying one, you'd better get an extra, extra large one.'

'Why's that?' she asked.

'Because,' I said, 'you'll have to live in it.' Thankfully, that was the end of that little episode.

At 2.15 p.m., I met Wub and Spoon outside the banqueting suite at the rear of the West Stand. We were given our clearance passes and led into the reception area. I chatted briefly with Paul Reaney and Don Warters and then met with Steve Riding, a mate of mine from way back. He was there to take photos for the *Yorkshire Evening Post* of the event. I was then interviewed by Yorkshire Television and filmed by their camera crew.

Wub and I were then escorted onto the lush green turf; it was almost 2.45. I had a chat with the pre-match announcer, and then, as I stood on the centre spot, he handed me the microphone.

I swallowed hard and uttered the words, 'Wub, I've been a Leeds fan for 40 years, and we've been together for almost 28 years.' I dropped onto one knee and asked, 'Will you marry me?' She was visibly shocked and replied, 'Yes, oh yes.' I saw Spoon walk onto the pitch with the flowers and, thankfully, the crowd was cheering. I gave Wub the flowers, kissed her and then said, 'Right, game on. Let's get kicked off.' I handed the microphone back and we left the pitch. In the tunnel, I said goodbye to them both, and they left the ground, as I took up my position on the Kop.

A couple of days later, the Trisha programme called again. They had got the pictures of the proposal from Yorkshire Television and wanted us to appear back on the show.

This time they put Wub and me up in a hotel, and we arrived at the studios in Elstree at 11.30 the next morning. We were told that we would be the last ones on and that it would be a long day. This time we were in a room together, with a lad from Middlesex: he was heavily tattooed. His wife was still with him, and Wub and I asked them what they were there for. The husband spoke first: 'I'm an alcoholic,' he said. 'I drink 36 cans of Stella and a bottle of vodka a day.' I thought I could shift some stuff, but this was incredible. I really hated him when his wife then said, 'Not only that, he goes out shagging most nights. He sleeps with five different girls, and I know them all, and then he comes back at six in the morning and makes love to me. It's got to stop, and that's why we're here.'

Wub and I were stunned. Just then, they came to take her husband away into another dressing-room. Wub asked, 'Does he keep it up OK?' I was a little surprised at Wub's forwardness but listened for the answer. 'Oh yes, no problem,' came the reply. 'The problem is that I'm knackered after three hours, so he stops for a can and a fag and then returns to his duties. He can keep it up all night, but there's no fireworks at the end.'

I felt a bit sorry for him: he had a good job at a factory and did his job well, despite having about eight or ten cans before work. When he went to his first detox to combat his drink problem, he went two weeks without a drink. When he went into work during this time, because he was sober and acted differently, his bosses thought he was ill and enquired if he felt OK. He told them the truth: for the past nine years he had been coming to work after consuming large quantities of alcohol. When he went back to work, he was back on the beer, so they fired him.

When my turn came to appear on the stage, I was ready for Trisha and her 'red' chair. This time, I had borrowed a Leeds United cushion from my mate Daz Gunga, and I smiled at Trisha as I placed it on the chair before I sat down.

All this publicity was a huge shock to Wub. Although she was once part of an audience at a circus scene on the television series *Follyfoot* in the '70s, this was big time. For example, only recently we were both on a plane bound for America when a lady came over to us and asked, 'I'm really sorry to bother you, but are you on your way to Las Vegas to get married?'

'No,' answered Wub, 'we're not getting married until next June.'

Just then, I leant across Wub and said to the lady, 'During the World Cup in Germany.' Wub looked at me and shook her head.

Not long after that, we were in a restaurant in a remote part of Scotland when a girl came over and asked if we'd been on the *Trisha Goddard* show. 'My mum's a big fan of the show and watches it all the time. You were both great!' she said. Wub was speechless. Even the popular magazine *Bella* came knocking and paid Wub £300 for her exclusive story.

I am a bit more used to the attention as refusing to paint anything red and going to every game everywhere does attract quite a bit of publicity, as well as the odd bottle of whisky. After several radio and television interviews, the whisky manufacturers Whyte and Mackay thought it would be a good idea to involve me in an advertising campaign they were running for Leeds United. They were the team sponsors and wanted to involve fans from different backgrounds. When I agreed to be involved, I had no idea what to expect.

Three fellas arrived at my house armed with note pads and loads of cameras. We had a chat over a cup of tea, and they said they wanted to photograph me from a different angle. Bizarrely, I ended up with three men pointing cameras at me, wearing only a Leeds United towel around my waist. I had to get out of the shower, and, with my hair all wet, they began eagerly snapping, as I stood posing at the bathroom door. I must admit that I had never felt like such a jerk, and I questioned whether they really were from Whyte and Mackay and not three blokes from a woman's glossy magazine (not that my bulky torso would excite many females out there). After about four hours, the end result was an image of me bending over the sink brushing my teeth, still with my towel on and holding in my belly for dear life! More embarrassing still was that the photograph appeared every week in the Leeds official match-day programme and in the official Leeds United magazine, *Leeds Leeds Leeds*.

I also recently appeared in a four-page article in a German football magazine, but, quite bizarrely, it was all in German. Legsy's sister came to the rescue and translated it for me word for word. The problem was that something got lost in the translation at the German end. Apparently I have attended every single Doors concert everywhere in the world.

Towards the end of the 2003–04 season, with relegation almost inevitable, a handful of fans were invited to take part in a campaign designed to spice up season-ticket sales for the following season. The campaign 'Love Leeds' would hopefully raise the profile of Leeds United during those troubled times. It was always going to be difficult, after relegation to the Coca-Cola Championship (a fancy name for the second division) became a reality.

It was raining heavily as I arrived at Elland Road on that Saturday morning. I had no idea what lay ahead. I was shown into the bar area in The Pavilion on Lowfields Road. The bar was closed, but there was an endless supply of tea, coffee and biscuits available. As I looked around the room, all I could see was five-year-old kids running about with balloons, whilst their doting parents, wearing Leeds shirts, looked on. What on earth was I doing there? More fans began to arrive: most of them families. I looked around desperately for someone I knew. I had made the decision to leave quietly when a bloke arrived and sat at my table. His name was John Fozzard, and he was obviously as embarrassed as I was. We both looked on nervously as a girl arrived and began setting up her little stall in the corner. She was to be known as the 'Face Painter'. The kids loved it, and when their name was called out they would skip happily towards her and sit motionless as the famous blue, white and yellow club colours were expertly painted onto their tiny faces. Then the parents were called, and they too had their faces painted. I looked at John and he instinctively knew what I was about to say. 'No,' he said, 'they won't be doing our faces – will they?' We were both hovering around 50 years of age.

'Nah,' I replied, 'they're only doing the kids and their families – surely?'

As the organisers went around the room, busily picking out the next victim, they came to our table. John and I both looked away, and they snatched a young lad who was about 20 years old. Sheepishly he was led to the Face Painter.

Things were beginning to get desperate when a call came from the door: 'Anyone who would like a complimentary tour around the ground can you come this way, please?' It was highly unlikely that two old fossils like us would be called to have our faces painted, but, 'just in case', we hurriedly made our way to the door.

'Stix' is a well-known figure behind the scenes at Elland Road, and in the absence of the normal tour guide, ex-player John McClelland, he would be showing us around. I had been on the tour before with my nephew, Scott, but this seemed like an ideal opportunity to escape the Face Painter, so we grabbed our loaned brollies and joined the back of the tour queue. Stix is an interesting character, and his love for the club is clearly evident. After showing us round the dressing-rooms and the dugouts, he led us up the stairs towards the boardroom. We paused on the stairs, as he showed us the many framed shirts of all the European teams Leeds had faced over the years. 'Almost all clubs happily leave a signed shirt as a souvenir of their visit, with one notable exception – Deportivo La Coruña. For whatever reason, the respective managers did not particularly get on with each other so you won't see the Deportivo shirt up there.' We then followed Stix to his very own 'cupboard'. In it was a very impressive collection of memorabilia that he had collected over the years, including personal items given to him by opposing teams. Someone asked, 'What happened to our old mascot, Ellie the Elephant?'

In response, Stix opened another cupboard and said, 'Do you mean him?' Inside was the original Ellie suit. It was a huge grey elephant wearing the Leeds kit and sporting the coolest of sunglasses. He looked a poor reflection of his former glory days, with the life literally drained out of him. It was sad to now see the remains of Ellie hanging in a cupboard, deep beneath the West Stand, but at least he was still at Elland Road.

It took me back to the very first time I met Ellie. It was the mid-'90s and Ellie the Elephant was at the height of his career. He would entertain kids and parents before, during and after games at Elland Road. At that time, we used to enjoy our pre-match drink in a bar in the stadium beneath the 'Captains Corner', between the Revie Stand and the West Stand. We would grab a final pint from the landlord, Ken, before taking up our seats at around 3.02 p.m. On one particular Saturday afternoon, we were just finishing our last pint when in walked Ellie the Elephant. He had just done his stint out on the pitch and had made his way directly down the corner tunnel leading to the bar. We all watched in amazement as he sauntered up to the bar, removed his massive furry elephant's head and placed it on the bar. We all looked at the tiny head that protruded from the neck of the costume and couldn't help but smile. He then unzipped his paws and picked up a pint of lager waiting for him on the bar. He took a huge gulp of his beer and lit up a cigarette. He drew in the smoke and blew it into the air. 'Fuckin' kids,' he said and continued with his pint. We just fell about laughing.

After the tour with Stix, we returned to the rest of the group. As we entered the room, my heart sank: everyone in the room had their faces painted in Leeds colours. It sank even further when they began calling out the remaining names. John and I were the last two to be done, and with our faces painted brightly we both sat there dumbfounded. Three players – Alan Smith, James Milner and Mark Viduka – were also there, and even they didn't escape the Face Painter. Weeks later, all three had left the club: Milner went to Newcastle; Viduka went to Middlesbrough; and Smith just went.

The following season, our painted faces were everywhere. My mug appeared on everything, including every match ticket. After one game at Elland Road, Wub had picked me up in the car, and we were cutting through the back streets of Beeston. As we pulled up at the junction with the main Dewsbury Road, a double-decker bus went by. On the side of the bus was a huge picture of yours truly staring back at us. We sat there speechless for a few seconds, before Wub burst out laughing so loud I thought she was going to have a heart attack. Over the next few weeks, my picture emblazoned on buses around the region caused quite a few of my mates to almost lose their no-claims bonuses.

I was back at Elland Road in April 2005 to take part as an extra in a new movie that was about to be released. Bryony Stokes from Twin Track Films rang me with details of a scene they were about to shoot at Elland Road. I gathered outside the ground, with a number of other selected Leeds fans, as we were briefed on our role. The movie, called *The Penalty King*, centred around a Leeds United supporter who was gradually going blind and this was to be the final scene. I was part of a crowd of fans who were to sit near to the two main characters: Leeds fan Lee Vaughan, played by the actor Nick Bartlett, and his wife, Maddie, played by Samantha Beckinsale. Lee was attending his last game before going totally blind. It was quite a star-studded cast: Nick had appeared in movies such as *Fierce Creatures*, *Gangs of New York* and *The 51st State* as well as television programmes *Tipping the Velvet*, *Trial and Retribution*, *The Bill* and countless others. Sam, of course, is the daughter of Richard Beckinsale from *Porridge* and *The Lovers*, but she is a star in her own right, having appeared in *London's Burning*, *Time after Time*, *Coronation Street* and, more recently, *Duck Patrol.* We, the 'crowd', had to imagine that we were watching a Leeds game back in the late '90s. The cameras were on us as we watched one of the film crew running up and down the track along the side of the pitch. Our eyes had to follow him and imagine that we were watching Alfie Haaland pass the ball to Lee Bowyer who then passes it to Jimmy Hasslebaink. Then we were all to jump up in anguish as if Hasselbaink had fired the ball way over the crossbar. I was sitting next to Alison and Mark Durant, who had travelled up from West Sussex to take part in the filming. It was all a bit of fun but a bit weird at times. For instance, we had to chant the crowd favourite, 'We all love Leeds, we all love Leeds, we all love Leeds' and so on, but we had to sing it to a different tune than usual, because of copyright infringements.

Also in the crowd that day was Leeds favourite Peter Lorimer. He had been persuaded to take part, and it was comical to see him there decked out in a big coat, Leeds scarf and an old flat cap. Alan Smith was also invited to play a cameo role, but, after his defection to Old Trafford, director Chris Cook thought it would be inappropriate for him to take part.

I have been fortunate enough to be invited to various parts of the country to talk to audiences about Leeds United and my experiences of supporting them. One such occasion was when I was invited to speak to the North Wales Branch of the Leeds United Supporters Club in Wrexham. Wub and I were put up in a quaint little hotel, close to the venue where I was to address the Welsh Leeds fans. Leaving Wub in the car, I went and checked in. As I made my way to the stairs with the rather effeminate landlord, Colin Forbes walked in. He was the secretary of the North Wales Branch and had come to see if everything was OK. He then walked outside and had a few words with Wub. The landlord then showed me to the room. On the way upstairs, I asked (at Wub's request) if it was a double or a twin room. 'Oh, don't worry, it's a lovely big double bed, you'll be fine,' was his rather strange reply. As we came back downstairs, Colin said, 'Right, I'm off for a quick pint at the club, see you in there.' He put down our bag, which Wub had given him, and left.

When the landlord disappeared into the back of the house, Wub came in and we went up to the room. Wub wanted to lie down for a while, so I went and joined Colin and some of the other lads, including Butter, originally from Kippax but now a member of the Wrexham Branch. The following day we had to leave fairly early, so we skipped breakfast. Wub went out to the car first, and I followed shortly after. As I was leaving, the landlord came out and said, 'Oh, are you off then? Hope the two of you enjoyed your stay. Come again, bye.'

With that I went out to the car, which was parked out of sight of the front door. Some of the lads had been telling me the night before that the landlord of our hotel was gay. This got me retracing my steps. When I had checked in, the landlord only saw Colin and me. He never saw Wub at all, not even when we left. I suddenly realised why the landlord had been disappointed when I told him we wouldn't be having breakfast.

I was recently asked to give a talk at Wealstun Prison. I was met at the gate and escorted through at least six locked gates and doors, before arriving at the prison library, where the talk was to be held. I had a cup of tea with the librarians, and shortly afterwards a group of inmates arrived. The discussion was basically about *Paint it White*, which was available in the library, but the talk eventually moved on to Leeds United's current plight and football in general. It was a good atmosphere, and the lads were very responsive. Just before I left, a warder called Nobby, a Brummie Leeds fan, showed me to the inmates' recreation room. On the walls were impressive Leeds United murals done by the prisoners themselves. Leeds fans here, Leeds fans there, sprung to mind. As I left the prison, with the gates slamming behind me like a scene from *Porridge*, I contemplated my next port of call: a talk at a local primary school. From cons to kids: it's funny how my stories seem to appeal to everyone.

15

Coach Daze

> I often take a few minutes out of my day and look down at Elland Road from the back streets of Beeston. I feel so proud to be part of this movement.

I much prefer to travel to away games by train. Before the days when certain pubs had 'continental' hours, Leeds fans would meet in cafés for a hearty breakfast before boarding the 'football special' to the next away game. The Golden Egg on Boar Lane, near to the station, was a favourite; so too was The Olympic on Vicar Lane. The Egg has now been replaced by a posh coffee bar, but The Olympic is still surviving the upsurge of trendy 'bagel bars'.

That said, the coach is much more convenient than the train, and, providing you get the right driver and the right set of lads, it can be a right laugh. We've kept the same backbone of troops for over 15 years, but, obviously, some of the clientele come and go.

Many Leeds supporters clubs have run coaches for many years, and, once you get a regular travelling party, it makes so much more sense. It is said, for instance, that the Fullerton Park and Griffin branches allow their members to take games on the coach for the last day of the season. For this one special day of the season, they get to wear their normal clothes and indulge themselves with that old favourite 'Fuzzy Felt'.

Getting the right coach company is crucial. We made a mistake, sometime in the early '90s, of switching companies. Leeds were to play at Everton in a mid-week fixture and we were drinking in the 'Mucky Duck' – otherwise known as The White Swan – in The Calls in Leeds. Nearly 50 lads were due to board the bus, provided by the new company, at 5.30 p.m., for the trip to Merseyside. By 6.15 our coach still hadn't arrived. The owner of the company assured me over the telephone that the coach had already been to the pick-up point, directly outside the pub, but there had been no one there, so the driver had returned to the depot.

I had been in the pub since 3 p.m. and, as you can clearly see outside through several large glass windows, I knew this not to be true. The owner told me he'd send the coach back within the next quarter of an hour. At nearly ten minutes to seven, the coach still had not arrived, and, with the kick-off at 7.45 p.m., urgent action was needed. Therefore, I rang the nearest taxi firm. 'Good evening,' the girl at the taxi firm said. 'Can I help you?'

'Yes, please,' I replied. 'Can I order a couple of taxis, please?'

'Certainly, sir,' she said. 'How many taxis do you want, and where are they going?'

'A dozen, please,' I said. 'They're going to Liverpool.' This was met by a long silence.

Talking to someone else in the office, I heard her say, 'Someone here wants 12 taxis to go to Liverpool.'

I then heard the other voice reply, 'They're taking the piss; give me it here.' 'Where are you going from?' said the second voice to me.

'We're just around the corner from you, at The White Swan. We need to get to Everton's ground in the next 45 minutes. We'll pay you up front: how much will it be, one way.'

'Seventy-five pounds.'

'Start sending 'em round. We need to set off now.' With that I hung up and told the lads to sup up.

Ten minutes later we were in a fleet of taxis hurtling westwards across the M62. Our driver seemed slightly intimidated by us. He then seemed very intimidated, as Danny Shipley, who was in the front, said, 'Get your foot down, mate. You can do better than this.'

'I need a piss, Snake,' John Robertshaw said to me, after we'd only gone a few miles.

'Christ, John!' I said. 'We've only gone 15 miles.'

'Soz, mate,' John replied. 'You know what it's like, once you break the seal: you're forever pissing.'

'I'll pull off at the next roundabout,' said the driver.

'OK,' I said, 'but don't stop. He'll piss out of the door. We can't afford to stop.' John looked at me. 'I'll hold onto your belt. Just aim it away.' Seconds later, we were screeching round a roundabout and then back down the slip road, with me holding on to John, who was three-quarters of the way out of the car. By now the driver was petrified. 'We'll give you a bit extra at the other end, mate,' I assured him. 'Just keep going, old pal.'

He asked how long we would be at Everton. 'Oh, you can get straight back,' said Russ Townend. 'We'll jump on other coaches to get home.' We entered Goodison Park at precisely 8 p.m.

Trips to Everton are rarely short of incident. In 1980 we were on the coach making our way away from the ground. We had just kept Everton down to a 5–1 victory. Tempers were a little frayed when, with a bang, our coach ran into the car in front. Brian, our driver, shouted, 'The stupid twat slammed all on: I'd no chance.'

The driver got out of his Volvo estate and walked towards Brian's window. I say walk: it was more of a stagger.

'He's pissed,' said Frank Rounding.

Davy Patrick shouted at him, with his strong Scottish accent, 'Hey up, ye pissed up old get. Wot ye fuckin' playin' at?' To our surprise the man turned out to be CID and we were right outside Walton Lane Police Station. His station.

'You're in the wrong, mate,' he said to Brian, 'but we'll let it go this time. On your way.'

Bernie Heaslip, with a can of beer in his hand, took his turn at the window. 'You ain't got much choice, mate, you're steaming,' he shouted to the copper. The policeman then replied to Bernie, but it was all in vain. Bernie had collapsed face down in the aisle, with his can still in his hand. The copper got back in his car and, with his Volvo lurching like a jumping kangaroo, he drove into the police car park.

A lot of the lads on our bus in those days were from all over east Leeds, and, after a couple of jars on the way home, we would drop them all off and head for Kippax. One time, as we approached the end of his road in Kippax, Martin Barrett shouted, 'Anywhere here,

Brian. Cheers, mate.' It was about 3 a.m., and there was no one about.

'See ya Saturday, lads,' Martin shouted, as he jumped off the bus and ran straight across the front of the coach to get to the other side of the road.

'Hold it!' Brian shouted, but it was too late.

A car overtaking the bus hit Martin head on and knocked him straight over its bonnet. 'Where the hell did he come from?' shouted Tim Thorpe, as we all scrambled off the coach.

Martin lay in the road motionless. 'He's dead,' said Tony Denton. However, he then moved and rolled over.

'Quick, he's still alive!' shouted Gary Levitt. Mark 'Cockbird' Clayton moved his finger from side to side in front of Martin's eyes, as if he was a paramedic or something.

The car had stopped, and the driver came back to help us sit Martin on the wall. 'I never saw you, mate, I'm sorry,' he said. He looked around at us as if he was going to get a good hiding. Despite getting a right whack, Martin seemed OK. This was possibly due to his large consumption of alcohol.

'It was his fault, mate, yer alright,' Steve Topping said.

'We're all insured, Mart, you'll be OK,' I said, as Rolf helped him down the street. The following day, it was my solemn duty to tell Martin that the very second he stepped off the coach his insurance ceased.

Our coaches have always had a cosmopolitan feel to them, with lads from all over Leeds mixing together. During the late '70s, Frank and his brother John brought together different sections of east Leeds. Lads from different estates would enjoy a fight with each other on a Friday night and then, the next day, enjoy a beer together. Gary Barrett and Carl Cooney, engaged in combat 24 hours earlier, would now be sound asleep in each other's arms. There was also Steve and Simon Duffy and, of course, Tony Duffy. Tony became the youngest Leeds fan to ever get arrested when he kicked a manchester united fan who had spat at him, when he was 12. He would have escaped, too, if he hadn't been wearing his elder brother's Doc Marten boots, which were too big for him and prevented him from running off fast enough.

Tony Denton from Kippax had also been quite unfortunate, a few years earlier. On the day in question, he had been in trouble with the police and his dad had ordered him not to go to Elland Road. But Tony defied him, and, when he returned home after the game, his dad was none the wiser. However, Tony had once again fallen foul of the law during the 1–1 draw with Luton, but, as he had only been ejected from the ground with no charge against him, his father would never know. Would he? But Tony's bad luck continued, and, as he and his dad watched the game that evening on *Match of the Day*, the camera panned in on the new Leeds manager, Brian Clough. The view of Clough was momentarily obscured, as two police officers walked past the dugout with a handcuffed Tony.

There was, and always has been, a smattering of travelling Hunslet lads on our coaches. Sandy Hamilton has remained a loyal fan throughout the years, and we all shed a tear when a special Hunslet lad died a few years back from cancer. Steve 'Gadge' Gardner knew he was dying, and the only things that bothered him were what would happen to his kids and the fact that he would not see Leeds lift the European Cup. There was many a quiet moment set aside for Gadge during our memorable European Cup run in 2001.

We were once involved in a small altercation with some Liverpool fans after a game at Anfield. Above all, our aim was to have a good laugh, drink a few beers and watch Leeds win. That particular day our resolve was put to the test. We had been invited to the Liverpool Supporters Club by some Liverpool fans who were known to some of our lads. Some other Liverpool fans took exception to this and that was that. A right old scrap took place in the middle of the street, on the corner outside of The Arkle pub. To be fair, our lads stuck together, and we even received praise from the local constabulary; they had seen us stay together and repel the attack with the minimum of fuss. After this incident, a certain bond grew amongst our members. As Frank put it to me recently, 'I think it was that day that everyone on the bus became real friends and had respect for each other. If we had not stuck together that day, I think we could have had someone killed.'

But even that day had a rather amusing end to it. While we were at the Liverpool Supporters Club, our coach had two windows smashed. As we drove off, we only just managed to pick up a very drunk Barry Mortimer, who was propping up the nearest lamppost.

As we drove out of Liverpool along the East Lancs Road, we knew we were coming to a well known 'ambush spot'. 'Get the piss-pot ready,' shouted big Steve Lavis, 'we're nearly there.' The 'piss-pot' was a large five-gallon drum that, in emergencies, we used to piss in. As we pulled up at the traffic lights, a cheeky Scouser 'surprised' us and threw a bottle through the already missing window. John Rounding and Russ Cooper picked up the piss-pot and threw five gallons of mixed piss over the unfortunate attacker. The other funny thing was that it was a windy day, so poor old Barry, who had staggered into the seat near the broken window, got absolutely drenched.

Over the years, Leeds and Liverpool have enjoyed a special bond. Don Revie used to speak with Bill Shankly on the telephone every Sunday morning to discuss the previous day's events. Much, of course, is said of that memorable night when Leeds clinched the League Championship in 1969, thus earning a huge appreciative ovation from the Liverpool Kop. The majority of Liverpool fans are tremendous; however, it has to be recorded that they have their bad element too. Leeds fans only have to fart, and it hits the national headlines.

Bramley, of course, was always well represented on the coach, as we moved into the '80s. Sid and Titty, both Bramley lads, had to be pulled apart one morning, when they were wrestling in a Leeds shop doorway, and we hadn't even set off for the match.

A mixed bunch of renegades, gathered from the four corners of Leeds, used to hog the middle of the coach, and their antics were legendary. Graham Rostron once turned up in a bright yellow fisherman's smock and hat. He never said a word to anyone all day about why he was wearing it, as if it was the norm. The following away game we arrived to pick his renegades up. He and six others boarded the coach: this time they were all dressed as yellow fishermen, complete with big yellow hats. Dave Hyde and Graham sat beside each other and discussed trawlers all the way to Sunderland. Gordon, Kev, Steve and John Glynn were more interested in the shipping forecast for the following day. Mark Slater was seen spitting on his handkerchief and quietly buffing up his bright yellow wellies. In sharp contrast, Mick Teesdale and John Hollington were sat behind them in smart trousers, white shirts and shiny shoes. They had got on the bus direct from a nightclub.

At the next game, Graham and his mob were much more sensible. They sat for the entire journey sporting the Wallace Arnold seat covers on their heads.

Whilst returning from Plymouth in the mid-'80s, we pulled up at a motorway service station. It wasn't long before a group of us were having our customary 'kick-around', with a cheap football from one of the shops. A heavy bout of can tipping had taken place on the coach, and quite a few unsavoury tackles were flying in. Very soon there was blood, snot and teeth everywhere. Apparently, watching the 'game' were a small group of American tourists, and, as they chatted in the toilets afterwards, Steve Morley heard one of them say, 'Jeez, wait till we tell them back home that soccer is not a ladies' game over here.'

Further up the motorway, we noticed that two of our members hadn't had quite enough to eat. They hadn't been travelling with us very long, but we were all surprised when we turned round to the back seat to witness one of them on his knees receiving from the other what can only be described as a 'mouthful'. It was apparently to pay off a debt! We never saw either of them again after that night.

On the first day of the 1984–85 season, we took two coaches to a pre-arranged pub on the outskirts of Nottingham: we were on our way to play Notts County. The pub was called The Bull and Butcher, and we had been there on many previous occasions. The landlord always made us welcome, and this time was no different. That was until an hour into our stay, when some unwelcome guests decided to pay us a visit. Notts Forest were playing at Hillsborough that day. (Apparently Forest fans hate being called Notts Forest as opposed to Nottingham Forest.) So, anyway, NOTTS Forest were playing at Hillsborough that day and, after seemingly being tipped off about our presence, decided to drop by. Peter behind the bar tried to reason with the Forest fans, but they were there to cause trouble and nothing else. A scuffle ensued as we took the fight outside and told Peter to shut the doors behind us, but it was over in about ten minutes. One enduring memory of that day was Stevie Priestley, hidden beneath a large spinning beer-garden umbrella, seeing off the last of the fleeing Forest contingent as they disappeared up the road. Charlie and the other Bramley lads were just returning to the coach when I noticed

Steve Mortimer bent down shouting through the pub letterbox. Seconds later, through the letterbox, he was handed his glasses and false teeth that he had removed before the clash.

The Kippax Branch certainly has a thing about false teeth. Kev 'Mouse' Broadbent, one of our senior members, used to leave his teeth in his pint when he visited the toilet so no one would 'nick it'. This was all very well, but why he had to eat a sausage roll before he left his teeth baffled me.

As we boarded our coaches to leave The Bull and Butcher the police arrived. The fracas was over and done with when they arrived: like the US Cavalry, they were half an hour late. Unbelievably, we were told we had to go to the police station to 'clear things up'. Despite pleas from the landlord, they escorted our buses to the local station. As we all drove into the compound, I turned to Gary Sharp and said, 'They're gonna keep us in here until after the match, you watch.' Time was getting on, and we were still on the coaches with nothing happening. Then, at about 2.30 p.m., they ordered us to file off the buses. I was sitting on the back seat and looked out of the back window. Instinctively, I jumped out of the rear emergency exit and walked over to one of the officers who was closing the huge compound doors behind us. To this day I don't know what I said to him, but, as I got within inches of him, I made a dash through the closing gap between the doors. I was off like shit off a stick, and, although I could hear them running behind me, I didn't look back. I also didn't know where the hell I was going. After what must have been a mile, I could still hear loud grunts and footsteps behind me. I was tiring.

Just then a recognisable voice wheezed, 'For fuck's sake, Snake, stop running.' I had been running away from Gary Sharp for a mile.

As we both bent over, puffing and panting, I said, 'Why didn't you say something earlier, you wally?'

'I couldn't run and shout at the same time. I'm knackered!'

We didn't have a clue where we were, so the logical thing was to jump in a taxi. We arrived at the ground with seconds to spare. The rest of them were released, without charge, at 4.15 p.m.

Apparently, they had lined our lot up against the wall and said, 'All those who were not involved in the fight go to the left. Those involved, go to the right.' As the lads shuffled about, unbelievably two of our lads went to the right. I won't embarrass them by naming them – let's just say it was Doom and Geordie.

We had a couple of clashes with Forest fans in the '80s. On one occasion, our coach was being driven by my brother-in-law at the time. Big Dave Walker was an imposing 6 ft 4 in. figure with a skinhead and tattoos. A Transit van loaded with Forest fans drew up alongside us and, unbelievably, tried to force us off the road. Instead of swerving to his left, Dave swung the wheel to his right, and we all watched in amazement as the Transit had to brake violently before it bounced onto the grass central reservation and ground to a halt. It was a very effective solution to a potentially dangerous situation.

A similar thing happened as we travelled down to Selhurst Park in London. We were visited by another Transit van, this time carrying Middlesbrough fans. We had two coaches travelling down that day, and the van pulled alongside the other coach, which was in front of us. Just then, Barney from Garforth shouted, 'They've just bricked our boys! Stop!'

The Transit van pulled off onto the next slip road, as the first coach came to a stop. We pulled up behind them to check they were OK, and, like a scene from *Die Hard*, some of our lads ran up the banking to head off the Transit that was approaching a roundabout. The driver of the van panicked, and, as he overtook the stationary cars in front of him, he lost control. The van ended up on its roof, with the shell-shocked passengers scrambling from the back. Believe it or not, we had our very own paramedic, Paul, on board, and he quickly assessed the situation. Seeing that all the occupants were sitting about dazed and confused on the grass, he decided that no first aid was required. So, anxious to avoid the police, we got our party back on the coaches and sped towards London, whistling innocently.

Looking back, we've had a number of professionals on our coaches over the years. We've had a pilot (James), a paramedic (Paul), a paratrooper (Dave) and quite a few paralytics.

Those paralytics got a good chance to flex their muscles in the early '80s, when we came up against Middlesbrough at Ayresome Park. It was during the Christmas period, and long-time Leeds fan Kenny Young from Middlesbrough had arranged an early drink for us. Surprisingly, Leeds have a strong support in that neck of the woods, and Kenny's brother Graham and veteran Leeds supporter Jim Newell joined us as we filed into The Lambton Arms. We were soon joined by a large number of Leeds fans from the North East. That pub has long since been demolished, but, at the time, it was a great watering hole and full of character. We had left Leeds early to partake in some festive cheer, and, as we sat down to our first beer, there were seven hours to go before kick-off. That was probably just as well, because also enjoying a beer was none other than Boro star Craig Johnston. He was sharing a joke with some of the locals and, eventually, came over to chat to us. Before he left to report to the ground, the cheeky old so-and-so signed a Middlesbrough fanzine and handed it to John Petch. It read, 'To the Kippax lads with my condolences. Craig Johnston.' 'Biggles' fired some uncomplimentary words in his direction, as he disappeared out through the back door. Andy Cockx and Kenny Dobson also noticed through the pub window that Johnston and his pals were having more than just a little difficulty getting into their car. When we arrived at the ground, Tony Leeds and 'Grandad' from the West Midlands Whites told us they had just seen Johnston being whisked into the stadium by two stewards. Perhaps his pre-match drinks would not go unnoticed, after all.

Something quite strange happened the following season. We were travelling to a game at Swansea when our coach broke down. The driver informed us that it would take over an hour for a replacement to arrive. Within minutes, the police arrived, but we had already made a dash over the field in search of the nearest pub. There was a certain familiarity about the whole scenario. When we reached the pub, it was the exact same spot where we had broken down two years previously, whilst travelling to the same venue.

Two years later, I was travelling in a car to Somerset with Pete Dillon. We decided to take a break and turned off at the next exit. It was not planned and we did not know where we were, but we had taken the very same turn-off at which we had broken down twice in the last four years. How bizarre is that?

Later that same season, with no league game on the calendar, Leeds were set to play Chester away in a Friday-night friendly. We decided to make a weekend of it, and so, on the Friday morning, Wub and I set off for the west coast with Pete and Jo Dillon, in our big old Chevrolet. It soon emerged that the game, for whatever reason, had been cancelled, but we had already arrived in the lovely city of Chester. Leeds reserves were scheduled to play the following day at Whitby Town. Whilst the girls got ready for our night on the town, Pete and I had a beer in the hotel bar. We deduced that, with the game cancelled in Chester, it would make sense for the first team to fulfil the fixture at Whitby the following day. How could we break this to the girls? Our pleas fell on stony ground that evening, but we both persisted, and the following morning, after servicing our respective partners in our rooms, we grabbed a quick breakfast and dashed from one coast to the other. The Chevrolet was a great old beast, and we shot over Fylingdales and arrived in Whitby in just over two hours. Leeds romped home 9–0, even though John Sheridan missed a penalty. On the bench for Whitby that day was a mate of mine called Tony Ward, originally from Garforth. Tony is a big fan of Leeds and now runs The Plough at Sleights near Whitby.

We were heading for Newcastle one season, and, as we entered the county of Durham, we pulled off the A1 into a village called Coxhoe. It was a regular stopping-off point for our coach, and the landlord of the local pub, The Kicking Cuddy, was always glad to see us. That particular morning it was snowing heavily, and the game at St James' Park looked in serious doubt. However, at that moment, it was the least of our worries, as, 500 yards from the A1, a police motorcyclist pulled us up. I got off the coach with Big John Martin and Collar to speak to the officer. It's fair to say he wasn't a friendly fellow. 'Where are you going, lads?' he asked.

As usual Collar took charge. 'We're off to the pub just down this road, mate,' he said.

'I don't think so,' said the officer. 'What do they call it?'

'The Kicking Cuddy,' John said. 'They're expecting us.'

He seemed a little surprised that we knew the name. He wiped the snow from his petrol tank and picked up the telephone that was fixed to it. He flicked through his notebook and dialled a number. After a brief conversation, presumably to the pub, he replaced his phone. Apparently they had confirmed what we had told him and he wasn't too pleased. He climbed onto his motorcycle. 'OK, on your way, and if you cause the slightest bit of trouble . . . '

'No worries there, sir,' interrupted Collar. 'They're old friends of ours.'

Within half an hour of our arrival at The Kicking Cuddy, it was announced that the game was off. The snow outside was getting thicker, and, as the welcoming coal fire burned bright, we all settled down to watch Leeds v. Castleford in a crucial rugby league game on television. 'I usually close at three,' the landlord told us a bit later, 'so if you want to stay here drinking, one of your lot will have to serve behind the bar. I'm away upstairs for my dinner.' We duly nominated Big John as our 'landlord' and with a remarkable show of trust, the real landlord left Big John behind the bar to serve 50 thirsty Leeds fans.

At around 8 p.m. we said our farewells and headed slowly down the snow-covered A1, leaving a very healthy profit for The Kicking Cuddy.

We were back in Coxhoe the following season, when big Webby walked into the pub. He had overslept and missed the coach, so had to come up in his car. When the time came to leave for the game, Ian 'Skippy' Marsden and I went to the game with Webby in his old Ford Sierra.

I must have been to every ground dozens and dozens of times, but I still couldn't direct you to any of them. As we approached Newcastle, none of us knew the way. Just then, Skippy noticed a car in front with a black and white scarf hanging out of the window and the familiar 'Howay, the lads' sticker in the rear window. The driver was on his own, and it wasn't too long before he noticed three 16 st. blokes behind him in hot pursuit. He picked up speed, and, in order to get to the ground, so did we. He put his foot down some more. So did we. Then he took what we presumed to be a crafty short cut through a housing estate. We were still up his arse when he pulled into a driveway and got out of his car.

'Come on, lads, what do yers want?' he asked, looking pretty scared.

Diplomatic Webby put his head out of an open window. 'We're following you to the ground, ya Geordie get. Where the hell are we?'

'Oh,' said the man, 'I live here. I'm not gannin' to the game. You want to be straight doon there and left.'

'Stupid twat,' Webby shouted, as he reversed out of the drive and sped off, leaving the man scratching his head.

Sobriety wasn't exactly in abundance on our coaches, and the camaraderie that existed, and still does, is phenomenal. I'm often asked what makes me go to football week-in, week-out, season after season. Well, occasionally, the 90 minutes at the game gets in the way of a cracking day out. Fifty lads will sit there contentedly consuming cold beers and watching classic videos such as *Debbie Does Dallas* or *The Return of the Turd Chewer*. A particular favourite of Lunge's is *Sluts with Nuts*.

I often like to take time out and relax with my can, whilst idly looking out of the window, as the rolling countryside goes past.

One of the saddest sights one could ever see is that of a cattle truck full of poor animals en route to meet their end. I try to get over this by imagining that when I see an empty cattle truck it is returning from Heathrow Airport. It has just dropped off all the cows, and, heavily disguised, they have all passed through Customs and are now on a one-way flight to India, where they won't be eaten.

Although I'm not a vegetarian, I am a huge animal lover. I have my name on a plaque at Panda House, the headquarters of the WWF (World Wildlife Fund), and I am a life member. I am also a member of the ILPH (International League for the Protection of Horses), the LACS (League Against Cruel Sports), the EIA (Environmental Investigation Agency), the Hunt Saboteurs Association and the Dogs Trust.

I was once in a Chinese restaurant with Wub in Pontefract. We were reading the menus before ordering our meal. I was fancying duck, when I just happened to gaze out of the window. Outside there was a pleasant little stream set in the gardens that ran around the restaurant. Making their way past us were two ducks. I looked at the menu and decided to order something else instead. I would not have been able to forgive myself if I had ordered duck and the next time round there was just one duck minus his mate.

My mate, and staunch Leeds fan, little Mick Hewitt is a vegetarian. I was walking down to Elland Road one evening and there was Mick at a hamburger stand. 'Hey-up, Mick,' I said, 'I thought you were a veggie?'

'Don't worry, Snake,' he said, 'I've ordered a cheese burger without the burger and with extra cheese.' I walked down to the ground with him as he tucked in.

That truly was a strange night. Leeds were playing Swindon Town in the Carling Cup. In the dying minutes of extra time, our goalkeeper Paul Robinson came up for a corner and scored the winner. That night, the game finished at about 10.30 p.m. It was not unusual, of course: evening cup games often finished hours after kick-off. I still remember, though – and it's not that long ago – when evening games kicked off at 7.30 p.m. and finished at ten past nine, with only ten minutes for half-time.

One sight I love is when we pass a pig farm near the motorway. They look so happy on their own little estate. They seem to have their own little houses and communities, and rumour has it that some even have local pubs and shops that the pigs go to. I'm not particularly convinced of the rumours that some of the pubs are called The Pig and Whistle or The Hogs Head, though. And I'm fairly certain they wouldn't be served pork scratchings.

Talking of which, over the years, our boys have clashed with the West Midlands Police Force on many occasions: we always find them very provocative. In early December 1986, we got off our coach to walk to The Hawthorns to play West Bromwich Albion. There was a fracas ahead, between some Leeds fans and the local constabulary. Although we had nothing to do with it, we soon found ourselves being harassed and beaten by a frenzied police force. Big John was kicked to the ground and severely beaten up. As our lads tried to intervene, half of our coach party was arrested in a matter of minutes. Afterwards, in the police van, 'Sid' Johnson and Stevie Priestley were handcuffed to their seats. As the police left the vehicle, in search of more victims, Stevie – who doesn't exactly resemble Charles Atlas – simply eased his wrists out of the cuffs, opened the back door and fled to his freedom.

We returned to West Brom the following season. It was the end of January, and I was with Dick and Paul Hazelgrave in The Hawthorns when I was approached by two of our friends from the West Midlands Police Force. Apparently, I appeared drunk, and they promptly arrested me. Leeds were well in control of the game, and goals by Andy Williams, John Sheridan and John Pearson had virtually put the result beyond doubt at 3–0. As I was being led around the pitch in handcuffs, West Brom pulled one back, but, as if to salute my disappearance down the tunnel, Bobby Davison restored Leeds' three-goal cushion.

It was never made clear to me why I had been arrested, but I was detained in a police cell for about four hours. As I sat in my cell, with a couple of other unlucky Leeds fans, I produced a balloon from my jacket pocket that I had put there the night before at a party. We were soon having our own game of 'football' with the balloon, and the police hated it. I was eventually charged with 'Entering a designated sporting arena after consuming alcohol'. Now, this law leaves a lot to be desired. Firstly, the word 'designated' leaves it open to police interpretation. I am a member of Yorkshire County Cricket Club, and alcohol is allowed inside the stadium. I regularly attend horse-race meetings where, of course, alcohol is legal. The word 'designated' allows the police to discriminate between football and other sporting events. During the season of my arrest, many football grounds sold beer within the confines of the stadium. As my arrest was made inside the ground, how could this 'law' apply to me? After enquiries by my solicitor, the answer was, 'because it's designated'. Basically, the police can choose which arena they 'designate'.

At my subsequent court appearance, I had summoned the help of Ray Clowes and my old mate Doctor Doom (Dave Green). They were in the vicinity when I was hauled away, and I hoped they would help me out of the tricky situation that I found myself in. It soon became apparent that I stood no chance. Despite declarations that I was innocent from my witnesses and despite the differing accounts of the arresting officers, who had absolutely no idea why I had been arrested, my charge was upheld, and I had a football exclusion order slapped on me. However, I was expecting this beforehand and subsequently, because of instructions from my solicitor, I escaped with a fine and no ban.

The outstanding moment in court that day, though, was when a Leeds fan was being cross-examined by the prosecution. After being told to remove his chewing gum, the Leeds lad in the dock looked at his opponent. She was a very smartly dressed blonde lady, probably about 50 years of age, with an incredibly posh accent. The lad in question had been arrested for foul and abusive language. The prosecutor read out the charge: 'During the game between West Bromwich Albion and Leeds United you were heard joining in a chant of . . .' she then coughed and, in the most upper-class voice you will ever hear, said, 'Andy Gray! Andy Gray! Andy, Andy Gray! When he gets the ball he does fuck all! Andy, Andy Gray!' She blushed as she sat down, and I swear that even the judge had to stifle a smile.

One occasion when we did surprise the police was at Old Trafford. We had decided to take a double-decker bus there for an evening fixture. As we arrived at the back of the scoreboard end, we were met by a very small number of police officers who were actually quite surprised to see us. I suppose their surprise was understandable, given that it was only a reserve fixture. They gave us our own little 'pen' in the seats in the main stand.

After our return to the old First Division in 1990, our coach passenger list altered slightly. Stuart Smythe joined our ranks, but, one time, he had to be disciplined by the committee when he boarded the coach wearing a bright red T-shirt. Ten miles down the M1 I relieved him of his offensive attire and threw it out of the coach skylight. Someone gave him a spare shirt, and he soon forgot his loss, as we settled down to our regular game of 'What's in the Tin?' This was a little pastime the 'back seaters' had devised, as we hurtled to all four corners of the country. The idea was that each one took on board a tin of something bought from a supermarket – but with the label removed. Each tin was opened in turn, and everyone had to eat whatever was in it. It was fun at first, and we soon became used to eating cold beans and sausage, and cold alphabet soup. Many of our members were often caught putting letters aside for future reference: spelling was not their strong point. However, the game soon turned sour, mainly due to the exploits of Craig 'Pencil' Woods. Pencil thought it would be a good idea to spice things up, in more ways than one, and began introducing chilli beans and such delicacies as red-hot peppers. Pencil soon took over the title of 'Poison' from Chris Archer, and the game was cancelled shortly afterwards: many of the lads had begun passing out and some suffered difficulties in breathing. It was back to the much more sedate pastime of 'See who can drink the most beer before Sheffield'.

One regular traveller who may have been worse affected by the intake of the more exotic foods was Andy 'Shag' Brunton. He seemed to get more and more distant as the weeks passed, and, after a while, he stopped coming altogether. We eventually found out from his brother Wayne that 'Shag' had suffered a minor breakdown. He was admitted to a specialist unit at the famous Jimmy's hospital in Leeds. Collar, Big John and I went to visit him one afternoon. After being shown to the building at the back of the hospital, we were met by a man dressed in pyjamas who showed us upstairs to a room where Shag was watching television with some other patients. They were watching *Quincy, M.D.* As we began talking with Shag, we were shushed by the others, who were glued to the set. So too was Shag. When we continued to whisper to him, Shag turned to us and, with his finger to his mouth, gave us a very loud 'SSSHH!!' The three of us slipped out unnoticed. We had lost Shag for good.

By the mid-'90s, the Kippax Branch had been 'incorporated' into the Holbeck Branch, and a healthy mixture of fans emerged. Ralph and Phil Benson were at the helm, and young, impressionable lads from the Holbeck, such as Benjy and Jonno, got a chance to rub shoulders with their Kippax 'heroes'. Benjy and Jonno had just discovered such vintage beverages as Thunderbird and Blue Nun and were talking fluent Swahili by the time we had reached Nottingham, on one away trip. Benny Jordan, a good friend of my cousin Graham, was an ever present and was often accompanied by his sister Carmen, who could easily match any man on the bus 'can for can'. Relatively new recruits, Rob Hirst, Brazza and Paul Abrahams from Kippax, have been assimilated nicely into the fold and, along with the new-look Mathew 'Stan' Standish, always lead the chant of 'Dom Matteo in the San Siro' on our return journeys.

New faces began to appear, and slowly some of the old guard dropped out of the scene over the years. One of those 'drop-outs' was our very own 'relic' John Scanlan, a top fan since the '60s. Unfortunately, John never seemed to re-acclimatise when we returned to the dizzy heights of the top division. He once told me that it was much better fun travelling during the '80s. I and many others agree with him. Although now much in need of a heavy dose of Grecian 2000, John still regularly attends games at Elland Road. I also sport more than the odd silver lock, and, as I look around these days, it's more like looking at a Saga holiday than a football trip. Many of the lads can just remember when they had their own teeth. There's often a moan from the young apprentices at the back of the coach when Radio Two replaces Radio One over the airwaves. On journeys back from away games, many of us senior members can be seen hunched over our mobile phones, as we squint to read our text messages, before surrendering and reaching for our reading glasses purchased from the £1 shop.

COACH DAZE

Stalwarts such as Barry Mortimer and Paul 'Robbo' Robinson have been with us, it seems, since dinosaurs walked the earth. They can often be seen reminiscing about the thousands of miles we have travelled together. Over the years, most of our travelling band of merry men have encountered trouble of some kind or another. During 40 odd years of constant travelling, the odd skirmish is inevitable. The younger lads listen intently as one fossil recalls: 'I remember back in '76. We had our backs to the wall as hundreds of [possibly about 20] Man City fans charged towards us. Of course, we saw 'em off.' Or another old-timer tells them: 'Coming out of Goodison Park one night in 1970, we had a right battle on Stanley Park [a small altercation involving about six people]. I was knifed, and blood was pouring out of my arm.' The truth is, he probably caught his arm on a jagged fence close to the coaches. An old favourite is: 'Back in the '70s we [the Leeds fans] took the Shoreham End [Sheffield United] three years on the trot.' (Actually, this last one is true.) Due to illness, veteran supporter Eric Barnes's appearances are now sadly limited, but I'm sure he was there when the first FA Cup final was contested in 1872.

One of our other older members, Pete Conway, is confined to a wheelchair, and he figured prominently on a trip to Norwich in 1994. We had decided to make a weekend of the trip by staying in Great Yarmouth in readiness for the Sunday afternoon fixture. Now, 'The Kippax' is infamous for missing kick-offs, but even we surpassed ourselves on that particular trip. We had left Leeds on the Friday evening, and, after two nights at the seaside, we missed the kick-off at Carrow Road by twenty minutes. Returning home afterwards, Pete was sitting at the front of the coach, with the driver just in front of him. Without warning Pete sneezed very loudly and surprised the driver so much that the coach veered across all three lanes before he managed to bring it back under control. Tommy Hyde spent the remainder of the trip wiping the blood from Pete's forehead, which had been badly gashed when his head hit the chrome bar across the front of his seat.

Pete's sneezes were legendary and once, when we had returned from a trip to Ireland, we were all in The Nags Head in Leeds. Once again, without any warning, Pete was attacked by a huge sneeze. It was so forceful that it flipped Pete and his wheelchair upside down. The wheels were still turning as we all struggled to help get him back up, fighting back tears of laughter.

16

Ales and Tales

> In 1643 the Earl of Newcastle headed south with the intention of capturing the city of Leeds. Thankfully, his plan was thwarted by Sir Thomas Fairfax.
>
> It is truly horrifying to think that had it not been for the intervention of Sir Thomas and his gallant troops, us Leeds folk could all be walking around today talking in a silly northern accent.

Leeds is fast becoming one of the most vibrant cities in Europe. It now boasts literally hundreds and hundreds of bars and restaurants. Of course, Leeds has never been short of pubs and bars, and I much preferred the atmosphere back in the '70s and '80s. There was no better way to round off an away day watching Leeds United than to sink a few pints of classic hand-pulled Tetley's Bitter in traditional pubs such as The Scotsman, The Nags Head, The Templar, The Whip and countless more. In 1982, Tetley's Brewery introduced the famous Tetley Pub Hunt. Every time you bought a pint of Tetley's Bitter, you would get a card stamped. Collect 20 stamps, and you would be awarded with a commemorative T-shirt. During the close season, we would regularly do the 'hunt' in one day, with all the pubs within easy walking distance. And this was at a time when the pubs would close between 3 and 5.30 p.m.

The Queens Hall was the depot of the Leeds tramcar network

until 1954. In the '60s and '70s it became a venue for almost anything. A huge football tournament took place there in the early '70s, but it was a football tournament with a difference. It was a 'Head Tennis' competition, and, out of around 40 competitors, the unlikely winners were Peter Lorimer and Johnny Giles.

Another event held at the Queens Hall was the annual beer festival, which we would often indulge in. Live wrestling was another huge favourite at the venue. Or you could experience one of the best Northern Soul 'all nighters' in the country. Live music was also a favourite with Leeds fans returning from a game, be it home or away. The world's top bands would play the Queens Hall on a regular basis. AC/DC, Whitesnake, Rainbow, Ozzy Osborne, Thin Lizzy, Black Sabbath and many more entertained the hordes of fans who would pack into the hall every Saturday night.

To round off yet another victory at Old Trafford, this time in 1981, we clambered into the Queens Hall to watch one of the top bands at the time, the Boomtown Rats.

Their set got off to a frenzied start and soon the packed crowd, swelled by the celebrating Leeds fans, were swaying and bouncing up and down, doing the 'pogo'. At the front, many fans, dressed in punk gear, were spitting at the band. This was a normal activity at punk concerts. A year or so earlier the Sex Pistols were drenched in gallons of spit – and they loved it.

At the 'Rats' concert that night, the 'pogoing' continued: hundreds were now bouncing up and down to the music. The band appeared uncomfortable with the situation, and, after about 20 minutes, they stopped playing. The lights went up. All eyes were on Bob Geldof as he addressed the crowd: 'For fuck's sake, Leeds!' he bellowed. 'That spitting thing went out years ago. Come on now. Stop it.' The crowd remained silent. All eyes were on Geldof. The lights went back down, and a solitary spotlight shone on Geldof, as he went down on one knee and sang into the microphone, 'A silicon chip inside her head had switched to overlo . . .'

Just then, the biggest, greatest glob of phlegm ever witnessed flashed through the spotlight and, as if in slow motion, landed smack in the middle of Geldof's left cheek. Immediately, the crowd resumed bouncing up and down in defiance. Geldof wiped the phlegm from his face onto his jeans. He continued with the song, as the crowd continued to pogo and spit to their hearts' delight. The Rats continued with their set, albeit a seemingly shortened one.

The Leeds audiences always seemed to be in the driving seat. I remember a time when Public Image Limited, the follow-up band to the Sex Pistols, appeared at the Fforde Grene on the outskirts of Leeds. Front man Johnny Rotten commented that it was like playing in front of a bunch of statues. He was referring to the apparent lack of enthusiasm from the crowd. Suddenly, the band were taken aback as the audience, a huge percentage of whom were Leeds fans, responded with an impromptu, 'Come on Leeds, Come on Leeds, Come on Leeds . . .' An empty beer bottle whizzed past Rotten's head and smashed against the back wall, showering the drummer with broken glass.

On our return from a game at Ipswich one year, a few of us left the train station and were walking past the Queens Hall. Rod Stewart was in town. I'm not a fan of his, although most of my mates are. I used to like him, until I found out that he was a manchester united supporter. That didn't help his cause at all. He's also a fanatical Scotland fan. Nothing wrong with that – apart from the fact that good old Rod is a cockney. Anyway, we were walking past when one of the security guards called us over. He was one of the stewards at Elland Road. 'Are you coming in, Gary?' he asked.

'No, I'm not bothered, Ronnie,' I replied. Glenn Parkinson, who was with us, suggested we go in. As he'd parked his Lambretta at my house, I didn't have much choice. Ronnie took us around the back of the hall and opened one of the doors. As we entered, I looked across the car park and noticed a bloke with spiky hair leant up against a wall having a right good piss. It was Rod Stewart. I couldn't really blame him: one downside to the Queens Hall was the toilet facilities.

Sometime around 1970, Country met Jazz in Leeds. My dad, the celebrated Country and Western singer Eddie Stevens, was singing in a club near to the picturesque surroundings of the abattoir. The club was a relatively small place and, as Dad was singing, a black lady joined in with him. The audience loved it, and they rattled out a few songs between them. It was only afterwards that he discovered that his special guest was none other than the one and only Ella Fitzgerald. She was appearing in Leeds herself and had dropped in to watch Eddie Stevens. The mutual appreciation continued for many years.

ALES AND TALES

During the Don Revie regime, players were, by and large, restricted in their activities around Leeds city centre. They were allowed to drink freely with the Leeds public, with the proviso that they only had 'one or two'. Revie was strict about his rules, and his players weren't allowed to have long hair and, for a time, weren't even allowed to sport sideburns. The players became famous for their bingo games and indoor bowling.

Of course, the Leeds public weren't shy about entertaining themselves, and pubs like The Duncan and The Pack Horse would often be crowded with drunken senior citizens, each actually believing that they were Frank Sinatra. Another favourite haunt for budding singers was the infamous Robin Hood on Vicar Lane. Bands would play there every Saturday night, but they would be upstaged on a regular basis by the wobbling 'Roy Orbisons', who looked like they were made of jelly. The place was usually filled to capacity after home games, and, on one particular Saturday night, Terry Hibbitt and Mike O'Grady, who were Leeds players at that time, were in the house. The evening's band had long since left the stage, and it was now occupied by a very drunken old man, blasting out his own unique version of Elvis Presley's 'Wooden Heart'. When he'd finished, he spotted the two players in the audience, and he slurred into the microphone, 'Ladiesh and Shentelmen, tonight we are joined by . . . *hic* . . . two players from Leedsh United. Pleash give a round of applaushe for Sherry Hibbitt and Michael O'Toole.' Even the players laughed as the 'compère' fell backwards into the drum kit, before pulling down the glittery curtains – that still adorn club stages these days – with him. As he disappeared behind the drums, he was heard to gargle, 'Thanksh for coming. Goodnight and God Blesh.'

In April 1978, Leeds played West Ham at Elland Road. The night before, a band called the Four Skins were appearing at a great music bar called Brannigan's. Long since closed, Brannigan's was a large cellar bar situated near where Break for the Border now stands. It attracted many top underground bands – both local and national ones – and one of our favourite bands from Leeds called The Sneakers made regular appearances there.

The Four Skins were from London: they were West Ham fans and, of course, they were skinheads. Word spread quickly around Leeds, and, long before the 'Skins' took to the stage, the place was absolutely packed with Leeds fans, including many members of the Leeds Service Crew, a group of football hooligans. I was with a group of lads from Kippax, and Mally King pointed out a group of skinheads in the far corner of the bar. Everyone presumed, rightly, that they were Hammers fans. Inevitably, not long after the band took to the stage, the place erupted. A big gap appeared in the middle, and blows and punches were swapped at a furious pace. Mick Rhodes warned that the fighting was getting closer to us, and Dave 'Gladys' Gladman suggested we order some more beer before the bar got closed. Geoff Mosby removed his glasses and put them in his shirt pocket. This usually meant business, but without his glasses, Geoff won't mind me saying, he is as blind as a bat!

Unlike in the movies, the band stopped playing as the fighting continued. It was edging closer to us. Geoff was like a boxing kangaroo. The only trouble was that he was punching anything that came near him, and sometimes that happened to be a Leeds fan. We took it in turns to guide him by his hips, directing him away from his own 'side'. Eventually, the Keystone Cops arrived and order was restored, but that was the end of the evening's music.

During the late '70s we would often make our way to a great watering hole on Vicar Lane. The Gemini was another downstairs pub and full of character. It was home to one of the top scooter clubs in the area, Gemini SC. Although the pub has now disappeared, as with a lot of the old places in Leeds these days, I'm glad to say that the scooter club is still thriving. Other scooter clubs would meet there after Leeds games, amongst them our own Kippax SC and Central SC. Matty Sherlock, the former landlord of The Royal Oak in Kippax, still rides with Central today.

Back in the '70s, however, all scooter and football talk came to an end at The Gemini every Saturday night at 9 p.m. The star of the show was a man by the name of Horace Glitter. He was a strange character, to say the least, but the place would be absolutely crammed full when he took to the small stage. He would be dressed in a kilt, a silly hat and a pair of silver Wellington boots. His act mainly consisted of him singing songs extremely badly, eating candles and, for some inexplicable reason, he would end his act by eating a full loaf of dry bread. Some people would stare in disbelief, while others would be crying with laughter, but, whatever the reaction, Horace Glitter could be sure of a full house the following Saturday.

After a short trip down to Bramall Lane one Saturday, Wub and I went with Dad and Barbara, his partner and manager, to a Country and Western night. I had never been to one of these sorts of evenings before, and I'll never forget it. We arrived at Torre Social Club on the outskirts of town to find the place swarming with people dressed as cowboys; there was also a contingent of 'Indians' roaming around the place. The participants all take it very seriously and have personal gunfights in which, thankfully, the only thing that gets hurt is a balloon. There was a cowboy walking around the room with a badge pinned to his leather waistcoat. He took great exception to being called 'sheriff', instead claiming that he was a 'marshal'. His badge was home-made and handwritten with the word 'Marshill'. The funniest sight was all these cowboys queuing for taxis outside the club afterwards. Barely half a mile up the road, the city-centre streets were full of people fighting, yet here was a posse of 55 year olds, wearing cowboy hats and carrying enough guns and rifles to defeat the entire native American population of the 1800s.

The following week, Dad was performing at a special birthday event. It was my mate Gary Page's family's do, and the night was going well. Gary was a former teammate when I played football and was a very reliable defender, with not much getting by him.

Later in the proceedings, Dad was rendered helpless by fits of laughter as Gary took to the dance floor with his mother-in-law. It was a particularly fast number, and Gary decided it would be a good idea to hoist his partner high into the air and, in true John Travolta style, flip her over his shoulder. Of course, the pair of them fell quite heavily to the ground. With his mother-in-law sprawled unceremoniously in the middle of the dance floor, Gary winked at me and shouted, 'See that, Gaz? Just like the old days. Nowt gets past me, kid!' Of course, Gary was promptly red-carded from the dance floor.

Afterwards, Dad told me that it was one of the funniest things he'd ever seen. Even funnier than the sign he once saw in his dressing-room. He had been playing at a club in what was probably one of the less safe parts of town. The sign read: 'No turn left unstoned'.

17

Forever Leeds

> I am convinced that Leeds United have more oddballs watching them than any other team in the world.

Ex-paratrooper Dave Brown is a Falklands War veteran aged 44. His father was serving in Malta in 3 Para, when he took nine-year-old Dave to watch the 1970 FA Cup final against Chelsea in the 3 Para's Sergeants' Mess. All Dave's uncles, on his dad's side of the family, were from east Belfast and were supporters of Chelsea, Liverpool and manchester united. They all tried in vain to get young Dave to support their respective teams. His mum's side of the family were from Glasgow, and the Leeds team at that time was full of Scottish legends such as Billy Bremner, Peter Lorimer and Eddie Gray. That inspired young Dave to support Leeds. As a nine-year-old boy growing up in Malta amongst the Parachute Regiment, he decided that he was going to be a Para when he was old enough. Leeds United, though, had already captured his heart.

A year later, the family moved back to England, and he saw his first live game: a 3–0 Leeds victory over Southampton. Living in Wiltshire, he was eager to see his heroes play at Elland Road, and for his 11th birthday his dad drove him up to Leeds to see the Whites entertain Liverpool. His dad was a Liverpool fan, and the only time Dave got to watch Leeds was when they played Liverpool or when they played near to Wiltshire. A few years later, his dad was posted out in Malaysia, so it was to be some time before he saw Leeds again.

He vividly remembers one Christmas when his uncle in Belfast sent him a manchester united kit. After telling his mother, in no uncertain terms, that he didn't want it, she went out and bought him the famous all-white kit of Leeds United. Although the kit doesn't fit him any more, he still has the famous 'owl badge' from that very shirt.

His love for Leeds United was rekindled in 1977, when his parents moved to south London. His very first match unaccompanied was against Arsenal at Highbury: he was 16. He got his first job at 17 and was then able to travel to Leeds with the London Whites, who were run by the popular Marion Fudge, now sadly passed on and still very much missed. It was around this time that I first met Dave. He was fascinated by Collar and me 'splitting the Gelderd End in half' after we had both climbed onto the barrier. At half-time, Dave introduced himself to us, and we have remained firm friends ever since.

In 1978, Dave joined 2 Para in his beloved Parachute Regiment. One of his first encounters with the enemy was when he traded punches with a manchester united fan during a smoke break. Instead of being marched to jail, they were taken to the gym, given boxing gloves and let loose on each other. This was the way the Paras dealt with misplaced aggression amongst recruits. Afterwards 'Para' Dave thought that was the end of the matter, but, a couple of nights later, he heard the manchester fan come into his billet. Thinking he had come for revenge, Dave dived in first and administered another sound beating. In fact, the guy had only come in to borrow an iron from one of the other lads.

In 1979, Dave was sent to Northern Ireland, which meant that his opportunities to watch Leeds became very limited. But he did get to matches whenever he could, and it got slightly easier during a parachute course at Brize Norton, in the middle of the Oxfordshire countryside. In his billet one night, he decided to make his way up to Leeds for the following day's match against Tottenham Hotspur. It was very cold and was snowing heavily as he hitch-hiked to Oxford train station. As he walked head-on into a howling blizzard, a taxi pulled up and, after the driver heard he was in the Paras, he gave him a free ride. After a couple of freezing cold hours in the station, Dave boarded a train for Birmingham. There, he had to wait another three hours, before arriving in Leeds at 9 a.m. on Saturday morning, only to find that the game had been postponed.

After another short spell in Northern Ireland, Dave returned with 2 Para to Aldershot. He managed to get to the games almost every week. Sometimes guard duty would present an obstacle, but this was overcome by 'selling' it to another bloke. The going rate in the 1980s was £20 for a weekend: a lot of money on a private soldier's wage. The free train tickets given to servicemen were an added bonus. Then, during an Easter break in 1982, the Falklands conflict came to the surface. Argentina had invaded the Falkland Islands and 3 Para were sent on ahead of 2 Para, who were confined to barracks awaiting orders to move out. They were allowed to go home at weekends as long as they could return to barracks within four hours, but even then they had to take all their heavy kit with them, minus weapons, of course. Leeds were playing at Birmingham, and Dave jumped on a train hoping to leave his kit in the railway station lockers, but, because of potential IRA attacks, all the lockers were sealed off. He walked up to St Andrew's Stadium with his entire kit on his back. After explaining the situation to a steward, he was led through to the police control room. He once again explained the situation, produced his ID card and left the kit with them. Unaware that Dave was a Leeds fan, he was then escorted into the ground by the steward for free. The gates hadn't even opened yet, and he passed the time away in the bar beneath the main stand. Once the gates opened, he made his way round to the Leeds section.

Dave and his comrades left Portsmouth in late April 1982, on the North Sea ferry MV *Norland*. The *Norland* was based in Hull and a lot of the crew were Leeds fans. The lads on board were rationed to just two cans of beer a day, but the crew had their own secret stash and even their own bar, so Dave was well accommodated. He was able to keep tabs on the football through the ship's main radio. Listening to one game during the voyage, he heard that Leeds had gone one up at Shrewsbury, and there were only about twenty minutes left. When the final scores finally filtered through, Leeds had lost 5–1.

When the ship arrived at Ascension Island the troops encountered a little problem. How do you get 750 men onto a landing craft from a roll on, roll off ferry? They were going to have to jump off, one at a time, into a very flat sea, bathed in tropical sunshine. They all thought that someone was taking the piss. That couldn't be right. The mood changed slightly as news reached them that the *Belgrano* cruiser was in the area. To a man, they then realised that they were on a North Sea ferry and that the Argies had submarines and Exocets. Bunked up below the water, Dave said that it was 'like waiting in a tomb'. They were then told that landings would be made soon, and they snaked down the steps in darkness.

It was now 21 May, and it was Dave's 21st birthday. It was then that Dave thought to himself, 'I am celebrating my 21st birthday with a bunch of nutters going to war!' 2 Para were the first troops, behind the Special Forces, to land on the Falklands, and, seven days later, they were fighting for their lives.

At Goose Green they found themselves outgunned and outnumbered. A close friend of Dave's was killed. He had tried to keep him alive, but the friend had been too badly injured. It is only when you speak to Dave, and people like him, that you realise the trauma that these brave young men went through. Many suffered broken backs and legs, as they repeatedly dived onto landing crafts in blackness. They were paratroopers, and, having been trained for something quite different, all this was alien to them.

Daylight brought constant pounding from Argentinian Mirage jets. On 26 May they did a recce on a farmhouse on Goose Green. The BBC World Service then announced that the Paras had successfully attacked Goose Green. However, this was news to the Paras! With their cover blown, 600 men scrambled from the area and were met by incessant fire from hundreds of Argies, who were embedded in bunkers. Moving up to Darwin Ridge to support A Company, they took a hiding but were told to 'hold back'. Commanding Officer Colonel H. Jones and a four-man team tried to outflank some strategic Argentinian positions. 'H. Jones knew he wasn't coming back,' Dave told me. 'He wasn't prepared to ask the lads to do something he wouldn't do himself. In all, we lost seven officers at Goose Green.'

A couple of days later, English newspapers were flown out to the men. A couple of days out of date, Dave read that Leeds had been relegated at West Brom, and loads of pictures of his mates were in the paper, being chased across the pitch by mounted police. Considering what Dave had been through the last couple of days, this was unbelievable: not only was he in the middle of a war, but his team had been relegated. That said, he didn't have time to reflect on it, because there were more battles ahead. Obviously, staying alive was now the top priority. In particular, one memory from the Falklands War still lives with Dave. He recalls, 'We were sitting on top of a mountain in a blizzard on 12 June. We were watching all the other firefights taking place amongst the mountains, such as 3 Para on Mount Longdon. We were cooking food, making hot brews and cleaning weapons. A journalist from the *Daily Mail* had been with us throughout the whole campaign, ever since the landings, and he was asking us what our thoughts were about home, girlfriends, etc. I asked him if it was true that Leeds United had been relegated.' Dave's comment made the front page of the following day's *Daily Mail.*

Para Dave spent his final three years in the armed forces with tours of America and Belize, before returning to Ulster. When he left in 1985, he moved to Leeds and resumed watching his team every week, home and away. Whilst his parents lived and worked in the Far East, Dave lived on his own and slowly came to terms with how the Falklands conflict had affected him. Leeds fans now replaced his comrades from the Paras.

Just a year later, Dave travelled with a coachload of lads from Leeds to Anfield to support York City in an FA Cup tie in which, incidentally, my mate from Kippax, Mick Astbury, was the York goalkeeper. When the coach returned along the M62 to Leeds, two lads jumped off the coach near to Elland Road to go to The Peacock pub. Almost immediately, one of the lads was banging on the coach window screaming that the other lad Gav had been hit by a speeding car. Dave, a trained medic, jumped off the bus, but, as he got close to his mate, he knew there was nothing he could do.

This incident clearly affected Dave, and he began drinking heavily and found it difficult to sleep. All he looked forward to were the Leeds games, where he could escape from the memories of the Falklands and Gavin's tragic death.

Dave is now heavily involved in helping Falkland veterans and their families, through an organisation called the South Atlantic Medal Association, and freely admits that his fellow Leeds fans have helped him greatly to overcome his experiences. Amongst those was a group of Leeds fans from Stockholm. Paul Sodermark, a manager of a sports chain store in Stockholm, is a supporter of AIK Stockholm but became a Leeds fan in the early '70s. His first venture to a live Leeds game was in 1982 at Burnley. Paul travels regularly to watch his English team, with friends and fellow Leeds fans Stefan, Ricky and Bengt. It was during a home game against Brighton that Dave met Paul for the first time. Dave just couldn't believe that fans would travel all the way from Stockholm to watch Leeds in the Second Division against Brighton! They have remained firm friends to this day.

Paul and his mates were over in Leeds recently, and their trip coincided with the fifth anniversary of the tragic deaths of Kev Speight and Chris Loftus, who lost their lives in Istanbul. The Stockholm lads and Dave went to lay flowers at the memorial to Kev and Chris at Elland Road, before a home game with Wolves.

As is well documented elsewhere in this book, the Leeds support in Scandinavia is nothing short of incredible, but Leeds support comes from far and wide across the entire world. Flying the Leeds flag from Key West in Florida – my favourite holiday destination – is Perry Ferguson. Perry moved from Leeds to the most laid-back place in the world almost 20 years ago, but the millions of miles between him and his beloved team have done nothing to dampen his enthusiasm and he regularly travels back to watch his team. In fact, Leeds fans come from all over America. Andy Smith and 60 other members of the Leeds United Supporters Club – North America (LUSCNA) met in Chicago for the England game in May 2005. LUSC branches are all over Australia. Leeds fans spring up in Hong Kong, China, Gibraltar, Italy and Canada. Even in Brazil!

Ian Bloom has been a Leeds fan since the minute he was born in Hull in 1961. After a career of watching Leeds, he made a career out of teaching English in Brazil, moving out there in 1986. However, his support is still clearly evident and when his daughter was born he had her christened with a Leeds badge on her white dress pocket, whilst Ian wore his Leeds United shirt throughout the whole ceremony. Whenever he is teaching English to his students, he uses Leeds to illustrate his lessons, explaining to the students everything they need to know about Leeds, footballing or otherwise. These days his trips to watch his beloved Whites are limited, but he regularly travels to São Paulo, 40 miles away, to watch games in the three 'English' pubs there.

An old friend of 'The Kippax' is Ziggi from Belgium, who continues to support Leeds, along with dozens of others from Belgium. Another 'new' Kippax recruit is Ines Hoehbauer from Germany, where support is particularly strong. Tom Berekli from Norway has been a Kippax member since its formation in 1978, along with the two Geirs, Jensen and Magne Fjellseth.

Hilary Attard is well known to Malta's Leeds United supporters and is widely thought of as 'one of the most passionate Leeds fans in Malta'. Hilary is a good friend of mine, and I try to meet up with him whenever he travels over to watch his Elland Road heroes. On one of his many visits, the then Leeds chairman Peter Ridsdale introduced Hilary to the Lord Mayor and Lady Mayoress of Leeds.

Costas Karberis features prominently in the Hellenic Branch of the Leeds United Supporters Club. Based in Athens, the foundations for the group were based on the strong bond forged between the Greeks and Leeds fans during the 1973 European Cup-Winners' Cup final against AC Milan on the Greek island of Salonika.

Leeds United Football Club is blessed with some of the most loyal supporters anywhere in the world. The Doctor is one of the zaniest characters I've ever met. When we all meet up at half-time in The Revie Bar beneath the Kop, you instantly know when the Doctor has arrived. In the crammed surroundings, you suddenly become aware of a warm intrusion in your back pocket: the Doctor's friendly greeting is to place his manhood in your pocket. He then menacingly challenges anyone to a 'cock-fight'; however, I've yet to see anyone take up his challenge.

John Hartley of Whitby is a close companion of the Doctor and has run the Whitby Leeds Branch since long before the days of Captain Cook and even Dracula – both Whitby legends. John Hartley is often in The Revie Bar. Whenever I am in there, and I have a look around at all the familiar faces, it becomes abundantly clear to me that I am among an elite bunch of supporters. For example, my old Scottish mate 'Jock', complete with kilt and 12-in. dagger.

Another fan who tends to stand out slightly from the rest in The Revie Bar is Robin. He speaks in a very quiet and articulate way, yet most people give him a very wide berth indeed. Robin's head, face and neck are completely covered in Leeds United tattoos: he looks as though he has just arrived from the circus as the 'world's most tattooed man'. On his forehead, he has the Leeds United shield tattooed alongside the England football shield. What makes his permanent collection of Leeds United artefacts even more satisfying is the fact that Robin actually lives in manchester!

Across at the other side of the bar always stand two of the finest Leeds fans you will ever have the privilege to meet. The one and only Mick Hewitt (well one of two actually) from the Vine Branch and Keith Gaunt. Keith's one annoying attribute is that he can still wear his 'Leeds Tour of Marbella 1984' T-shirt. Mine won't even pull up over my wrist.

The Kippax lads always stand in the same corner, beneath a large framed dedication to Kevin Speight and Chris Loftus. The bar itself is always full at half-time, but on the occasions when all is not going well on the pitch, it looks more like a 'New Year's Eve' celebration, as many of the fans prefer to watch the rest of the game on the televisions situated all around instead of from their seats in the stands. The 45 minutes' 'extra drinking time' is probably just as well, as it usually takes that long for Paul Mathews and Jed to decide whose round it is. Whenever I am in, Big Ian from Tingley always comes over for a chat and Daz Stoker can often be seen busily squeezing in between the hordes of fans, selling his Leeds badges.

Another fantastic Leeds supporter is Kev Gaught. On 1 May 1965 a young Kev settled down to watch the FA Cup final on television between Leeds United and Liverpool. He was at the house of his uncle, a staunch Liverpool fan. To support 'the opposition' seemed the obvious thing for Kev to do. But afterwards, Kev stuck with Leeds, and on seeing his first live Leeds game (against Ipswich) in 1968 he was hooked for life. What made this unusual was that Kev lives in Bury St Edmunds – 180 miles from Elland Road. Over the years, Kev has become a permanent fixture at Leeds games all over the world and in 1990, with his brother Popeye, he formed the popular East Anglia Branch.

Of course, veteran Leeds fans go way back in time. Supporters Chairman Ray Fell saw his first Leeds game during the season following the end of the Second World War. His colleague, Eric Carlile, probably saw his first United game *before* the First World War.

Another of Leeds' notable followers is Kev Morgan and his best buddy, Clarkey Richardson. Clarkey, a massive fan of Tony Hackworth, fell out with the club in the '90s following a personal disagreement with Howard Wilkinson. He then fell out with Peter Ridsdale and vowed to withdraw his support for the club. Clarkey is a gem of a Leeds fan, but he is also a man of principle. He stopped supporting the team – the first team, that is. He travelled to every reserve game, home and away, throughout the rest of Ridsdale's term in office. Clarkey only returned when Ridsdale left.

I had a nice drink with Kev and Clarkey in Morecambe in May 2003. Kev had invited Wub and me to his daughter Catherine's wedding to Brian. It was a grand affair, and after the ceremony we returned to our hotel to get showered and dressed for the evening reception downstairs. It was packed with members from both sides of the two families, with a generous smattering of Leeds fans also present. The bride and bridesmaids looked gorgeous as they danced around the floor in beautiful silk dresses, tattoos and trainers.

The traditional wedding just wouldn't be the same without a good old punch-up, and this one was no exception. Members of both families exchanged punches, but, in this particular bout, it was the women who took centre stage. The lads from both sides just sat around, casually drinking and smoking until the women burnt themselves out. The root of this particular fracas, however, was most unusual. Catherine and Brian had been married at Lancaster Cathedral, or so they intended. Brian assumed that the priest would order the marriage licence, but when the priest asked Brian for it he didn't have a clue what the man of the cloth was talking about. With a packed cathedral looking on, panic set in, and the couple agreed to pay £100 so that they could proceed with a mock wedding to appease the guests – followed by a mock wedding reception. The following morning, a small party, complete with sore heads, attended the real wedding.

In 1989, Phil Cresswell suffered a serious illness that required nine operations. After the third of those, he was given just 24 hours to live. Phil is a staunch Leeds fanatic, and his determination to live meant that he not only pulled through, but within three years he was a Leeds United steward. Since his first United game in 1967, Phil from Bramley in Leeds has seen every transition that is possible at a single football club occur but has remained loyal throughout. His first game as a steward was on my birthday (28 March) in 1992, although I'm certain that that was just a coincidence. He was appointed Supervisor Steward in 2000, and these days he operates in the dangerous waters of the East Stand's lower tier, otherwise known as the Family Stand. His 'thumbs up' gesture is legendary amongst fans, and, although it started out as a security thing, it is now an obligatory part of his match-day activities, as fans return the gesture all through the game.

Phil has only missed a handful of games in almost 40 years, both as a fan and as a steward, and no one could put it better than Phil himself when he says, 'It's an honour and a privilege to serve the club I've supported for so long.'

18

Sun, Sea, Sand and More Sangria

I noticed that this particular village had quite a few families that looked as though they could be inter-bred, and said so to Wub – aka Lesley Edwards, B.Sc.

She replied, 'What do you mean? Are they all bakers?'

In August 1984, the 'Millionaires' Playground', Marbella, suffered a slight earth tremor. Leeds United had rolled into town. As most people will know, Marbella is slightly upmarket, with Sean Connery, as well as many other celebrities, amongst its residents. For this reason we decided to stay at the more affordable Fuengirola. Seizing the chance for a week in the sun, Wub went along for the ride, and, to celebrate his birthday, Big John Martin also made the trip. We spent the first few nights in the many bars around Fuengirola and then, on match day, once all the millionaires' yachts had been placed out of harm's way and all the luxury homes padlocked, Leeds fans marched into Marbella. Even the cockroaches had on bow ties and monocles.

Leeds were taking part in a four-team tournament, and, as you'd expect, the weather was gorgeous. Keith Gaunt was dressed in his famous Marbella T-shirt, and everyone in the ground was in high spirits. Even when the beer prices started going up every half-hour the Leeds fans remained in a calm and happy mood. At half-time, several Leeds fans spilled onto the pitch and, after commandeering one of the footballs, had a kick-around with some of the reserves who were out having a stretch. Big John had joined them, and the sight of this nigh-on 20-st. giant running around in huge khaki shorts is one that I shall remember forever.

I was sitting near to Brian from Halifax: he had his favourite yellow Leeds shirt on, with number 13 on the back. He was with the other two stooges, Tez and John. Brian was also sporting some rather nifty white trousers. Brian is of a similar build to Big John, and I watched in amazement as he stood on top of a dividing wall soaking up the intense sun rays and swigging a beer. Not that I was paying much attention to his nether regions, but I noticed a small brown patch appear at the top of his legs, and it appeared to be getting larger. It appeared that I wasn't the only one who had noticed. 'Brian!' someone shouted. 'You've shit yourself.'

'I haven't,' Brian replied, indignantly.

'Yes, you have,' someone else shouted back at him.

'I haven't.' Brian was adamant.

'You have, mate,' I said.

'Gary,' he said, 'I haven't shit myself: I'm shitting myself. I haven't finished yet.' He had a whole section of the stand to himself for the entire second half, and, after the game, he casually slipped into the sea to do his 'washing'. We watched and squirmed as unsuspecting swimmers swam by him, spitting out the seawater as they passed.

A few days later, we arrived back in Kippax at around 3 a.m. It was dark, but there were several police vans in the area, each one full of officers. Our taxi was waved through a cordon at the edge of the village. As we approached the top of the hill where we lived at that time, the word 'SCAB' was daubed over several walls. It was during the miners' strike, and we discovered next morning that two lads living in Kippax had 'broken the strike' and had gone back to work. This had angered the mostly mining population, and the police had been brought in to protect the two men around the clock. Welcome home.

Overall, I think that Wub is happy for me to continue my world travels, but, obviously, there have been one or two minor disagreements. Ironically, one of the biggest altercations we experienced was about a game that never actually took place.

It was June 2002, and Leeds had arranged to play a friendly in Seville, Spain. But before all that, Wub and I were setting off to spend our usual fortnight in Oban on the west coast of Scotland. We were greeted by beautiful sunshine on the Scottish coast, and along with Wub's sister Julie, her partner Paul and their young son Jacob, we all began to unpack and settle into a cottage nestled in the sloping hills and mountains. Minutes after our arrival, Wub's dad Harry and his wife Maureen walked in. The two of them spend half of the year up there, and they were on a campsite a little under half a mile away. Both of them have been coming to this part of the world for around 40 years, and we all look forward to our annual get-together. On that occasion, Harry announced that the barbecue would commence in one hour, before he and Maureen returned to their site.

They have their own little permanent corner of the campsite, which over the years has become known as 'Harry's Ranch'. Shortly afterwards, we arrived carrying enough food to feed a whole regiment. The fires were lit, and we all relaxed with a cold beer.

The Scottish national flag flies proudly over the site, but on my visits there I'm given permission to hoist the Leeds United tricolour flag in its place. This flutters on the pole for the whole fortnight we are there. It's a bit like when the Queen flies the Royal Standard at Buckingham Palace to announce that they are in residence, I suppose.

After our feast, we drank and talked into the wee small hours. The following day was spent roaming around the town of Oban, and we all went into a pub for Sunday lunch. Two hours later, Harry returned to his ranch, and we returned to our cottage arranging to meet up in a few hours' time.

Everything was so tranquil. Wub and I were in the lounge. She was in the big comfy chair, with a large cup of coffee and her nose in the biggest, thickest book I've ever seen. I opened a can of Stella and eagerly flicked to the first page of the latest edition of *Viz*. We both smiled as we heard Jacob's infectious laugh through the open window. He was playing in the garden with Paul and Julie. Suddenly the peace was shattered as 'Marching on Together' blasted from my mobile phone, perched on the table beside me. I picked it up, but, as the reception was pretty poor in the hills, it cut off. Seconds later I received a text message. It was from big Mick Hewitt. It read: 'Leeds in Seville 26/6. Flights from Luton. Shall I book you on?' I shuddered. This meant that Leeds were playing in Spain four days from then and not the following month as first thought. I was only into the second day of my two-week holiday. I gulped as I texted back to Mick, 'Yes.'

'Who was that, love?' Wub asked, as she turned the page of her book without looking up. She has a knack of always appearing so friendly just before a storm is about to erupt. I came right out with it.

'It was Mick Hewitt,' I said. She looked up at me. She seemed to anticipate what was coming. Her blinking eyes and the slight cock of her head asked the question for her.

'Leeds are in Seville. He wanted to know if I was travelling with them,' I said. Then, as quietly as I possibly could, I said, 'It's this Thursday.'

'WHAT?' she, quite understandably, shouted. 'What do you mean "this Thursday"?' She began to turn white. It was not a good sign. It doesn't happen often, thank goodness, but when she gets angry it is very unpleasant. She starts to cough, and her left eye drops slightly (a bit like Jim Morrison's used to when he was on stage). Her face was now pure white. Her eye had dropped, and she had started to cough. She was now shaking, and her book was on the floor. 'What are you going to do? What have you told Mick?' she asked.

In a feeble attempt to defuse her, I asked, 'Don't you fancy a week's holiday in sunny Spain?'

'In case you hadn't noticed,' she snarled, 'we are on fuckin' holiday!'

I certainly wasn't gaining any ground here. 'I'll leave you the car, and I'll get the train back to Leeds. You'll be all right here with Julie and Paul; it's no good spoiling your holiday.' I knew instantly that this was making it much, much worse. Needing a quick exit, I said, 'I'll go up the hill, see if I can get a reception and speak to Mick.'

'And just what exactly are you going to say?' I heard her ask, as I left the cottage.

Meanwhile, Julie and Paul had tried unsuccessfully to pretend that they hadn't heard us arguing. Jacob just stared at me as I scaled the steep hill in search of a good reception for my phone. 'Mick, it's me,' I said eventually. 'I got your message.'

'Yes,' Mick said, 'it should be a good trip. Eight days.'

'You know I'm up in Scotland, don't you?' I asked.

'Yes, why, what's up?' he replied.

'Well, we only arrived here yesterday. I'm going to have to come home tomorrow.'

'Why?' Mick was puzzled.

'Well, the 26th is this Thursday.'

'No, it's the 26th July when we go.' I reminded him about the text that he'd sent me.

'Oh no,' he said. 'I've just got back from the World Cup [in Japan and Korea]. I'm a bit jet-lagged. Sorry about that.'

I hung up and scrambled back down the hill to the cottage. I walked into the lounge and noticed that Wub had picked up her book, but I could see that she wasn't really reading it. Taking my life into my hands, I casually sat down and returned to my copy of *Viz*. I could feel her eyes burning right through me. 'Well?' she asked.

'Well what?' I replied. I was still feeling scared, but quite relieved at the same time.

'You know damn well what!' she said, raising her voice again.

I almost heard myself say, 'I was only kidding,' but instead I told her that Mick had got the wrong month. A couple of hours later, we were both ready to live happily ever after again – till the next time.

Unbelievably, after all that major confrontation, the game in Seville was cancelled. However, Wub and I were soon heading to the sun again together. Because of their close affinity with and affection for Leeds United, the people of Thessalonika were delighted when Iraklis FC were lined up to play Leeds at the opening of the newly revamped Kaftanzoglio Stadium, where Leeds had played back in 1973. This was September 2004, and the close bond between the Greeks and Leeds was soon rekindled. That close bond was witnessed by Leeds fan Jon Nuttall, who was working in Athens at the time and travelled by train for seven hours to Salonika. He and his mate met up with the Leeds team and manager Kevin Blackwell at the team's hotel. The 'neutral' Greeks were soon won over by the friendliness of the team and all left proudly wearing Leeds badges given to them by the manager.

Our group arrived late at night, and, within yards of our hotel, we witnessed a horrific car crash. The collision between a car and a moped left the rider, a young man, lying motionless in the road with blood pouring from his head, and, more worryingly, there was what appeared to be brain tissue spilled onto the ground beside his head.

Not the greatest sight to be greeted with. Those who had seen the incident were still visibly upset by it as we checked into the hotel.

It didn't take us too long to set up a bar as our 'local'. The Note Di Notte across from the hotel was perfect, and while Wub grabbed a couple of hours' sleep in the room, I joined the lads. An added bonus was the two beautiful young girls behind the bar called Vaso and Helen. Of course, within seconds, Ralph Benson was drooling like a huge St Bernard dog. Clarke Richardson and Kev Morgan from Lancaster arrived about an hour later. They had travelled up by train through Bulgaria and were both wearing genuine army tin hats from Sofia. Of course, the hats ended up on the heads of Vaso and Helen, as they acted out a kind of lesbian scene for the pleasure of the growing band of Leeds fans converging on the bar. Just in time, I spied Wub walking into the bar, and by the time she came to sit by my side I was deeply engrossed in a newspaper – a Greek newspaper.

Lee Farrer and the Mavericks were next to enter the fray and were soon followed by the Doctor and Whitby John. We were running up quite a hefty bar tab, but the girls held us all in check, and all the drinks were paid for and then some. Inevitably, the Doctor thought it would be a laugh to introduce his trouser snake to the two girls. Like a big school kid, he was ordered to stand outside the bar for 15 minutes. This he did and returned to the bar fully zipped up and sheepishly apologised to our hosts for his over-exuberance. Little Mick Hewitt was busily circulating amongst the locals, both inside and outside of the bar, with sheets of paper and a pen in his hand. Thousands of miles away, Big Lil's Saloon Bar in Leeds city centre was in danger of being closed down, and Mick was gathering signatures to protest against its demise. The ever-reliable Greeks were only too happy to assist in Mick's quest. Ever-present Leeds fans, Phil and Chris Beeton, walked past the bar with Eric Carlile, and they too lent their support to the cause. Much later, as we began to make our way back to the hotel, Pete Southam collapsed in the middle of the road and was about to be whisked away in an ambulance. While Mick engaged the police in a meaningless conversation, Pete was helped away from the scene, unnoticed by the law. Lawrence Daly then appeared on the scene, swaggering all over the road, before tripping head first across a waste bin. The police looked at each other and shrugged their shoulders, before driving off in silence.

The following day we all boarded the coach and headed for the stadium, flanked by an unnecessary police escort. We arrived at the ground, and, mistaking ours for the team bus, a group of Greek fans rushed for our autographs. I think the different proportions of our collective bodies were enough to convince them that none of us had kicked a football for quite some considerable time. Of course, we then headed for the nearest bar. The landlord was extremely happy to see us and provided us with several complimentary beers. Mozzer and Ralph rallied some of the locals for a great 'team photo', with the obligatory Leeds flag in the background, and everyone, including the landlord, left in high spirits. Once inside the ground, I have to say that the game was fairly low-key, but Jeff was certainly interested and leapt to his feet when 'we' scored. Leeds were playing in their newly acquired sky-blue shirts, and Iraklis were in white. Slightly confused and helped along by well over a gallon of Irish coffee, Jeff had inadvertently cheered their goal. Butler pulled one back for 'the blues', and we all returned to our drinks a little happier.

Another summer trip of note was one deep in the Rhine Valley in Germany. The year was 1996 and Leeds were up against SC Freiburg. We were all camped out in the hospitality tent as Bill Fotherby, the then managing director, tried in vain to stop us getting free bottles of wine. The bottles were supposedly only available to so-called sensible people who didn't know the first thing about football but ran the local hardware store or the local garage and had sponsored the game with a personal donation of about £10. Our 'Formation wine-snatching team' consisted of Jeff, Kev Morgan, Clarkey, Doctor, Whitby John and me. Half the team would distract the front-door keepers, including Fotherby, while the other half would sneak into the back of the tent, where the wine table was conveniently situated. To be honest, it became too easy, and we ended up with enough wine to floor Keith Floyd, Oz Clarke and Jilly Goolden put together.

An extremely biased German referee – who refereed the game as if he had donated £10 and had been given a free licence to do as he pleased – totally controlled the game, and, unsurprisingly, Leeds were beaten. The Leeds players were so incensed that after the final whistle they stormed off the pitch without waiting for the Freiburg team to receive their winners' trophy. As it turned out, the formalities took that long that the home side drifted off into the dressing-room without collecting the cup. Kev seized the opportunity and donned a Leeds tracksuit that had been discarded near the touchline and walked onto the pitch. As he approached the huddle of old gentlemen in the centre circle, he told them that he was the Leeds manager. With the 'committee' wishing to bring the farce to an end, Kev was subsequently awarded the trophy and posed for photos by the German press, whilst clutching an additional prize of a huge bouquet of flowers.

As we left the small ground to head into town, we noticed the Leeds players boarding their team bus. It was a bright red double-decker. We chatted with some of the players, and I got the unlikely striking trio of Tony Yeboah, Ian Rush and Brian Deane to sign my baseball cap. In the bar we discussed the prospects of the current team for the forthcoming season. It was during what I call Howard Wilkinson's 'Martian' period. Howard had done a great job initially with Leeds, but, at that time, some of his decisions left a lot to be desired. Like signing an 80 year old by the name of Ian Rush. 'Rushy' had been, without doubt, one of the game's greats, but now he was past it. Allegedly, Rush was on a £1,000-a-goal bonus for Leeds. He left the club with a £2,000 overall bonus!

In July 2005, our two dogs Jack and Jill peered through the windows of our Jeep, as we sped over the dry, dusty dirt-track to what would be their home for the next week. Wub and I were travelling to Norway for two Leeds games. Keith Kirby was one of the original Kippax members but now ran the Hartley Wood Dog Kennels with his wife Debbie at Micklefield. Jack and Jill were to be their latest guests.

The trip to Norway was a sort of celebration. A week earlier, I was a proud member of the audience at Harrogate Conference Centre to witness Wub receive her Bachelor of Science degree from Baroness Betty Boothroyd. It had been a pretty good year for my girl. In April, she achieved a distinction as a Technician in Cellar Management at Carlsberg/Tetley Brewery and followed that by successfully retaining her annual First Aid Certificate.

I got to thinking to myself as we drove to the airport that she could provide the perfect drink to get me absolutely shit-faced; when I fell over drunk and badly hurt myself, she could adequately tend to my injuries; and she would be clever enough to understand why I did it in the first place.

19

I'm a Leeds Celebrity, Get Me Out of Here

During the Don Revie era, the celebrities were on the pitch; these days, the celebrities are on the terraces.

The first Leeds-supporting celebrity I knew was Peter Moth. He was my religious education teacher at Garforth Comprehensive School in 1967. He left teaching to become part of the news team at the regional magazine programme *Calendar*. From then on, in my eyes Mr Moth became a celebrity – and he was a Leeds fan.

Leeds United's colours were already running freely through my veins and, unfortunately, my school reports (which, quite sadly, I still have) reflected this:

> If Gary showed as much commitment to his work as he does to his worship of Leeds United Football Club, it would be a major advantage.
>
> Mr Frazer – English.
>
> Although very good, Gary has spent the entire course making a metal ashtray and stand dedicated to a football team.
>
> Mr Thompson – Metalwork.
>
> Gary's work has been good and neat. He has a very pleasant nature but does sometimes tend to appear pre-occupied about where his football team will be playing at any given weekend. I have spoken with Gary about

> the situation, and he must really begin to address his future.
> Miss Yates – Form Teacher.

And this one from Mr Edwin Scott, head master:

> There seems to be no doubt that Gary has great potential, but it is also clear, however, that certain distractions do not appear to be helping. It is good that he has a healthy interest in sport, but it is important that it should be channelled in the correct manner.

Of course, over the years, Leeds United has become the chosen club for many top celebrities. Colin Montgomerie, one of the world's top golfers, is an avid supporter of the Whites. He started supporting them when he was six years old, back in 1969. Obviously, the Scottish connection with the club was a major factor, but he is in no doubt whatsoever that he would have been a fan anyway. His family lived in Ilkley, and his dad's business used to have season tickets at Elland Road. Worryingly, Colin now lives closer to Stamford Bridge than Elland Road, but he insists his loyalty is as strong as ever. A mate of mine, Dave Shack, recently met Montgomerie in an airport VIP lounge. 'Shack' was flying out to America on business when he encountered the European golf team who had just arrived back from their historic Ryder Cup victory at Oakland Hills. Europe had clinched the victory thanks to a putt from Montgomerie, and he was happy to pose for a picture with Shack, which, incidentally, was taken by Paul McGinley, Montgomerie's teammate from Ireland.

Shack is the author of *Elland Road E-males*, and his book launch in Leeds was a huge success. It was attended by many of the club's players, past and present, including Peter Lorimer, Eddie Gray and Dominic Matteo. Also there that evening was another massive celebrity Leeds fan: Radio One DJ Chris Moyles, who was on hand to lend his support, as he had figured prominently in the book. Just for good measure, Shack is married to ITV presenter Nicki Chapman, who is of course a Leeds fan. As a result of his many contacts in the music and television industries, Shack has managed to seek out many Leeds celebrities from all over the country. He was once attending a TV Hits Awards show that Nicki was presenting, and it just so happened that at his table was the actor Ralph Ineson. As the two began chatting, it emerged that Ralph was a huge Leeds fan, and they forged a friendship there and then. Since then, through Shack, I have been lucky enough to meet Ralph, and on one occasion he walked into a pub that we were at in Southampton. He happily chatted with fellow Leeds fans and posed for photographs. I also took advantage of the 'photo opportunity' and had my picture taken with him, along with Andy and Ben Starmore from Bournemouth.

Ralph has featured in countless television series, including *Emmerdale* and *Heartbeat* but is best known for his role as 'Finchy' in the BBC sitcom *The Office*. Ralph once told me that his co-star in *The Office* Ricky Gervais is slightly eccentric and could quite easily be a secret Leeds fan. Well that's official, then. Ralph was also the main character in the TV series *Playing the Field*, and throughout every episode he appeared in a Leeds United shirt.

After the game against Southampton, at which we had met Ralph, he and Shack met up with Bradders from Radio Aire at the Leeds' team hotel. With them were Paul Dews, from the *Yorkshire Evening Post*, and former Leeds favourite Tony Dorigo. They were discussing where to go for something to eat, when someone suggested a top Italian restaurant in the centre of Southampton. After Dorigo left Leeds, he spent some time with Southampton and so readily agreed. When they arrived at the restaurant, Dorigo was the last out of the taxi and was saddled with the fare, as the rest of the gang trooped in to be greeted by the excitable owner. However, seconds later, the manager went berserk as Dorigo walked into the restaurant. The proprietor continued to shout and gesticulate at Dorigo, and Shack's group jumped to their feet to ensure that there was no trouble. The owner's language was alternating between Italian and English and no one, except Dorigo, knew what the hell was going on. By now, Tony was cowering in a corner looking slightly embarrassed. Eventually, the manager started to calm down, and, although still obviously angry, he was now more jokey and relaxed. As the group listened intently, he explained his outburst. The manager was a proud fan of the Italian team Atalanta, and, a few seasons previously, his team had been battling against relegation. The situation at the foot of the table was tight. So tight, in fact, that it went down to the last minute of the season. Atalanta were awarded a penalty: a penalty that if scored would preserve their status and send their nearest rivals plummeting to the second division. Up stepped the Atalanta full-back, an experienced footballer who had joined the club only the season before. He placed the ball down on the spot, stepped back a few yards and ran up to take the kick. With the Atalanta fans holding their breath, the full-back sent the ball over the crossbar. That full-back was, of course, Tony Dorigo, and he had just, against all the odds, walked into the Italian restaurant owned by the biggest Atalanta fan in England.

Shack once told me his own story of footballing disappointment. It was at Elland Road in 1975, and Leeds had just beaten Barcelona in the first leg of the European Cup semi-final. Shack, aged about eight, checked with his dad, jumped over the wall and ran over to Joe Jordan, armed with his little autograph book. Jordan, sweating heavily, looked down at Shack with his outstretched book and pen. 'Please Joe . . .' young David begged.

Jordan's look still haunts Shack to this very day. Through the hole where two teeth used to be, Jordan hissed, 'No, fuck off, kid!' In floods of tears David trudged back to his dad in the West Stand.

'Did you get it?' his dad asked.

'No,' replied Shack, 'I couldn't catch him.'

The celebrity chef Brian Turner CBE has been a Leeds United fan since 1955. He vividly remembers sitting outside The Peacock pub with his dad, before going into the ground and being passed 'over the heads' to the front. In 1957, he went to Hillsborough to watch Leeds. It was during the days of John Charles, and, as Brian stood with his dad behind the goal, King John let fly with one of his famous pile-drivers. The ball soared narrowly over the bar and hit Brian straight in the face. The ball was made of leather, soaked in the afternoon's rain and threaded with old laces. Brian recalls, 'It didn't half hurt, but boy was I proud!'

As far as I am concerned, Brian Turner is one of the top two chefs in the country. The other one is *Ready Steady Cook*'s Paul Rankin. Irishman Paul is fiercely proud of his support for Leeds and has followed them since boyhood. The actor Ardal O'Hanlon, another Irishman, is also an elite Leeds fan. O'Hanlon, better known as Father Dougal from the sitcom *Father Ted* and the star of *My Hero*, lists Johnny Giles as his favourite player of all time. He met Giles once at an event in Dublin and described it as 'one of the greatest nights of my life'.

The music industry also contains many Leeds fans of all descriptions. 'Philthy' Phil from Motorhead is a Leeds fan. Jonny Cragg of Spacehog, another great drummer, is an ex-pat Leeds fan living in New York. In the mid-'80s Andy Dickinson discovered the magic at Elland Road. Andy is still a top fan and, in his spare time, is the singer with the Lo-Fidelity Allstars. In the booklet accompanying the album *Don't Be Afraid of Love*, the acknowledgements end with thanks to 'Rod Stewart and all on the LUFC European Tour'. Thankfully, it's the real Rod Stewart and not that spiky-haired, tartan-clad singer who still sings 'Maggie May'. No, this Rod is the Rod who Andy met on the official Leeds United club trip to Valencia in the Champions League.

It is rumoured that Madonna's drummer is a Leeds fan, but one thing is for sure: Tim Booth, the lead singer with James, most definitely is. Shutty and the rhythm section of Terrovision, Nicky from Westlife and Kelly from the Stereophonics are all bona fide fans of the club. Hugo Speer, who appeared in *The Full Monty*, has been a fan since his early childhood. Top cricketer Nasser Hussain has pledged his undying love for the club, and so too has Peter Stringfellow – I wonder if he can lend the club a few bob? Stefan Edberg, the legendary tennis player, has been a fanatical season-ticket holder for many years. The fine actresses Liz Dawn and Lisa Riley are fully fledged Whites along with Carol Vorderman. Richard Whitely, who unfortunately suffered his final countdown recently and will be sadly missed, confessed to being a Leeds fan.

The film industry lists Barry Skolnick, director of *Mean Machine* – starring Vinnie Jones – and Chris Cook, the director of new release *Penalty King*, as major Leeds United fans. Jeremy Dyson, the man behind the popular comedy series *The League of Gentlemen*, counts himself as one of the Leeds faithful. That jolly TV presenter Jeremy Paxman reluctantly admits to being a Leeds United fan, although he gets 'fed up with everybody having to have a favourite football team these days'.

The world-famous author Caryl Philips first visited Elland Road in 1963. He was just five years old, but West Indian-born Caryl said he had found his spiritual home. Philips, a critically acclaimed author and one-time nominee for the Booker Prize, emigrated from St Kitts-Nevis to Leeds with his family when he was just 12 weeks old. Big cricket fans, his parents were horrified when Caryl asked if he could go to watch Leeds United that first time with his babysitter. Although he obviously can't recall much about the game, he knows that Leeds beat Leicester 3–1, and, from that moment on, he was hooked. Despite working as a teacher at New York's Columbia University, he still returns to Elland Road at least half a dozen times a season.

James Brown, the Editor-in-Chief of *Leeds Leeds Leeds*, disclosed recently that the actor Russell Crowe – yes him – is a Leeds fan. James had been talking with an old photographer friend who travels the world photographing famous stars. The subject got around to Russell Crowe. 'Oh, you'd like him,' said the photographer, 'he's a Leeds fan.' Crowe said that he had always been a fan of 'Dirty Leeds', claiming, 'That was the team I liked in the '60s and '70s. Always hard and skilful.' You can't argue with that.

20

Brighton Revisited

To most Leeds fans, the league division you're in is irrelevant. It's just as well, really.

After the dizzy heights of the Bernabéu Stadium in Madrid and the splendour of the San Siro Stadium in Milan, Leeds fans eagerly flicked through the fixtures for the 2004–05 season. Their mouths watered at the prospect of visits to such places as Rotherham United's Millmoor, Gresty Road at Crewe and the amazing Withdean Stadium, home to Brighton and Hove Albion. What the hell happened?

You hear tales of Second World War veterans being found after living alone for 30 years on a remote island with no outside contact who have returned to witness fewer changes than those suffered by Leeds United during the three years since their dramatic fall from grace in 2002. Undeterred, Leeds fans took a deep breath and got on with life in the Coca-Cola Championship. I wouldn't have missed that trip to Brighton for all the tea in China.

Brighton's previous ground, the Goldstone Ground, was just about acceptable, but how the amazing Football Association can allow a football team in that division to play at a ground as appalling as the Withdean Stadium is totally mystifying. The away section is limited to around 600, and those unlucky enough to get a ticket witnessed a bewildering experience. For the entire game, we were perched precariously on a temporary structure that wobbled and swayed with every movement. If Leeds had scored, it was debatable whether or not the structure would have withstood the pressure. As it turned out, this was never put to the test, with the mighty Brighton running out easy 1–0 winners. Another temporary structure ran along one side of the pitch, whilst a small stand on the opposite side represented the only permanent structure in the ground. The opposite end to us was just a grass banking. Oh, and a tree. A bungalow sat atop the grass banking, and its occupants were treated to a free game every other Saturday. If this isn't the ultimate motive to take up shopping I don't know what is. Three people and a dog watched that particular game from the bungalow end, and then it began to rain. The game was so enthralling, it seemed that everyone in the ground noticed one of the occupants nip into the house for an umbrella. Then we all watched as the dog disappeared inside – and they say they're not intelligent. The game continued to be played in a dull fashion, and suddenly we all noticed that the 'crowd' in the garden had swelled to five. However, this must have been deemed unsafe, because minutes later they were joined by a ground security guard in a bright-green jacket. I kid you not!

Thankfully, the nightlife in Brighton was pretty good, and, after booking into a hotel for the night, a few of us spent the evening in a bar on the main pier. There was a karaoke taking place, and it wasn't long before our lot got involved. First up was Sally Moorhouse, who delivered a perfect version of 'Mustang Sally'. The audience was rocking as big Kev McGowan and Stuart 'Kosovo Joe' Steven pranced around the stage with air guitars. A few years ago, I performed my karaoke special in Doncaster. I got up on stage with a silver cardboard cut-out FA Cup and sang the Three Degrees classic 'When Will I See You Again?' Without my cardboard cup in Brighton, I refrained from entering the stage.

Our section of the audience then began to chant the name of our 'leader': 'Raaallpheyy Benson!' As is his wont, Ralph played hard to get for a few seconds and then a trail of bodies lay in his wake, as he charged to the stage, knocking all before him for six. He belted out his favourite 'Sweet Caroline' and then another Neil Diamond, and then another, and then Gene Pitney's '24 Hours from Tulsa'. The next day, as our coach left the hotel, we had to make a small detour to the pier to get Ralph down from the stage.

BRIGHTON REVISITED

To be honest, I prefer the long coach journeys. The atmosphere on the coach is second to none, as we return from games. Our official 'Entertainments Manager' Mick 'Danny Mills' Halliday warms up the coach audience and, one by one, introduces a string of performers that would, quite frankly, blow your socks off.

One such long-haul trip was the trek down to watch Leeds play Plymouth Argyle. A fantastic display by the phenomenal Leeds fans contributed to a Leeds victory, and, when we returned to our hotel after the game, the landlord told us in the bar that he was a season ticket holder at Home Park, and he had never seen away support like it – ever. After a few nightcaps we retired to bed and were soon loitering in the bar area again the next morning after a hearty breakfast. The landlord generously agreed to open the bar, and, although later than we were used to, 9 a.m. was quite acceptable. I chatted with Andy Starmore from Bournemouth. Andy is a big fan of the club and eagerly awaits Leeds visits to the south-west coast and attends the games whenever he can with his son Ben.

We really do have some amazing characters in the latest batch of travellers. Blonde Carol brings her sons along to every game despite continual threats by the authorities for taking the lads out of school early to get to mid-week away games. Phil Benson's two offspring, Pete and Amanda, also make the odd journey with us. Pete, aka Mr Bean, is the official coach joke teller. Sally Moorhouse's travelling mate Kathy Warren attends every away game, whilst her hubby Paul prefers to travel by train. Big Mal Stockdale is so tall that he sits on the back seat with his head sticking out of a specially constructed hole. Whenever Mal travels, Ralph has to check that there are no low bridges en route. The funniest thing about Mal is that he always wears a Leeds shirt with 'Giles' on the back. Johnny Giles was probably the smallest player ever to play for Leeds. Mally Johnson has started bringing his young lad along, as has Denny Mitchell: these young boys are apprentices for the future. 'Old Joe' always travels to away games with a lumberjack shirt on while Gary Barass, the landlord of The Royal Park in Leeds, invariably worries that the 16 bottles of Stella that he has brought with him will not be enough to get him to the match.

We still have a number of celebrity lookalikes who come to the games. Paul 'George Clooney' Trueman comes to matches in between acting roles, and Richard 'Screech' (from *Saved by the Bell*) Cooper constantly checks his mobile phone for messages when he travels with us. Of course, Stuart and Rob Hayward are constant fixtures at the front of the coach and have to continually keep our driver Jack in check. Jack steadfastly refuses to go any slower or faster than 20 mph. This prompts a constant outbreak of the song – to the tune of 'Grocer Jack', an excerpt from *A Teenage Opera* (1969) sung by Keith West – 'Grocer Jack, Grocer Jack, is it true what Ralphy says, you won't go fast, oh no, no,' repeated several times.

A few of our current members could be ex-members of the Leeds Service Crew. It's a bit of a strange 'organisation' and similar in many ways to the SAS: no one can publicly admit to being in it. I used to drink with one of the senior members, Pernod Harry. A splendid chap, was Harry. He would sit in the downstairs bar at the old Hogs Head after a home game, instructing his young troops as to their duties for the following week's game. Harry was heavily tattooed and always belied his unsavoury role by smoking a satisfying pipe.

These days, as I travel all over the world with Mick Hewitt Tours, I chat to numerous ex-members of the Leeds Service Crew. Before we go to away games abroad, and after we've picked up Mick and his son Alex, we travel around West and South Yorkshire picking up lads en route to the airport. As we do so, it is difficult to determine who is and who is not a former member of the 'regiment'. Could it be denim-clad Wayne Hewitt, or his mate Jimmy Keetley, as they struggle aboard with 150 cans of Guinness – each? Is quiet, unassuming Paul White hiding a violent past? Maybe Gary Challoner, with dyed-ginger hair, is trying to forget years gone by. Definitely looking the part are the 'Dynamic Duo' Ash and Al, Frank Bartle, Gaz Campbell, Paul Hayes and Mick Crow. Or is it just an act? Heavily disguised, Paul Johnson would be the next to board along with the heavily featured Brian Kinghorn. Simon Featherstone, well built and grinning broadly, always puts his bag above his head and cracks open a beer. Simon has obviously kept himself fit – why? The last call in that area is usually The Old Crown in South Kirkby. Known locally as 'The Top House' it is run by Leeds fan Ray Wellings. The walls are covered with past and present Leeds United memorabilia. Could they be hiding something? We would then pick up Matty Hindle and his mate Scott Baxter and head for Doncaster.

This always leaves just two more to pick up at the train station, before we head further south to pick up Terry and the rest of the Chiltern Whites. Little Frank Smith and Tim Lee get on at Donny station. Tim is known to always sleep in his socks: could this have at one time been in preparation for one of the regular dawn raids that took place many years ago by the police tracing Service Crew members? Three of the aforementioned are ex-Leeds Service Crew members. These days, of course, most ex-members have married, settled down and have their own chavs . . . er . . . kids.

Despite some of the violent pasts of our members, we don't get much friction between the lads, with the exception of a couple of minor scuffles. Big Kev and Butch once had a slight altercation on a trip back from a game against Queens Park Rangers and even Ralph got involved once, as we were on the coach waiting to travel home after a match with Crewe Alexandra. Chris Donahue arrived on the coach, and Ralph took issue with him for stopping off for a tray of sausage, chips and curry sauce. The fact that we couldn't move anywhere until the police gave permission had escaped Ralph, and Chris flew off the handle. In the mêlée that followed, Chris's sausage and chips ended up on the floor. It seemed such a waste, so, as the two lads tussled, I picked up the sausage and ate it, and I passed the chips back for Chris's son Steve to consume.

All differences are always put aside by the time we arrive back at The Viaduct. This is our sanctuary and the lads from other coaches who also go from the pub usually arrive back at the same time. The Hunslet Branch are usually first back to The Viaduct with Collar, Sean Etherington, Paul 'Eddie' Edwards and Paul (Snake). Moose is usually already at the bar with John Moran. The 'Cas Vegas' lot are always arguing the toss when we arrive with them. They argue constantly over whose round it is. Tico swears he got them in at the Wetherspoons we stopped at before the game at dinner time. Dr Doom will argue that he got them, and the charade continues with both Suede and Tony Green insisting that they bought the drinks last. No one is any the wiser as they all leave together to get the last train back to Castleford.

These days, although there is a steady rise in hooliganism, our seasoned troopers tend to just enjoy a drink and a day out. That was our sole intention when we stopped off at Spennymoor following a pleasing Boxing Day victory against Sunderland. We'd arranged to go to my mate John Baxter's pub in Durham, but the driver thought it was a bit out of our way. Instead, we pulled up at a rather nice, out-of-the-way pub. It was the ideal setting for our lads to take in a game of cards, throw a few darts and generally chew the fat after the game. In fact, Spender and I were so engrossed in football talk that we hadn't noticed that our lot had gone, and that the pub was filling up with Sunderland fans. Ralph had given the final call to get back on the bus, but the two of us hadn't heard him. Apparently, on their way out, our lads had encountered the Sunderland fans just entering the pub. After a little stand-off, our coach drove away, leaving the Sunderland fans shaking their fists and shouting at our lot about what they must have assumed was a moral victory. Spender and I were totally unaware of all this activity, as we were continuing to chat away at the other end of the pub. Suddenly, with the Sunderland fans still gesticulating at it, the coach stopped. Ralph had realised that the two of us weren't on the bus and had turned around to come and get us. That unnerved the Sunderland fans who retreated back into the pub. At that moment, Spender and I passed through them on our way out. It was then that the two of us realised something was going on. Another stand-off ensued. Again, nothing happened, and our branch, this time with Spender and me, went to board the bus. Not wanting to let the incident end there, the Sunderland fans regrouped and came back out to follow us to the coach. Yet another stand-off took place. I looked around at some of our young apprentices, many still holding snooker cues behind their backs. Ralph told everyone to get back on the bus, but that was quickly overruled, as we all held our ground. Then common sense prevailed. One of their group, a stocky lad with small glasses, stepped forward: he appeared to be in charge of the posse. 'Look lads, this is stupid,' he said. 'Give us our cues back, and we'll call it quits.' Then, like a scene from a Western, the cues were handed back, ever so slowly, as all eyes remained fixed on the other side. I swear that if someone had so much as sneezed, all hell would have broken loose. Then we all boarded the bus – backwards – and we were on our way.

Being out on the road following Leeds is one of the great joys of life, and I much prefer away games to home games. But, as yet another way of acquiring funds, Leeds United recently introduced a

20-year home-game season ticket. Of course, the club wanted to be paid in advance for this 'privilege'. I only know of maybe one or two people who took up the offer: Richard Roberts of Garforth and . . . er . . . no, only one actually. Whilst his commitment has to be admired, I've yet to see Richard wearing the obligatory pair of donkey's ears that must come with every purchase.

I could actually have done with those ears one evening, after an away game back in the late '70s. Wub and I had been invited to a 'pyjama party' at Gord Findlay's house in Kippax. Wub was still living in the East End Park district of Leeds, and I had volunteered to have a day of sobriety and pick her up in my old dark-blue Ford Transit van.

I had only known Wub for a few months and instantly knew we were made for each other, after we'd been on our very first date. Not far from her house was The Victoria pub on York Road. The Sneakers, my favourite band, were playing there, and so that's where I took her. That night, she wore a bright-red trouser suit, and I must have said something to her, because on our very next date she wore the same trouser suit, only this time it had been dyed black. It wasn't the most brilliant job of dyeing that I'd ever seen, but the thought was there, and that's what counts.

On the night of the pyjama party, Wub dressed in an old pair of men's pyjamas and drew on a moustache. I was wore a big old-fashioned woman's nightdress, a headscarf, a couple of rollers in my hair, a pair of Doc Martens and two large balloons stuffed up my gown. My Transit van was old and rusty and had sliding doors that were in such bad condition that, if I drove above 20 mph, the doors flew out at 45 degrees, and it looked like a small aeroplane. As I drove around the first corner, the van instantly broke down. I couldn't believe it. I started swearing and cursing for all I was worth. It was dark, and I noticed a car pull up behind me. There was enough room for it to overtake, but it just sat there. I slid the door open and, with an outstretched arm, signalled for it to overtake. It just sat there. I signalled again. Nothing. I'd had enough and, fuming, I jumped out of the van and charged towards the car. I stood over the bonnet, in front of the full-beamed headlights, and screamed and shouted at the car's occupants. Two frail old pensioners sat in the car absolutely petrified at the raving lunatic with a headscarf, hair rollers and a beard in front of them. Just then my balloons went askew, as I jumped up and down like Basil Fawlty. The car slowly backed up and tootled off down a side street.

Although I wasn't very amused that evening, I think I inherited my sense of humour from my ma. I can still remember one Christmas morning at Blackpool, when I was about 12 or 13 years old. We were on the sea front with our Julie, Dad, Auntie Ann (who unfortunately never got to read this book as she sadly passed away in July 2005), Uncle Frank and Grandma. Ma handed our dog Kim to Dad and started bouncing up and down on our Julie's pogo stick that 'Santa' had brought. It was a crisp and sunny morning and a bit windy. All of a sudden, Ma's wig flew off. I was gobsmacked. I had absolutely no idea that Ma wore a wig.

The next day, Dad and I went down in the car to Hillsborough, for the Boxing Day game with Sheffield Wednesday. It was quite a trek in those days, and, as we drove along the winding roads in our pale-blue Ford Cortina Estate, I mentioned to Dad that I hadn't known that Ma wore a wig. 'Son,' he said, 'there's a lot you don't know about your mother. She's got a wicked sense of humour. One day, whilst we were courting, we both slipped on some ice in the park. I suggested that we throw some dirt on it so that nobody else would slip. Your mother was having none of this and, within seconds, we were both crouched down behind a nearby hedge watching others do exactly the same thing that we'd just done.'

After a Johnny Giles penalty had given Leeds a 1–0 victory, we began the journey back to Blackpool. I was still thinking about Ma. When we were kids, she would disappear upstairs. As me and our Julie would sit watching television, she would walk in quietly behind us. When we turned around, we would both nearly jump out of our skins. Ma would be standing there wearing white face cream and looking for the entire world like a ghost. I would always be petrified.

When I was young, I apparently used to suffer from the odd gumboil inside my mouth. The remedy in those days was to put a poultice on the sore. A poultice was like a spongy clump of light-grey gooey stuff, and it was very, very hot. It used to hurt like hell. I never said anything to Dad, but I often wonder if I ever really did have a gumboil at all. A sense of humour is essential when following the fortunes of Leeds United, and I have Ma to thank for mine. She also makes the best apple pie in the world.

One evening in The Viaduct, I was at the bar chatting with Steve 'Student' Butler and our old mate Brad. Also in the pub that night were Slugger and Charlie from Bramley.

Joining the party half an hour later were little Quentin and Jack Slinger from Shipley. That little gang go back years to the old Kippax days, and we began reminiscing about some of the good old times. As we were talking, Mick Wilson walked in. Mick was an old mate of mine and had played in the same football game as me several years prior. It was between us – The Royal Oak, Kippax – and the Leeds United juniors. It was a prestigious match for us and was used as a warm-up game by the Leeds juniors for an upcoming European tour. The game at Fullerton Park was evenly matched, and Kenny Smith, our manager, had told us not to hold back in the tackle because 'they won't'. Late in the game, and, with this still in mind, I found myself in a one-on-one situation with Leeds' forward Rob Peel. A clever ball had been flipped over our defence, forcing me to come out of my penalty area. As we both raced closer to the ball, it was obvious that neither of us would back down. I clattered into Peel and managed to boot the ball into touch. Peel was on the ground for ages, surrounded by anxious Leeds United staff who kept glaring at me. I shrugged my shoulders. 'It was an accident,' I said. 'I'm a Leeds fan.' They continued to give me icy stares as Rob was carried off on a stretcher. I'm sure it was nothing to do with that tackle, but I never saw, or heard about, Rob Peel again.

In December 2002, the branch lost a good member. Chris Dawson was a great lad, and when he died suddenly, it was a shock to everyone. Obviously, 'Chuckles' received a good send-off from his mates at The Viaduct. I remember one rather drunken evening when Chuckles and I were propping the bar up. It was getting late and we were discussing every topic under the sun – literally. With the world forever getting smaller and smaller, the moon, we decided, was going to be the next favourite holiday destination. 'But we'll have to be quick,' I said to Chuckles. 'That Sea of Tranquillity will be the place to be seen, so we need to get a hotel built on the sea front as soon as possible, before the big rush.' I sometimes wonder if Chuckles has already accomplished our mission.

Jeff and Lunge always try and catch the 7.58 p.m. train back to Garforth, after a few after-match drinks in The Viaduct. One particular Saturday they'd 'overdone it with the sherry' and both fell asleep on the train. They missed their stop at Garforth and woke up at York station. They had to wait for another train to go back to Garforth. Hours later they boarded one such train. Determined not to fall asleep again, they sat with their eyes wide open all the way back. It was dark, and, as they approached their station, they got up. When the train stopped, they jumped off. As the train disappeared out of sight, they looked at each other. They had got off too early and were six miles from home. This particularly upset Lunge as he was desperate to get back to a club to meet his mysterious lady friend known only as 'Silver Pants'.

I had once been in the same club, around 20 years previously. A new comedian by the name of Roy Chubby Brown was fast emerging on the club scene. A bunch of lads from Kippax – among them Fish, Gibber and me – spent £1 to be in the sell-out audience. Before the peformance, I was in the toilet having a pee, while talking to Mick Rawson. 'I've heard that this comedian is shit hot,' I said to Mick. Just then, a bloke wearing a flat cap came to the empty urinal that separated Mick and me. Unzipping his fly and pissing hard against the porcelain, the bloke said in a broad Teesside accent, 'Well, I've heard that he's fucking shite!' We had just met Chubby Brown, the man who was to become one of the biggest names in British comedy over the next few years.

Les Hince, the landlord at The Viaduct, often travels to away games with us. Upstairs in the pub he has 12 or so rooms, which are always full. The rooms are fully equipped with TVs, but there are no Bibles. The thin texture of the pages of the Bible fascinates me, and there's no better way to round off an evening than to carefully tear out a page, wrap it around a comb, place it to the lips and rattle out a few tunes.

Leeds played Gillingham in the FA Cup a few years back. The kick-off was at 12 noon, and so, as we would be setting off in the very early hours, Lunge, Ralph, Richard Watson and I opted to take one of the rooms. It has to be said that we consumed a fair bit of alcohol. Lunge and I didn't go to bed at all and continued drinking right through the night, so we were a little delicate at the breakfast table. At 4 a.m. the rest of the lads who hadn't stayed the night began arriving for a quick pint, before the long journey south. Lunge and I forced a lager down, and we were back on track. This, coupled with a couple more cans on the coach, left us nicely ticking over by the time we arrived at the ground at around 11.45 a.m. I made the mistake of asking a policeman where the Leeds end was. Immediately, he asked me if I had been drinking. 'What? At this time. You must be joking,' I replied. It was clear to all concerned that I, of course, had been. Lunge and his brother Simon were standing close by as I said, 'Well you can't arrest me anyway, mate.'

He looked a bit bewildered by this and said, 'Why on earth not?' I fumbled with my wallet and produced a yellow card that I foolishly waved in front of his face.

'Because I have this,' I sneered. 'A get out of jail free card!' With that stupid remark, the copper grabbed my arm. 'Oh no you don't,' I thought and scurried off as fast as my drunken legs would carry me. Simon roared with laughter and he told me after that the sight of me, an overweight 47 year old, running away from the police was one of the funniest sights he'd ever seen. I managed to remain a free man and, once in the ground, quickly began to sober up.

I certainly needed to. Later that evening, Wub and I were going to see the comedian and West Bromwich Albion fan Frank Skinner in Leeds. When the time came, Skinner made a very cheeky entrance. He walked out onto the stage to huge applause, and then he stood waiting for it to die down. When it had, he simply looked out at the audience and said, 'It wasn't offside, you know. Either of them.' Almost everyone in the audience knew what he was talking about and burst out laughing. I had to explain to Wub that he was referring to a game between Leeds and West Brom at Elland Road in 1971. It is still talked about today. Referee Ray Tinkler ignored his linesman, who had flagged for two offsides, and allowed a goal by West Brom to stand. It caused a riot at Elland Road, and the ground was subsequently closed down for the first four games of the following season.

Many overseas Leeds fans regularly converge on The Viaduct prior to home games. Of course, the place is always full of Irish and big Ian Mackay and Alan Smith (the proper one and not that defector) from Belfast practically live at the pub. The Scandinavians are always out in force: Erik Sveen returns on many occasions, despite receiving horrific facial injuries when a lorry hit him in

Tottenham a couple of years ago. Recently, I was also re-acquainted with Oscar, an old friend from Sweden, who had made his way to Leeds for a game.

Another afternoon, I was having a pint with Jeff in The Viaduct. Regulars Dave, Phil and Tim were at the bar waiting to be served. 'What you doin' in here Snake?' asked Dave.

'Off to Cambridge, Davy boy,' I replied. Leeds were playing Cambridge in a testimonial, and, of course, we anoraks were going. Les was behind the bar, listening to our conversation.

'I fancy that,' he said. 'It'll be an afternoon out.'

'Well, we're not off for t'football,' Jeff quipped. Just then Les's wife Tammy arrived from upstairs.

'Can I go to the game with these lot, love?' Les asked. 'Leeds are down at Cambridge tonight. We're a bit quiet here, eh?' Tammy was holding the latest addition to the family (they have about 26 children).

'Yes, of course. If you take him with you,' she said, handing Les their baby boy, who was probably only about 7 or 8 inches high.

'Alright, go get his coat, the bus is going in an hour.' An hour later, three men and a baby were sitting on the back seat of the coach heading down the A1.

Supporters from all over the country frequent The Viaduct on match day. Durham, Leicester and Wellingborough are always well represented. Chris Tams, Dave Shack and Neil Jeffries make regular pilgrimages from London. Chris is a prominent member of the noted WACCOE brigade. Standing for 'We Are the Champions' Champions of Europe', this independent organisation was formed by Ian Fieldhouse, a Leeds fan from Scotland. Since the formation of its own website in 2003, membership has risen to over 1,600.

After a game at Ipswich one year, Chris was standing on the platform at the train station with hundreds of other Leeds fans. Chris told me, 'All of a sudden the Orient Express pulled into the station, with its dining car stopping outside the main group of fans. Of course, always keen not to look a gift horse in the mouth, all of us started asking the people on the train for alcohol. After a couple of minutes, we started seeing bottles getting passed out of the train – this obviously made everyone else's pleas louder. One of my friends Lyn was talking to one of the buffet-car stewards, so we were obviously expecting great things when he passed over a very large bulky napkin. The train pulled away, and we stood around Lyn, with smiles like Cheshire cats, awaiting the great unwrapping of the package. Was it a lovely bottle of Château Lafite or Louis Jadeaux, perhaps? Imagine our surprise when we found two packets of water biscuits and a large piece of very ripe and smelly brie!'

Two of the best-loved members of the Leeds United family, Elsie Revie and John Charles, both passed away recently. They were both regulars at Viaduct meetings and many Holbeck Branch events. Elsie was so approachable and friendly that she struck up friendships with many supporters over the years. I count myself as one of those privileged people. Les and Tammy Hince had lunch with Elsie on a regular basis and, along with Ralph and Joe, represented our branch at her funeral in Edinburgh. It was deeply saddening for all concerned, but the memories of those two unique characters will live on forever.

After Don Revie died in 1989, Elsie had become the president of the Leeds United Supporters Club and attended functions three, sometimes four, times a season. At one particular banquet evening, 500 black-suited supporters listened intently as she spoke with great wisdom about the current plight facing Leeds United. She turned to the table where the current squad of Leeds players was sitting and said, 'This football club is, and always will be, one of the great names in football. I'm sure you don't need me to tell you just how much this club means to these fine supporters here tonight. Goodness me, the boys [Revie's team] used to enjoy a drink or two. They were always out in the city centre. But they respected Don and the club.' The players looked nervous, as she continued, 'I realise that these days there is much more money around, and the temptation is so much greater, but please, boys, for the sake of Leeds United and its fans, let's make this a club we can all be proud of.' The audience rose to their feet and cheered and applauded Elsie loudly. The players had just been spoken to by their 'mother', and, what's more, if they didn't eat all their vegetables, there would be no pudding.

Elsie attended another memorable evening, sitting alongside Vicky, the widow of Billy Bremner. It was an evening to celebrate the 100 greatest Leeds players of all time. Leeds' fans, suited and booted in dinner jackets and bow ties, arrived from all over the globe, including America and Hong Kong. An emotional evening was perfectly rounded off when Billy Bremner was voted 'The Greatest Leeds Player of all Time'. There was hardly a dry eye anywhere, as images of Billy were shown on large screens around the room. As the haunting music came to a close, a tearful Vicky appeared on stage and accepted the award. Visibly moved, she said, 'I don't know what to say. I'm so emotional. But I'm sure Billy would have been proud to pick up his award tonight.'

Also there that evening was the towering figure of John Charles. An hour before the event got under way, I had been sharing a whisky with the great man, as we stood at the bar in The Viaduct. As testimony to his legendary standing at the club, Charles was voted the fourth greatest player of all time. And, probably fuelled with the whisky from the pub, he entertained the audience with an impromptu version of 'Sixteen Tons'.

The funeral of John Charles in Leeds was a major event, attended by mourners from all over the world. After the service at Leeds Parish Church, the hearse was driven to Elland Road where it took John around the pitch for the final time. Thousands had gathered, including all of the present Leeds United squad and many other members of the footballing world. Eddie Gray addressed the silent congregation. I stood alongside Richard Watson, Barry Hope and his son Nicky. None of us had seen Charles play, but we were drawn to the aura of the man who was a football legend in every sense of the word. As the hearse drove out of the stadium, I noticed a frail-looking figure standing alone to the side of the main gathering. It was Leslie Silver, the one-time chairman of Leeds United.

Following the successful response to the greatest players night, the 100 greatest Leeds goals of all time soon followed. As before, the voting was conducted by the official club magazine, *Leeds Leeds Leeds*, and, once again, suitably attired fans converged on the Conference and Exhibition Centre behind the East Stand for the award ceremony.

Wub and I were at a table with Big Mick Hewitt and some of his troops, one of whom was Tony Short. Tony is quite a unique character because, although his sight is severely impaired, he attends every game. His sense of humour is legendary, and he can often be seen watching the game through a small telescope. At that evening's event, he was having a small argument with one of the waitresses. Whyte and Mackay had sponsored the event, so, consequently, several bottles of whisky were placed on each table of 12. The Leeds United officials and staff didn't seem to appreciate the generous gesture. They had a point: people were satisfying themselves with the complimentary spirits, and, as a result, business at the bar was relatively slow. That said, it's not a good idea to try and remove a bottle of whisky from a blind skinhead: not one who has already drunk a full bottle and especially not one who used to be in the Leeds Service Crew. Sensibly, the staff backed down and the whisky drinking continued. However, we did begin to get the odd lager from the bar – it seemed only right.

The winner of the 'greatest goal' wasn't a huge surprise, but what was a surprise was the fact that Tony Yeboah was there in person to receive his award. The best-kept secret of the decade was unveiled as Tony walked out from an adjoining room. His legendary strike against Liverpool at Elland Road had earned him a place in the Leeds United history books. The ultimate football memorabilia dealer Dick Fenwick, a personal friend of John Charles, was also at our table and is not one to miss an opportunity. He reached beneath the table and brought up an old plastic carrier bag. From it, he produced an old pair of football boots. 'I had an idea he might be here,' he winked. Afterwards, as Yeboah posed for pictures and gave autographs, Dick pounced with his boots to be signed. Not to be outdone, I got a snap of the 'Goal King' and me.

By way of a celebration of the 100 greatest goals, I forwarded my own contribution to Neil Jeffries, the editor of the official Leeds United magazine *Leeds Leeds Leeds*. Every single one had been scored by Leeds against manchester united. About a week later, I was taking a trip around Edinburgh Castle with Wub when my mobile phone rang. It was Neil from the magazine. 'You twat!' he said.

'Hello mate, just hold on a minute,' I replied, walking outside to finish the conversation. 'What's the matter?' I asked.

'I've received your "100 goals", and I've had to spend over an hour to check that they were all correct,' Neil said.

'Oh,' I said, 'they are all genuine goals, mate. I thought I may have to use a few penalties and own goals, but there was plenty to choose from.'

'Yeah, I know. Well done. They'll be in the next edition.'

Our return coach trips back from the airport are themselves legendary. Everyone enters into the spirit of things, as we all embark on what can only be described as a 'vodka frenzy'. Once, after I had consumed quite a large amount of firewater, I was perched behind the coach driver, singing and dancing to 'My Sharona' by The Knack. When the track had finished, I asked the driver to rewind it and play it again. As I wobbled about slightly, he said, 'It's the radio, old mate, I can't rewind it.' Just then, unbelievably, 'My Sharona' began again. Momentarily, everyone stopped drinking. Quite bizarrely, someone, somewhere else in the country, had telephoned the radio station immediately and asked them to play the song again.

Despite all of our European adventures in recent years, we had to wait until the summer of 2004 to witness Leeds winning our last piece of silverware to date. Leeds overcame a 'strong' Hibernian side at Easter Road to capture the 'much sought after' Whyte and Mackay Trophy. Not that the hordes of travelling Leeds fans saw the presentation. Due to quite a lot of unrest between rival fans and because of security reasons, the police wouldn't allow an official presentation of the trophy that had eluded Leeds for over 90 minutes. Only a handful of people, mainly journalists from the world's press – well, the *Daily Record* – witnessed the momentous occasion.

To compensate for missing out on the historic spectacle, manager Kevin Blackwell agreed to come to The Viaduct the following night and show the trophy to the lads. We were the first Leeds fans to actually see it. A splendid night was had by all, as he and a couple of players chatted and posed for photographs.

To say Blackwell's hands have been tied at Elland Road is a gross understatement. I'm not going to harp on any more about the tragic events of the last few seasons, except to say that I feel Blackwell should be given a chance to see if he can build a team to get us back into the Premiership. Let's face it, we were going nowhere under Peter Reid. However, I did feel sorry for Reid: he too was forced to operate with both hands tied securely behind his back, which explains the record amount of loan signings and obscure purchases that he brought in.

One such loan signing was Roque Junior, the famous Brazilian now playing with AC Milan. No one could quite believe it when

Leeds announced that the club was to acquire its first and only World Cup winner. Now, Leeds fans have had a lot to put up with over the years, but this was just too hard to swallow. It was painfully obvious that the 'Roque' who made his debut at Leicester was an impostor. Rumours were rife that the real Roque (full name José Vitor Roque Junior) was kidnapped and tied up in the back of a car at a car-boot sale at Hull dockside. The man in the heart of the Leeds defence that evening at the Walkers Stadium was simply a circus clown on stilts.

Meanwhile, household names continued to be drafted into the Leeds set-up.

Lamine Sakho arrived from Marseille. Despite a promising start, he quickly descended into oblivion. Due largely to his lively hairstyle, these days he apparently holds down a secure job as the long, tall, thin air balloon seen spiralling skywards outside Ford car showrooms and the like.

Kevin Blackwell has also had to juggle with players he would not normally have included in his plans. When he brought over French trialist Dominic Gourville, Leeds' financial situation was made clearly evident. Obviously, as the arrangement might prove to be only temporary, Gourville was booked into a city centre hotel for the duration of his stay. Which hotel was it? The Marriott? The Hilton? The Queens Hotel, perhaps? No, Dominic Gourville was given his own room upstairs at The Viaduct.

Obviously, Les was delighted and looked after his star guest admirably. One morning in The Viaduct, we were quaffing rather large quantities of ale when bleach-haired Dominic came downstairs for his breakfast. He was absolutely stunned to discover around 100 lads preparing for yet another away game. A few days later, it got even worse for the poor Frenchman. We were boarding the coach to go to a midweek away friendly, when Les got a telephone call from Leeds United. Amazingly, it was left to Les to inform Dominic, who was downstairs having a coffee, that he wouldn't be playing that evening. Instead of getting a taxi to Elland Road for the team coach, he should instead get a taxi and go to Thorp Arch to report for a training session. It was a very strange feeling as Dominic stood at the pub door, and we waved him goodbye from the coach windows. Despite scoring a cracker in a pre-season friendly at Darlington, Gourville's services were not retained by Leeds United.

With the exception of Dominic Matteo and James Milner, there are so-called stars that deserted the Leeds ship at the first opportunity; their names don't deserve to go in these pages. However, one man who can have as many pages as he likes is Lucas Radebe. 'The Chief' commanded the highest gate of the season: almost 38,000 for his testimonial game against a World All Stars XI. Incidentally, it was also the highest gate of any Championship side that season and would have beaten the top attendances at half the Premiership grounds as well. I had spent a few days with the family at Center Parcs in Nottingham, before driving to our last away game of the season at Leicester. The following day, I then drove back to Leeds in order to attend the testimonial game at Elland Road. All the way back up the motorway, I saw droves of Leeds fans in coaches, vans and cars all travelling to pay their respects to a real hero. One car had in it a young lad who was possibly about 12 years old: he was hanging out of one of the back windows up to his waist, waving and screaming with Leeds scarves tied to each wrist.

I'm not a big fan of testimonials: I feel that these days, most so-called loyalty rewards are inappropriate. Of course there are exceptions. Gary Kelly had given Leeds United sterling service for over ten years and deserved his big day when Leeds awarded him a testimonial against Celtic at Elland Road. Kelly handed over all his testimonial funds to his cancer charity in Drogheda. Lucas Radebe also fully deserved his testimonial. When he was at the peak of his game about five years ago, Alex Ferguson came sniffing for the Chief. He was politely turned down by the modest South African, who said that Leeds had been good to him and that he wanted to stay. There aren't many footballers around who would act with such pride and dignity.

A host of stars turned out for Lucas, including old favourite Vinnie Jones. There was also a historic appearance by Leeds United Ladies' forward Lucy Long. Coming on for the second half, she scored a cracker at the Kop end, leaving goalkeeper Bruce Grobbelaar clawing at fresh air. Predictably, Vinnie was first on hand to help Lucy celebrate, jumping on her outstretched body, while she was lying on the ground; the crowd loved it. Actually, my cousin Jayne's daughter Jemima plays for the ladies' team, along with Kippax resident Jill Browning.

In the bar after the game, not many people knew what the final score was. Dave Stevens said it could have been '7–3 or something'. Nobody was really bothered, but everyone agreed that it had been a fantastic occasion for a fantastic servant of the club. I enjoyed a celebratory drink that night with 'Sycamore Sect' members Trev, Daz, Lee, Paul and Diane.

At the recent Holbeck AGM at The Viaduct I was with Big John Martin. He apologised for reading the *Daily Mirror* and handed me a small cutting from the newspaper. It was regarding an email sent to the sports letters page by someone from Newbury. It concerned José Mourinho's ungracious behaviour after the recent Liverpool v. Chelsea European Cup semi-final at Anfield. It read:

> Smell the stench of sour grapes. The truth is, if Anfield held a European semi-final between two English teams, every year for the past 40 years, you would not see a bigger character than José Mourinho.

Much against the grain for the *Daily Mirror*, the reply from them was:

> Well let me take you back to the last European semi-final between two English clubs I watched there. It was against Leeds in the 1971 Fairs Cup semi-final. After one pulsating Leeds attack, accompanied to the tune of 'We all hate Leeds and Leeds and Leeds . . .' the ball landed inches from my chin. As Billy Bremner picked it up, a youth with unfortunate features yelled, 'And we really hate you Bremner, ya ginger twat!' Bremner bounced the ball off the lad's face, smirking, 'Here's another reason to hate me. I've made you even uglier,' before running off to take a corner. It was a good one too. So was his goal that took Leeds to the final. Believe me mate, football used to be so full of bigger characters.

What this club would give for such a character now. Jermaine Wright can run about all day in his all-white kit in the muddiest, dirtiest conditions ever witnessed, and he would still walk off the pitch as though he had just been in a Persil advert. It's unfair to criticise players, really. For example, to say that the decision to bring in Kevin

Pressman after we've just had the last three England goalkeepers at the club is totally baffling. However, Pressman was on a rolling contract. That's just as well, I suppose, because I'm convinced that, due to his size, he could put out a large forest fire in minutes, simply by rolling over it.

These days, against all odds, I believe Leeds are slowly beginning to get back on the right track. It doesn't need an expert analyst to see that the team, as yet, is nowhere near as good as it needs to be, but, slowly and surely, I'm convinced we'll get there.

However, one thing *is* for certain: the best two words in the English language are Leeds United.